EXPLORING TOURISM AND HOSPITALITY INDUSTRY: ISSUES AND STRATEGIES

Editors
R.K. Gupta
Prashant Gautam
Arun Singh Thakur

NEHA PUBLISHERS & DISTRIBUTORS
DELHI

Publisher

NEHA PUBLISHERS & DISTRIBUTORS

4832/24,Prahlad Lane,S-207

Ansari Road, Daryaganj,Delhi-110002

Ph.: 43570976, 23278261

Email: nehapubdistributors@gmail.com

Edition: 2014

ISBN : 978-93-80318-52-3

Laser Typesetting

JEE-VEE Graphics

Delhi

Price : Rs. 1595.00

Printed by **Vikas Computers**

PREFACE

Tourism and hospitality industry provides principal economic development prospects for many countries and a means of improving the livelihoods of its residents and with the development of support infrastructure. This industry is seen as providing benefits to all the players of society. Both the public and private sectors involved in tourism depend on planning to achieve sustainable tourism development that respects the local community, creates appropriate employment, maintains the natural environment, and delivers a quality visitor experience. However, many tourism destinations have pursued development without proper planning and without considering the many impacts such development will bring to the community.

Many people are involved in the tourism development process and all these people have a stake in the destination's future. They voice their dreams, experiences, wishes and discontent, and tourism development can take these into account. Some voices are loud, others silent or unheard. Not necessarily because stakeholders in tourism want them to be so, but because the destination functions in such manner.

Untill the 1980's and 90's tourism was seen as a profitable sector of business with no obvious constraints to growth, few barriers to entry to the market, an almost universal welcome from governments and, for the most part, few effective regulatory requirements to take the environment into account. Organizations - large and small, countries, governments, everybody, even individuals were acting on the Dowkin's principle of self interest. They do not make significant changes to the way they do business because of exhortations or out of good intentions, but only in response to the pressure of external factors that cannot be avoided, or to seize a competitive advantage.

Even right now International tourism, despite of many jolts and fluctuations, has been going through a phase, in which the opportunities for making quick profits from exploiting what were regarded as freely available natural resources dazzled the eyes of Govt. and businessmen, as well as many local residents. But despite of this entire, there are certain limits to growth. This issue of limits to growth was come into existence after we saw decline of many destinations as tourist destinations.

It is widely acknowledged fact that the strategic planning is crucial to successful tourism development and management; and strategic planning has been a widely adopted principle in tourism development at both regional and national levels. Arguably, the merits of strategic planning can only be possible given that a plan can be implemented in the first place.

Suggestions are offered in the literature to help planners and researchers develop more integrative and less reactionary approaches to strategic planning. While some have been adapted from business models and focus on product formation and issues of supply and demand, new research in the field contends that approaches to tourism, particularly in rural areas, must be inclusive and emphasize meaningful public participation.

The present book 'Exploring Tourism and Hospitality Industry: Issues and Strategies' organised itself as per the spirit of the introductory quote of this preface. Editors are feeling very happy to bring this book on the occasion of 'HOSTOCON 2014' at Panjab University, Chandigarh.

This book is a collection of assorted researches that addresses a large vista of tourism related issues. The research articles are all, in their own part, notable scholarly contributions documenting diverse aspects and studies related to the tourism. This book offers an inclusive glance into issues related with the status and development of tourism and hospitality industry. The tourism and hospitality industry is well on its way to becoming one of the most powerful growth engines in the coming time, thus these research studies are relevant for a number of stakeholders like governments, destinations, tour operators, travel agents, tourism workers, developers, tourism researchers, students and travellers themselves. This book seeks to fulfil the needs of planning for the industry.

Editors acknowledge the valuable research of the contributors and believe that this publication is a significant contribution towards future development and planning purposes not only for tourism industry but also for other tourism related activities and those who are interested in the tourism research. Editors sincerely believe in the standards of academic integrity and highest levels of scholastic conduct, thus declare that the respective authors would be responsible for any kind of plagiarism found in their contribution.

R.K. Gupta
Prashant K. Gautam
Arun Singh Thakur

Chandigarh
08.02.2014

LIST OF CONTRIBUTORS

Amit Katoch	Research Scholar (Tourism), Central University of Himachal Pradesh, Dharamsala, Kangra, Himachal Pradesh, M No +91-9418385084, amitkatoch2007@gmail.com
Anu Jhamb	Assistant Professor, Deptt. of Management. UIET, Panjab University, Chandigarh. anujhamb2000@gmail.com
Anupama Srivastava	Lecturer, Institute of Tourism Studies, University of Lucknow
Anushree Banerjee	Research Scholar Institute of Tourism Studies University of Lucknow. 08anushree@gmail.com
Arun Singh Thakur	Assistant Professor, University Institute of Hotel Management and Tourism, Panjab University, Chandigarh. arun.tourism@gmail.com
Gaurav Kashyap	Assistant Professor University Institute of Hotel Management & Tourism Panjab University, Chandigarh gauravkashyap@gmail.com
Jaswinder Singh	Assistant Professor, University Institute of Hotel Management and Tourism, Panjab University, Chandigarh. jaswinder_chef@yahoo.co.in
Kalyani Singh	Faculty, Food Science and Nutrition, UIHMT, Panjab University, singh.kalyani26@yahoo.com
Kulwant Singh Pathania	Professor, Faculty of Commerce and Management Studies, H. P University, Shimla-5
Lakhvinder Singh	Research Scholar, Department of Tourism & Hotel Management, Kurukshetra University, Kurukshetra lakhvindersingh.kuk@gmail.com

Lipika Guliani	Assistant Professor, UIHMT, Panjab University lipika_b@yahoo.com
Pallavi Thakur	Research Scholar- CMT&HS HNB Garhwal University, Srinagar, Uttarakhand Pallavithakur.tourism@gmail.com
Pardeep Jain	Professor, Department of Management, SLIET, Longowal, Punjab, India.
Pooja Rajput	Research Scholar (Geology), HNB Garhwal, Srinagar (A Central University), Uttarakhand. M. No +91-8988159173. poojakatoch2011@gmail.com
Prashant K Gautam	Assistant Professor, University Institute of Hotel Management and Tourism, Panjab University, Chandigarh. Prashant.k.gautam@gmail.com
Preeti Madan Sharma	Manyawar Kanshiram Institute of Tourism Management (MKITM) Kusum Kunj, Behind Hydel Colony, Prag Narain Road, Lucknow-226001. preetimadan@rediffmail.com
Punit Gautam	Associate Professor Dept. of Tourism & Hotel Management North-Eastern Hill University (NEHU), Shillong, punitgautam@yahoo.co.uk
R K Gupta	Director, University Institute of Hotel Management and Tourism, Panjab University, Chandigarh. rakeshdcs@yahoo.co.in
Rajesh kumar Jhamb	Lecturer, Govt. Polytechnic for Women Sector-10, Chandigarh. jhamb.rajesh@gmail.com
Rajpreet Kaur	Research Scholar, Department of Management, SLIET,Longowal, Punjab, India.
Ram Mehar	Assistant Professor, Department of Education, USOL, Panjab University Chandigarh, India.
Ravi Bhushan Kumar	Professor, Department of Tourism & Hotel Management, Kurukshetra University, Kurukehetra. ravibhushankumar1999@rediffmail.com
Rohit Garg	Professor and Director, Hindu Institute of Management, Sonepat-131001, rohit.teacher@gmail.com
S.Mehdi Hasan Rizvi	Computer Programmer, Institute of Tourism Studies, University of Lucknow

Sandeep Walia	Assistant Professor, Maharaja Agrasen University, Baddi, Himachal Pradesh. Sndp.walia551@gmail.com
Saurabh Rawat	Research Scholar Institute of Tourism Studies University of Lucknow. vicious_saurabh@yahoo.com
Shefali Saini	Assistant Professor, Department of Tourism, Hospitality and Hotel management {THHM}, Punjabi University, Patiala, shefalisaini1988@gmail.com
Shikha Misra	Research Scholar, Punjab Technical University, IITTM Centre, Gwalior. profshikha@gmail.com
Shikha Sharma	Research Scholar, Institute of Vocational Studies (MTA), Himachal Pradesh University, Summer Hill, Shimla, 171004. Himachal Pradesh. ssharma.shimla@gmail.com
Sunil Upadhyaya	Assistant Professor, Manyawar Kanshiram Institute of Tourism Management (Uttar Pradesh Tourism). sunilupadhyaya@gmail.com
Suyash Yadav	Research Scholar, Institute of Tourism Studies, University of Lucknow, India; yadav.suyash@gmail.com
Syed Ahmad Rizwan	Assistant Professor, UIHMT, Panjab University syedahmadrizwan@gmail.com
Tanvi Beniwal	Assistant Professor, UIHMT, Panjab University, tanubeniwal@yahoo.com
Tek Chand	Ph. D Scholar, Faculty of Commerce and Management Studies, H. P University, Shimla-5
Varinder Singh Rana	Assistant Professor (School of Hotel Management & Tourism) Lovely Professional University Jalandhar-Delhi G.T.Road (NH-1), Phagwara, Punjab-144402 varinder.rana@lpu.co.in
Vijay Kumar	Dept. of Tourism, Hotel, Hospitality and Heritage Studies, Jamia Millia Islamia, New Delhi 110025, India vkumar@jmi.ac.in
Vishal Srivastava	Faculty, Manyawar Kanshiram Institute of Tourism Management (Uttar Pradesh Tourism) Vikalp Khand-II, Near CB-CID Office, Gomti Nagar, Lucknow-226010, U.P. vishal@up-tourism.com

CONTENTS

INTEGRATING GEOLOGICAL CONCERNS OVER TOURISM DEVELOPMENT: A CASE STUDY OF DHARAMSHALA, KANGRA, HIMACHAL-PRADESH (INDIA)

Pooja Rajput

Research Scholar (Geology), HNB Garhwal, Srinagar (A Central University), Uttarakhand. M.No +91-8988159173, poojakatoch2011@gmail.com

Abstract: Tourism Development at any Tourism destination should consider the geological aspects of the location i.e. the rocks, soil profile and plate tectonics. As, they help in understanding of soil mechanics & rock mechanics of the place. These aspects are very important prior to developmental and construction activities in a destination. Also, the proper understanding and knowledge of geological aspects are important in the forecast and understanding of natural hazards like landslides, earthquake, floods and volcanic eruptions. This paper points out to the massive construction developments going on in the tourist destination of Dharamshala without considering the geological aspect of the place.

Keywords: Geology of Dharamshala, Tourism, Hazard, Geotechnical Engineering.

Aim of Paper: The purpose of this research paper is to integrate geological concerns of Dharamshala with the tourism aspect. Dharamshala is a tourist destination and undergoing phenomenal development in terms of Infrastructure. A large number of Hotels, buildings are being constructed in the hill station, but no importance is given to geology of the place. Dharamshala is tectonically highly disturbed area which comes under seismic zone V and surely the uncontrolled construction activities can lead to the very destruction of the place.

Research Methodology: This study gives an inclusive view of Tourism with regard to geological aspect of the place. It also involved review of literature from journals, books, magazines, websites etc to support the argument that developments should be done after proper understanding of geological elements of the place, to avoid catastrophes such as calamity in Uttarakhand in 2013 etc.

Introduction

Himachal Pradesh is a beautiful state of India having wealth of natural resources. The mountainous state is known for its picturesque valleys, ferocious rocky ravines, flowering meadows and the inexplicable snow-clad Himalayan peaks. The hill station has beautiful topography, stands on the spur of the Dhauladhar range and is also known as Scotland of India. If we take a look at the history of this quiet little hilly town, then it once was also a British hill resort. But in course of time, it revived into a beautiful blend of culture. Tibetans' came to this place in 1959 after the Chinese invasion in Tibet. Dharamshala is also seat of Tibetan's government in exile and home to His Holiness the Dalai Lama. The place is visited by foreign visitors mainly due to Dalai Lama and the British lineage it has got from the pre-independence era. Also, a large number of domestic tourists visit the hill station due to the natural beauty and the religious circuit which is present in & around it. So, the main reason for which the tourists come here is primarily natural attractiveness and religious aspect. In order to fulfill this great demand of tourists, a large number of Hotels and other infrastructure have come up in Dharamshala and the effect of this massive & uncontrolled development is that both ecology & geology of the place is under great threat. Also, the place comes under seismic zone V, which is highly prone to earthquakes. The tourist place also has witnessed the most severe earthquake in India, the 1905 Kangra earthquake with an intensity of 7.8 magnitude killing 20,000 people, 53,000 domestic animals and destruction of over one lakh houses. Also, the place has been experiencing a large number of small tremors frequently. Scientific investigations reveal that most of the earthquakes which have occurred in the region are result of the movement of thrusts/faults and are located along three major thrust zones i.e. the main boundary thrust (MBT) separating shiwaliks from rest of Himalayas; the main central thrust (MCT) separating lesser and central Himalayas and the central counter thrust (CCT) separating central Himalayas from the Tibetan Himalayas.

Major earthquakes in Himachal Pradesh

Date	**Intensity**	**Place**
4th April 1905	8.0	Kangra
19th January, 1975	6.7	Kinnaur & Lahaul spiti
26th April, 1986	5.7	Dharamshala
15th June, 1978	5.0	Dharamshala

Figure-1 Major Earthquakes in Himachal Pradesh

(**Source:** National centre for Disaster Management, New Delhi.)

Besides earthquakes, landslides are the other geological hazards that are common and peculiar to the region. The fragile nature of rocks forming the mountains of the region, along with anthropogenic activities has made the place more vulnerable to the adversaries of nature. All these things clearly stipulate the need to focus on geological aspects, while developing infrastructure and tourism at such destinations.

Lessons to be taken from Past Catastrophes

There are numerous examples within and outside country, where non consideration of geological aspects have resulted in loss of lives and destruction of property. Heavy rainfalls in Uttarakhand & Himachal Pradesh in June 2013 lead to huge destruction to life and property. But, if careful analysis of the disaster is done, it would point out that anthropological activity in form of uncontrolled construction along the tributaries of Ganga was also a major reason for massive destruction. The tsunami disaster on Thailand in 2004 and Fukushima Daiichi nuclear disaster on Japan in 2011, also clearly point out that we should be ready for such seismic disasters through proper planning and taking geological factors in consideration. The proper understanding of geological concerns helps in proper interpretation of landforms and earth's process to identify potential geologic and related man made hazards that may impact civil structures and human development.

In the present time, we are giving more emphasis to infrastructure and superstructures without considering its implications on environment, particularly the already existing abiotic and biotic factors. The geology of a place plays an important role in stability of structures. So, it is very important to understand it and create economical and safe designs for structures. The knowledge about soil profile, character about the soil and strength of soil helps us to carry on structural developments which suite the biotic & abiotic factors of the place.

Dharamshala has undergone great infrastructural developments due to the tourism activity and being the administrative seat of Kangra district. But no importance has been given to geological and tectonic setting making it most vulnerable to Geo Hazards.

Figure 2: Kedarnath after big disaster (Source- http://all4youth.com/)

Tourism in Dharamshala

Dharamshala is a beautiful hill station and a tourist place located in the middle Himalayas in Himachal Pradesh. It is a tourist destination popular among tourists, both Domestic & International for variety of reasons such as scenic beauty, religious purpose, adventure etc. Recently, it has also been in news due to cricket Stadium, where international cricket matches are held frequently. Dharamshala is a nature lover's delight and offers its visitor overabundance of tourist attractions to travel around. This hill station is forested with conifer trees and snow capped mountains embrace three sides of the town while the valley lies in the front. The snowline is Infact very easily reachable at Dharamshala than at any other hill station and one can reach snowline just in 7-8 hours distance at Triund.

Dharamshala is the headquarter of the Kangra district. In 1905, this town had suffered a major catastrophe in form of a massive earthquake, in which thousands of people were killed and lead to huge destruction of property. But since then, the town has undergone reconstruction and flourished into a calm health resort. The tourist destination has flourished significantly. It is divided into two distinct parts- upper Dharamshala & lower Dharamshala. The upper Dharamshala has a number of touristic attractions such as BhagsuNag, waterfall, Dharmkot, Galu Mata temple, Buddhist monasteries and temples, Tsuglagkhang, Dip Thekchen Choeling Monastery, Triund, Dull Lake, Lord Elgin's tomb, St. John's in Wilderness, sunset view from Naddi and Tranquil forests of Deodar in Forsyth Ganj & McLeodGanj. While lower part of town is famous for Kotwali Bazaar, Kangra Art Museum, cricket stadium, Dharamshala college, Shaheed Smarak and All India Radio Dharamshala. Dharamshala is also headquarter of Government in exile of Tibetans since 1960's under the esteemed leadership of His Holiness The Dalai Lama. Dharamshala is also known as "The little Lhasa" and has added a new dimension to the cultural web of the place. The altitude of Dharamshala town varies between 1200m to 2600m and its temperature varies from 0o C in the month of January to a maximum of 380 C in the month of June. The annual rainfall of the place varies between 290 cm to 380 cm which is second highest in India. The best time to visit the tourist destination is January to June and September to December.

Dharamshala has a number of tourist attractions- Natural and Manmade. Primarily the tourist destination is famous for pilgrimage or religious purpose for presence of temples in and around it. But, the place is beautiful for its majestic Dhauladhar range, natural beauty and Deodar forests present in upper reaches of the town. The presence of His Holiness Dalai Lama makes the place extra special and attracts international tourists. The beautiful picturesque cricket stadium of Himachal Pradesh Cricket Association is the second most beautiful stadium in the world and most distinguished in terms of its gorgeous location and artistically made structure.

Also a number of tourist attractions are present around Dharamshala such as:

- Kunal Pathri Temple, near Sarah.
- Bhadra Kali Temple at Sarah, 450 year old temple at Sarah.
- Tea Gardens - Hodal Tea Estate, Tua Tea Estate etc
- Aghanjar Mahadev temple at Khaniyara, 5-6 Kilometres away from Dharamshala.
- Indru Nag Temple at Khaniyara, located Near Aghanjar Mahadev temple.
- Rock inscription, Khaniyara
- Norbulinga Institute, Norbulinga Institute is the premier Tibetan institute in the world which offers courses of study for Tibetan culture and arts located in Sidhpur, 5-6 Km away from Dharamshala.
- Chinmaya Tapovan
- Vidhan Sabha
- Gyuto Monastery
- Chamunda Devi
- Rock inscription, Pathiar
- Gopalpur Nature Park

- o Temple of Baijnath
- o Temple of Sidhnath, Baijnath
- o Buddhist stupa known as Bhim-ka-Tila
- o Brajeshwari Temple at Kangra
- o Toy train from Pathankot- Kangra- Jogindernagar.
- o Baglamukhi Temple at Bankhandi
- o Heritage village Pragpur
- o Rural village site at Baba Baroh and Nerti.
- o Jwalamukhi Temple
- o Tatwani near Rait
- o Kotla fort
- o Nurpur Fort
- o Monolithic rock cut temple at Masroor
- o Pong Dam and Rancer Island
- o Hill stations near Dharamshala- Dalhousie, Khajjiar, and Chamba etc.

The rich plethora of attractions present in and around Dharamshala provides huge opportunities to Tourists.

Dharamshala has got great accessibility by Air, road and rail. The nearest airport is at Gaggal (13 km); the Broad gauge railway link (85 Km) is at Pathankot and through road, it is accessible from Pathankot (85 Km), Chandigarh (250 Km), Delhi (526 Km). Roadways are primarily the lifeline of Dharamshala.

Geological aspects of Dharamshala

Dharamshala lies in the middle Himalayas. The altitude of Dharamshala varies from 1200 metres to 2600 metres above sea level. The geology of the Dharamsala region is an alternate bands of sandstone, shale and clay layer. The upper most part of the region consists of Dhauladhar Granite and the lower most part consists of Siwalik group conglomerates. The lineaments includes two active fault facing NW and SW direction, three thrust namely Chail thrust, Main boundary thrust, Drini thrust facing NE and SW direction.

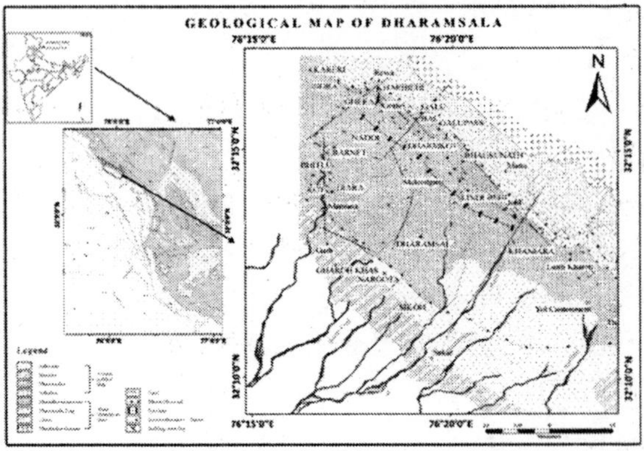

Figure-3 Geological Map of Dharamshala modified by Pooja Rajput (After Mahajan et al 1991)

The Dharamshala town falls in active seismic zone V indicating that the area is greatly prone to seismic hazard. The geology of the Dharamsala area which forms a part of lesser and outer Himalayas is characterized by the occurrence of the following formations/ group from north to south, viz., Dhauladhar granite, Chail formation, Dharamsala traps, Dharamkot limestone, Sabathus, Dharamsala group and Shivalik group. This area shows great diversity of lithology within a small area showing that the study area is tectonically very active (Mahajan et al., 1997; Mahajan and Virdi, 2000).

Also, the earthquakes which have occurred in these regions such as Kangra earthquake (1905); Dharamshala earthquake (1978) and Dharamshala earthquake (1986) are correlated with Main boundary thrusts, Subsidiary Drini Thrust and transverse faults.

The Dhauladhar range just on the back of Dharamshala town has a general east west trend due to tectonic movement, large steep walled stream canyon southern slope and contracted north south ridges. The Ganga plain lies to south of Dhauladhar range with undeformed alluvium and McLeodGanj was built on a prominent mountain ridgeline that extends from the ridge of Dhauladhar to the level of the Kangra valley. Below the ridge axis, the natural mountainside slopes range from 30 to 50 degrees. The geologic materials underlying Upper Dharamsala are a relatively strong bedrock unit with weak surface deposits. The bedrock is composed of strong, thick-bedded sandstone inter-layered with weak, thin-bedded shale and siltstone. Also the slopes of Dharamshala are covered with thick overburden materials including colluvial soils (meaning soils moving downhill under the force of gravity or deposited by downhill movement), which are vulnerable to seismic activity. The main McLeodGanj area till Tsuglag Khang (Main Temple) of Tibetans and main Kotwali bazaar is comparatively stable then the slopes due to the presence of main bedrock in the region. But all the roads leading to Dharamshala and increased construction in the town on the slopes has been done on the landslides without considering the seismicity of the area. Also, the stability of these colluvial slopes is unknown to earthquakes and monsoon.

Hazards associated with the place

The diverse geology of the Dharamshala and the history of hazards associated with the place strongly point out that the place is vulnerable to Hazards especially seismic Hazards i.e. earthquakes and landslides. The geo hazards international team based in USA & funded by Flora Family Foundation in 2006 conducted a study related to assessed regions geology and seismotectonic setting and clearly stated that the area is prone to earthquakes and landslides due to tectonic movement.

Figure1: View of McLeodGanj

(**Source:** http://www.downtheroad.org/India-Nepal-Subcontinent/images/2PICS_Dharamsala_Mcleod_Ganj/IMGA0002.JPG)

The development of world's highest mountains, Himalayan ranges occurred due to the collision of Indian sub continent plate with Eurasian plate & it started 50 million years ago. And it is believed that the Indian plate is drifting northward at a rate of 40mm per year and colliding with Eurasian plate. But at the same time, it also made the Himalayan region as the most earthquake prone belts in the world. The region has highly folded rocks and large active thrust faults. These faults act as energy reservoirs accumulating strains until their energy is liberated in the form of massive earthquakes. A large number of earthquakes have occurred in the Himalayan region 1803 (M8.1 Kumaon, India), 1897 (M8.3 Shillong, India), 1905 (M7.8 Kangra, India), 1934 (M8.2 Bihar, India and Nepal), 1950 (M8.5 Assam, India), and 2005 (M7.6, Kashmir). All these facts strongly point out that even larger events can occur leading to huge loss of lives and property. Also, several sections of the plate boundary have not experienced earthquakes since long and have been storing huge energy ever since seismic events have occurred in these areas. So, there exist "seismic gaps" which have potential to create huge calamities in form of earthquakes and landslides.

The scientist of Wadia Institute of Himalayan Geology estimates that buildings in McLeodGanj & Dharamshala have a 10 percent chance of experience shaking of 0.7 g (70-percent of the acceleration due to gravity), assuming a standard design life of 50 years. Probabilistic seismic hazard maps prepared by the Global Seismic Hazard Assessment Project (GSHAP), a worldwide earthquake hazard estimation project, give a lower estimate of 0.27g for the Kangra area, but many earth scientists familiar with the area consider the GSHAP estimates for the Himalayan region to be low. Also, the illegal mining activities for slates in Bhagsu Nag and Khaniyara is posing a great threat to environment, resulted in destruction of forest cover and erosion of soil.

All these aspects & heavy construction in lower and upper Dharamshala stipulates the need of great planning and proper understanding of the geology of the area, prior to developmental activity. Apart from the construction activities the region has also witnessed increase in population from 10939 (excluding Tibetans and visiting population) in 1971 to 22,586. There has been increase in Tibetan population from 8,111 to 13,701 from 1998-2009. There has been increase in tourist population from 1, 46,720 in 2006 to 1, 61,234 in 2011. Also, there has been mushrooming growth of Hotels throughout Dharamshala. As, a result the physical atmosphere of the town has changed due to great flux of tourists, population of the hosts & construction activities. Surely, these all aspects point that it is high time now to become wise and stop uncontrolled anthropological activities or it would be too late to face the consequences.

Construction in Dharamshala (Lower & Upper)

The majority of the buildings in Dharamshala have not been made keeping in mind the Seismicity of area. And, major importance has been to build concrete structures which consist of more concrete & steel. The geology of the place has been totally neglected. The buildings (commercial, residential & public) in upper and lower Dharamshala are susceptible to earthquake damage and entire population is on peril due to risky construction.

The deficiencies in construction and development activities:

- o The steel is used profusely on the top & not in the walls.
- o The tourism establishments & new buildings have been built profusely on slopes without any proper planning, prone to landslides & earthquakes.
- o The majority of structures being built is not considering the geological aspect and suffers significant seismic vulnerabilities.
- o The frame of the concrete structures does not have enough properly placed reinforcing steel to resist earthquake shaking without extensive damage.
- o Beams and columns are not continuous from the foundation to the roof or from one end of the building to the other.
- o While constructing structures no investigation of soil is done or help of geologists or Geophysicists is taken & everything left at the mercy of God.

- Most of the hotels and building are multistoried structures with no spacing from each other.
- The streets in local bazaars & town are narrow and congested.
- Most buildings have unreinforced brick walls.

Geotechnical Engineering

In order to improve the existing & building structures, earthquake protection measures should be taken in consultation with civil engineers, Architects & geologists. Earthquake protection measures can be taken with regard to architectural design; structural counter measures and construction & maintenance quality. For prevention of seismic damage first of all carrying capacity of the location & sustainability should be considered. Also massive & uncontrolled developments should be avoided. The buildings if constructed should have simplicity & symmetry in plan & elevations; small rooms; less height; lighter roofs; wood frames in between walls and presence of seismic bands-plinth band; lintel band; eaves/ roof band; floor/ceiling band and gable band.

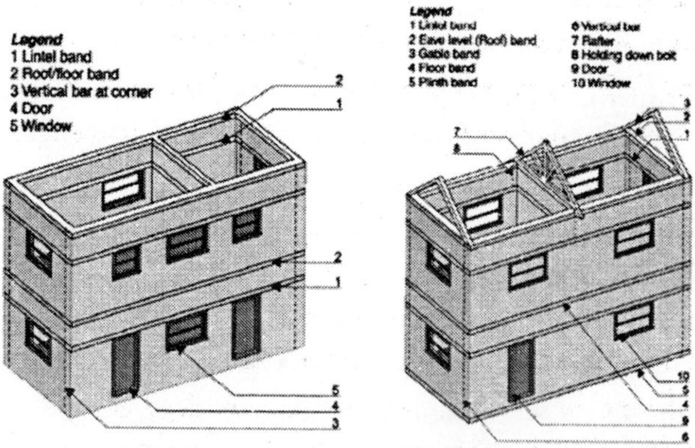

Overall arrangement of reinforcing masonry buildings (roof not shown)

Figure 4 & 5 - overall arrangement of the seismic bands in buildings

Source: Paper of Anand Arya (Professor Emeritus in Earthquake Engineering, University of Roorkee, Roorkee) of "non-engineered construction in developing countries -an Approach toward earthquake risk prediction"

Also, seismic retrofitting of should be done of existing non-engineered buildings to minimize seismic impacts of earthquakes.

Conclusion

Tourism development should incorporate geological concerns while developing the infrastructure and superstructure. Also, care should be taken to avoid over construction & uncontrolled development to minimize impacts on environment. Dharamshala town falls in seismic zone V and is largely composed of soft sediments. Also, the diverse geology & history of seismic hazards associated with the place strongly point out that the place is vulnerable to Hazards especially seismic Hazards i.e. earthquakes and landslides. So, massive construction in the tourist destination should be avoided to prevent calamity such as Kedarnath. We should take lessons from the catastrophe & adopt all means to prevent geohazards. Also, disaster mitigation for sustainable development should be done by means of public awareness, compulsory legislations, land use zoning, constructing earthquake resistant structures, retrofitting of the existing structures, constructing seismic hazard maps and seismic microzonation of Dharamshala Town.

Acknowledgement:

The author is grateful to Prof. A.K. Mahajan (1991; 1994; 2000 & 2001), Deepika Thakur (2013), Geo hazards international team (2006) based in USA & Flora Family Foundation (2006) from whose papers/research articles maximum geological information was taken to support the paper. The author is also thankful to Himachal Pradesh Remote Sensing Centre; State Council for Science, Technology and Environment, Kasumpti Shimla, Himachal Pradesh; Department of Tourism; District Statistical Office; Municipal Committee and Tibetan Secretariat, Upper Dharamshala, whose information was used to support the research paper.

References

(2006). A Culture at Risk: An Initial Assessment of Seismic Vulnerabilities in Upper Dharamshala, India. GeoHazards

International, Flora Family Foundation. Retrieved January 11, 2014, from www.geohaz.org

Aswathanarayana, U. (1995). Geoenvironment- An Introduction. Rotterdam: A.A. Balkema.

Chakraborty, A. (n.d.). AHP based landslide hazard assessment in a mountainous urban area of Dharamshala, Himachal Pradesh, India, using Remote Sensing Technique.

(2009). District Human Development Report- Kangra. CSK Himachal Pradesh Agricultural University, Palampur, Department of Agricultural economics. Retrieved January 1, 2014

(2013). Extened Progress of Progress Reports. Records Volume 145-146, Part 8, Geological Survey of India, Government of India. Retrieved January 8, 2014

(2012). Geology and Mineral Resources of Himachal Pradesh. Geological Survey of India. Lucknow: Army Printing Press. Retrieved January 6, 2014

(n.d.). Himachal Pradesh Development Report. Government of India, Planning Commission of India. Retrieved from https://www.google.co.in/search?q=Soil+gas+radon%E2%80%93thoron+monitoring+in+Dharamsala+area+of+north-west+Himalayas,+India+using+solid+state+nuclear+track+detectors&ie=utf-8&oe=utf-8&rls=org.mozilla:en-GB:official&client=firefox-beta&channel=np&source=h

Hrasna, M. (2002). Geoenvironment and Geofactors of the Environment - the Basic Concepts of Environmental Geology. Bratislava, 57: Acta Geological University. doi:Acta Geological Univ.Com

Indian Mountain Initiative- Sustainable Mountain Development Summit 2012. (25th - 26th May, 2012). Indian Mountain Initiative - Sustainable Mountain Development Summit 2012 (IMI SMDS2) (pp. 1-16). Gangtok, Sikkim: THE ECOTOURISM & CONSERVATION SOCIETY OF SIKKIM (ECOSS) and Central Himalayan Environment Association (CHEA), Nainital. Retrieved January 5, 2014, from www.imi-smds2.org

Kumar, A., & Sivaramakrishnan, J. (2008). GROUND WATER INFORMATION BOOKLET KANGRA DISTRICT, HIMACHAL PRADESH. Government of India, Ministry Of Water Resources, Central Ground Water Board. Retrieved January 1, 2014

Kumar, G., Kumar, A., Walia, V., Kumar, J., Gupta, V., Yang, T. F.,. .. Bajwa, B. S. (2013, October 1). Soil gas radon-thoron monitoring in Dharamsala area of north-west Himalayas, India using solid state nuclear track detectors. Journal of Earth System Science, October 2013, Volume 122, Issue 5, pp 1295-1301. doi:10.1007/ s12040-013-0344-5

Mahajan, A. K., & Kumar, S. (1994). Linear Features registered on the Landsat Imaginery and Seismic Activity in the Dharamshala-Palampur Region (NW Himalaya). GEOFIZIKA, VOL II. Retrieved January 1, 2014

(1979). Operation: Anantpur- A Multidisciplinary Integrated Project for an Appraisal of Natural Resources and Environment of Ananthapur District, Andhra Pradesh. Geological Survey of India. GSI Miscellaneous Publication No. 47,57.

R.N.Yong, Mullingan, C. N., & Fukue, M. (2006). Geoenvironment Sustainability. CRC Press Inc.

(2008). State of the Environment Report- Himachal Pradesh. State Council for Science, Technology and Environment. Shimla: SCSTE. Retrieved January 1, 2014

Sterleke, B., & Zurbrugg, C. (2003). Baseline study on Water Supply, Sanitation and Solid Waste in Upper Dharamshala, India. SANDEC Report 09/03. Retrieved January 5, 2014

Thakur, D., & Gill, G. S. (2013). SOME GEO-ENVIRONMENTAL HAZARDS IN DHARAMSHALA AREA OF HIMACHAL PRADESH AND THEIR MITIGATION. International Journal of Advancement in Earth and Environmental Sciences, IJAEES (2013) Vol.1, No.1, 41-53.

Thapa, R., Kumar, R., & Sood, R. K. (2008). Study of Morphotectonics and Hydrogeology for Ground Water

Prospecting using Remote Sensing and GIS in the North West Himalaya, District Sirmour, Himachal Pradesh, India. The International Archieve of the Photogrammetry, Remote Sensing and Spatial Information Science, XXXVII(B4).

(1978). Urban Geology of the Twin Cities of Hyderabad-Secundarabad and Delhi. Geological Survey of India, Government of India. GSI Miscellaneous Publication No. 42, Kolkata,43.

Wadhawan, S. K. (2010). Geoenvironmental Studies in India, Glimpses of Geoscience Research in India. Retrieved January 1, 2014

Walia, V., Mahajan, S., Kumar, A., Singh, S., Bajwa, B. S., Dhar, S., & Yanga, T. F. (2008). Fault delineation study using soil-gas method in the Dharamsala area. ScienceDirect. Retrieved from www.sciencedirect.com

MAKING OUR CULTURAL FAIRS ECO-FRIENDLY: A CASE STUDY OF LUCKNOW MAHOTSAV

Preeti Madan Sharma

Manyawar Kanshiram Institute of Tourism Management (MKITM) Kusum Kunj, Behind Hydel Colony, Prag Narain Road, Lucknow-226001, preetimadan@rediffmail.com

Abstract: Eco-friendly practices are the most critical need of the hour and must be followed with complete dedication. The gravity of the situation comes across whenever we see the dilapidated condition of our historical, cultural and natural heritage. Annual Cultural Fairs and Festivals are an area which has yet not been considered seriously enough to come under the scanner of eco-friendly practices and norms. The research paper proposes to identify areas which should be concentrated upon to make such events an asset to the community in all respects, whether it is cultural, ecological or economic.

There is much to be desired in the administration and management of such events, especially in the field of environmentally friendly practices. This could be initiated in the simple practice of banning polybags to planned development of green zones, pollution control and setting-up of proper garbage disposal units. The paper studies in detail the arrangements of the annual event organized by the Uttar Pradesh Tourism Department, the Lucknow Mahotsav. Efforts have been made to evaluate the existing arrangements and draw out the positive and lacking areas in the planning and execution of the eco-friendly practices.

The issue of bringing in eco-friendly practices in the tourism sector and facing the challenges thereof cannot be avoided any further and need to be resolved on urgent basis. Planning and managing such events on eco- friendly grounds is one of such challenge.The research paper strives to draw out an ecologically friendly model for such events so as to increase their environmental friendly quotient without compromising their intrinsic charm and commercial viability.

Keywords: eco-friendly practices, culture, pollution control, garbage disposal, green-zones.

Concept

It is becomingly increasingly important for event organisers to understand the environmental impact of their event, in the interest of sustainability, sound strategic management, cost effectiveness and maximizing sponsorship and funding.

In some cases, there may be an acceptance that an event will have some negative implications for the environment. Some event organisers may simply want to limit the scarce resources used in delivering the event and in so doing may put in place event management practices to demonstrate their commitment to limiting such consumption. Others will identify positive environmental impacts and, in these cases, developing a strategy to capture such impacts is critical.

Objective

- The aim of the study is to carve out a model for the ecological and economical success of annual cultural events.
- To study the management, coordination and practices adopted at Lucknow Mahotsav, the annual cultural festival celebrated at Lucknow, Uttar Pradesh.

Research Methodology

The first step was to collect background information. This was done through books, brochures and websites on the city and Lucknow Mahotsav. The next step was to take gain firsthand information about the event and its management especially with regard to eco-friendly practices. A questionnaire was prepared to gather information from the attendees, stall owners and management to get an insight into this area. All this helped immensely to understand the working and essence of the event and to develop a workable model for an eco friendly event.

Introduction

Hosting environment friendly events is the immediate need of the hour. Mere green washing the event for the sake of adhering to rules and policies will neither resolve the problem of environment degradation nor will it set the ground for others to follow green practices. The study aims to develop a step by step model for organisers of major events to ensure their event is both successful and more environmentally responsible. It outlines ways to develop and implement an environmental strategy and action plan, and offers practical tips, resources and checklists. It is critical for organisers to adhere to such models as it brings to the valuable source of ideas for reducing their event's environmental impacts in many key areas - from choosing supplies and contractors, to managing waste and resource use, transport, energy, water and greenhouse gas emissions (Allen,2005).

The first time that environmental concerns were raised by the public was at the 1992 Albertville Winter Olympics in France, which led to the first 'green Games' in Lillehammer, Norway, in 1994. The Lillehammer Olympic Organizing Committee received the UNEP Global 500 Award for setting environmental standards which were absent from previous Olympic games. Environmental Guidelines for the Summer Olympics were developed to guide Olympic hosts to ensure that facilities are constructed in a more environmentally friendly manner. Event greening is however not only limited to sports events,

Sustainable event management is the process used to organize and manage an event with particular concern for environmental, economic and social issues. Sustainability in event management incorporates socially and environmentally responsible decision making into the planning, organization and implementation of, and participation in, an event. It involves including sustainable development principles and practices in all levels of event organization, and aims to ensure that an event is hosted responsibly. It represents the total package of interventions at an event, and needs to be done in an integrated manner (Allen,2005).. Event greening should start at the inception of the project, and should involve all the key role players, such as clients, organizers, venues, sub-contractors and suppliers.

Event Greening

Event greening makes good business sense and can mean a better experience for everyone involved. Hosting a more environmentally responsible event can:

- o Improve the experience of participants. For example, a well-functioning public transport system will reduce travel time, traffic congestion, exhaust fumes, and parking issues. Good waste reduction policies and an efficient recycling system will reduce the amount of waste at an event.
- o Position you as a leader by setting best practice standards for more environmentally responsible events. Demonstrating environmental commitment can also enhance relationships with customers and stakeholders.
- o Save money by reducing the cost of waste disposal, energy and water.
- o Help meet international expectations. Managing the environmental impacts is regarded as a core component of staging a world-class event. Significant efforts to reduce environmental impacts are made by the organisers of every major event like the 2006 FIFA Football World Cup in Germany, the 2006 Melbourne Commonwealth Games, the 2008 Beijing Olympics, the 2010 Vancouver Winter Olympics, and the 2010 FIFA Football World Cup in South Africa.
- o Help protect reputation of the state/country. An environmentally friendly tourism brand puts environmental performance prominently on the radar for visitors. By demonstrating efforts

to reduce the environmental impacts of major events, organisers can help safeguard 'clean and green' reputation.

- Help meet the expectations of the locals. Most countries, today, are concerned about environmental impacts. They are aware of the significant environmental problems the world faces as a result of global warming. Many are interested in environmentally responsible products and services. As these proportions continue to grow, so too will public expectations for events that are more environmentally responsible.
- Create legacies by raising attendees' awareness, inspiring behaviour change, and influencing suppliers to adopt greener practices.
- Help the environment and local communities by creating new business opportunities, minimising greenhouse gas emissions, waste and the use of water and energy; and boosting local economies.

Levels of Impact

Environmental impacts have been broken down into three categories based upon the ease with which they can be measured.

1) Basic Impacts: The basic environmental impacts are in the real sense only about the presence (or not) of plans and systems to manage the way an event affects the environment.

Whilst this may seem simplistic, the presence of plans such as these would represent a big step forward for many events, and funders of events may therefore wish to simply measure whether events have these plans and systems in place.

Their presence is also seen as a valuable as these plans will typically involve a scoping and identification of more detailed environmental impacts that could be measured at an intermediate and advanced level.

2) Intermediate Impacts: Intermediate-level environmental impacts tend to focus around measurement of people's activities and perceptions around an event. If an event has tried hard to promote environmental best practice then it could be valuable to measure the impact this has had on spectators and attendees - firstly in terms of whether this has been noticed, and secondly whether people intend to change their own environmental behaviour as a result.

In terms of people's environmental activity around an event, it is relatively straight-forward to put in place tools which provide good benchmarks for organisers to measure year-on-year, for example total miles traveled by car/public transport. For certain events, organizers or funders may want to go one step further and translate people's responses into more formal measures of CO2 emissions.

Primarily these impacts will be secured through survey work. In the case of developing specific measures around areas such as carbon or waste, it will typically be necessary to use a specialist contractor who will be able to design appropriate survey tools, and who will be skilled in converting those responses into formal measures.

3) Advanced Impacts: Advanced environmental impacts are those which represent behavioral change on behalf of those connected to the event. Whilst these areas are difficult to measure, they represent a real area of opportunity for event organizers in that a positive environmental impact might be achieved through hosting. Offsetting the potentially harmful environmental impacts of an event might therefore be achieved not only through technical measures to address carbon or waste, but also by creating a positive impact on people's future environmental behavior

Phase of green event planning

The four key phases involved in developing and implementing the environmental strategy and action plan for a major event are as follows:

- o Planning the entire event
- o Before the event activities
- o During the event activities
- o After the event activities

It is important to start planning a greener event early; successfully implementing greening actions can require plenty of lead time. Another reason to start the planning process early is that an environmental strategy may be a minimum requirement to enter a bid process. It may also provide a compelling point of difference between competing bids. Given the geographic location, of many venues a good environmental plan could help counter concerns about the environmental impacts generated by participants travelling long distances to it.

Decisions made at the early planning stage can significantly influence the types of environmental impacts that arise from the event. For example, decisions about an event's location and venue can significantly affect the ability to reduce greenhouse gas emissions and impacts associated with transport, energy and water use. Wherever possible, those responsible for staging events should consider the potential environmental impacts of different locations and venues before making their final choice (Jones, 2010).

Charting out a green event

a. Mapping out the blueprint of the event this would bring the entire event and its requirements into perspective.

b. Identifying the crucial stakeholders some of them are listed below:

   Key stakeholders: Event organizer, venue owner(s), local government, central government, sponsors, suppliers/contractors, regional tourism operators, participants, spectators etc. Other stakeholders: Local community, interest groups such as local and international non-governmental organizations, sports and cultural organizations, advertising and merchandise providers, accommodation providers, transport operators, media and broadcasters.

   All of the above stakeholders can play an important role in promoting and endorsing greening actions associated with the event.

c. Drawing commitment from the event owner, event organizers and decision makers. Without the full commitment of the stakeholders it will not be possible to implement many of the initiatives needed to reduce environmental impacts. A commitment to greening initiatives by these key players also signals to other stakeholders to follow suit.

d. Assess and gauge the direct and indirect environmental impact of the event. Various factors which influence the environmental impacts that an event may have include:

   - o the type of event
   - o Whether it takes place at a single location or venue, or across a range of venues.
   - o the duration of the event - whether one day, one week or one month
   - o the time of year the event takes place
   - o where participants come from and how far they need to travel
   - o the food and beverages provided at the event
   - o Whether significant merchandising is involved.

   It may be possible for event organisers to have greater influence over certain environmental matters than they anticipate. For example by choosing venues, locations and suppliers that have organisational environmental policies and are undertaking greening actions, the event can utilise and build on these existing initiatives. This can save time and money. To help prioritise the environmental impacts, the strategy and action plan need to consider issues:

   - o with the most visual impact - eg, waste or traffic congestion
   - o with the most potential for cost savings or reductions - eg, waste and energy
   - o associated with the particular event - eg, water quality may be significant for a water-based event, whereas greenhouse gas emissions may be significant for a motor sport event

e. Determine the scope of the event and of the environment and an overview of identified impacts the event is likely to cause. For example:

   - o The focus areas that will be covered in the strategy (e.g. waste, transport) and those which are not included.
   - o What the strategy aims to achieve.
   - o The principles used when developing the strategy and action plan. These can be useful when communicating objectives, as

they prevent absolute statements which may be difficult to live up to (see below for examples).

- o How the aim of the strategy will be achieved. Ideally, there should be an objective for each chosen focus area (e.g. waste, transport, energy).
- o A measurable statement against which success can be measured (e.g. x per cent of waste diverted from landfill).
- o Key people (e.g., partners, suppliers) involved in ensuring the strategy is delivered.

f. Complete baseline assessment: If an event is held regularly and past data is available, it is useful to undertake a baseline assessment of the event's current and past environmental impacts. Used in conjunction with measurements taken while the event is underway, the baseline assessment can demonstrate improvements in environmental performance over time and provide the basis for success stories.

g. Green Purchasing: The materials, supplies and products used to produce an event all has the potential for negative environmental impacts. Through environmentally preferable purchasing reductions in these impacts can be achieved through the supply chain. Options to reduce environmental impacts of purchasing can be achieved through such things as; using products which have an eco-label, including organic, fair trade, FSC or other sustainable forestry products, VOC free, environmentally safer cleaning agents, PVC-free paints, sustainably produced foods, products made from sustainable and recyclable materials, etc.

h. Avoid Green washing means misleading consumers about a company's environmental practices or about the environmental benefits of a product, service or event.

i. Carving out the environmental strategy and action plan: The strategy needs to set out what is going to be done to reduce the environmental impacts of hosting an event, and why this should be done. The action plan sets out how the aims, objectives and targets identified in the strategy will be achieved. It needs to clearly link to the strategy each of the chosen focus areas. For example, why is it important to reduce waste at this event? Or certain venues may already have composting and recycling facilities in place. For each of the focus areas outlined in the strategy. The steps that must be taken to achieve the objectives and targets. The person(s) or organization(s) responsible for undertaking each action. When each action will be completed. How targets will be measured to demonstrate they have been achieved. The measurement may be quantifiable and/or qualitative.

j. Setting targets is essential for measuring success. It is important to consider the kind of measurement that will be possible, what data can be collected, and any systems that may need to be put in place at the outset to enable data collection.

k. Funding and sponsorship in adequate quantities for greening initiatives is crucial to ensure the objectives set out in the strategy and action plan can be implemented and achieved. However, it is also important to consider the cost effectiveness of proposed actions; otherwise, large amounts of money may be spent to achieve only small environmental gains. Spending on environmental actions needs to be appropriate and realistic for the event. Actions that have longer-term benefits (e.g. establishing permanent recycling facilities at a venue) may be more cost effective than one-off actions that may appear initially less costly. Considering the expectations of stakeholders may help determine whether to undertake an action.

Sponsorship is another potential source of funding. A growing number of businesses have well-developed environmental responsibility policies and seek to align themselves positively with such initiatives by becoming sponsors of, or suppliers to, major events that have a 'green' or community focus.

During this period, the targets and actions identified during the planning phase are investigated and - providing they are cost effective - implemented in readiness for the event.

The implementation phase is a good time to think about what training staff and volunteers may require. Ensuring these people understand the planned greening actions is important, as they are the ones who will interact with attendees or spectators. Training staff and volunteers to be 'green champions' on site can increase the likelihood of attendees participating in greening activities, such as recycling, and continuing such activities in their personal lives.

l. Green volunteers or green champions
    - o Selection - The ability to role-model green behaviour should be a criterion for selecting volunteers.
    - o Training- Ensuring volunteers understand the event's environmental strategy should be a key priority during training.
    - o Management - Staff who will manage volunteers also need to understand and support the greening initiatives.

m. Event delivery is the most crucial part where the event takes place and the benefits from the environmental strategy and action plan are realized. During the event, the focus should be on:
    - o Monitoring progress: Monitoring progress throughout the implementation process will provide confidence that things are progressing to plan. When and how progress is to be reported should be covered in the strategy and action plan; so too should the groups (e.g. venue owners, suppliers) responsible for providing necessary information.
    - o Overseeing activities - for example, ensuring recycling stations are working efficiently and being used correctly by attendees.
    - o Engaging visitors and the wider public through signage, loud-speaker announcements and promotions.
    - o Measuring impacts - capturing key data to demonstrate that targets have been met and aims achieved.

n. Adequate post-event analysis and assessment, it is difficult to determine how successful greening actions have been and what lessons have been learnt. During this phase, the focus should be on:
    - o Analysing the data collected against targets set in the strategy and plan
    - o Reviewing the action plan and receiving feedback from stakeholders about what worked well and what could have been done differently

- o Providing feedback to suppliers and venue owners so they can improve their services for future events
- o Communicating the results to the event owner, attendees, future organizers of the event, and other groups interested in the actions undertaken. It is important to share the greening successes and lessons learnt.

The Lucknow Mahotsav

The city of Lucknow, spread evenly on both sides of the Gomti offers a tourist plenty of places of historical interest. The legacy of the imperial splendor of Lucknow has always fascinated people all over the world. The ambience of Avadh has commonly been associated with leisurely habits, etiquette, architecture, food and refinement-the city has preserved this spirit of the bygone days. Lucknow took almost two centuries to grow to the size of a metropolis. The first hundred years of success belonged to the Nawab Wazirs who, in different degrees contributed to its growth and made it, what has metaphorically called, the "Shiraz of Avadh", & the "Constantinople of India". The Nawabs were responsible for imparting a distinct image to the city, which indeed is unique. They worked meticulously to dress Lucknow with religious and secular edifices of incomparable excellence. The city has the colour of culture in its every nook and corner.

Lucknow Mahotsava is organized every year to showcase Uttar Pradesh Art and Culture and in particular Lucknowavi 'Tehzeeb and Nazaakat' so as to promote Tourism. The year 1975-76 was observed and organized in South Asia as The Tourism Year. On this occasion, to promote Lucknow's Art, Culture and Tourism for national and international tourists, the decision to organize the Lucknow Festival was taken. Since then, with exception of a few years Lucknow Mahotsava has been organized every year. Lucknow Mahotsava is usually adorned with performances by the celebrities, famous artists' and on the other by renounced classical singers. In this program the upcoming local artists are provided a special representation on the cultural evenings. In addition, the national as well as local Shayars (Poets) are also provided due representation through Kavi Sammelans and Mushayaras.

An Agricultural Fair is also organized to accommodate the participation and representation of peasants. Crafts work from approximately 20 regions is displayed in the Crafts fair.

To give the Exhibition a grand outlook all the stalls have similar facials. Lucknow's Art and Culture is also portrayed through replicas of the various famous architectural monuments and mannequins; these are exhibited at different strategic points across the Mahotsava premises.

On this occasion, other attractions like 'Ekka Tonga' Race, Kite Competition, Boat Race, Vintage Car Rally, Youth festival and Drama Competition are also organized for public interest. Participation is invited from various age groups in these events.

The duty for cleanliness and the parking arrangements is done by Nagar Nigam. For public convenience extra buses are arranged by the Uttar Pradesh State Road Transport Corporation. In addition auto, cabs etc are also arranged and specially tagged for Mahotsava purpose. For security maintenance CCTV cameras have been placed strategically across the ground, nearby police stations are also kept on alert and security agencies are hired to provide guards. All the routes to Mahotsava venue have active police patrolling on it.

Lucknow Mahotsava Samiti installs Gas Balloons, Public Hoardings and Banners etc. all over the city for the publicity of this Grand Event. Other Departments like Tourism, Local District Administration, Police Department, Lucknow Developmental Authority, Jal Nigam and Electricity Board are the helping hands of Lucknow Mahotsava Samiti.

Green Planning the Lucknow Mahotsav

There are many areas where the organizing committee can have a positive impact when hosting an event. Greening practices are practical things that can be done to encourage sustainable living and the Mahotsav can raise its standard and take its reputation to another level by adopting the following greening practices while planning and executing the Lucknow Mahotsav:

- Green purchasing: This must be the thumb rule for the purchasing committee, all purchases whether tangible or intangible must be through organizations and institutions that believe and practice environmental friendly policies.

- Waste management: REDUCE, RE-USE, RECYCLE this must be the premier mantra to be followed in all practices related to waste management. Biodegradable materials should be used in every way possible. The use of polythene should be abolished and done away with altogether.
- Efficient energy utilization: The possible option is zero-emission resources like the solar energy. Annual events and venues that are used on a regular basis must work towards developing resources which are energy efficient, renewable and minimum in producing harmful emissions.
- Water conservation: this can only and only achieved through no-tolerance policy for water wastage. A system for minimization of sewage and grey-water must also be put into place for conserving this very precious resource.
- Emissions reduction: The carbon footprint of an event is the total impact of the event relating to the total amount of CO2 emitted due to the consumption of fossil fuels. This would include aspects such as the energy consumption, the waste generated, marketing, transport, flights, accommodation, and other actions that would contribute to climate change. This must be given proper attention and requires all-round surveillance to reduce emission. Although this cannot be completely done away with but can certainly be reduced drastically if the organizing committee put in control systems at various levels and stages.
- Biodiversity conservation: The scheme for planting trees in and around the venue must be the all year round agenda for the organizers. The organizers must give back to the environment whatever they take through protecting, conserving and developing the flora and fauna of the event destination, in this case the city of Lucknow.
- Social and economic development: Event greening is not only about the environment, but needs to consider the social and economic benefits to the local community as well. By stimulating

the local economy and social development, the whole community will benefit from the event, and this will support poverty alleviation in the long term.Initiatives to stimulate the local economy and empower the host community should be incorporated into greening activities whenever possible. This can be done by purchasing local products, skills training and job creation.

Greening the Lucknow Mahotsav

As, the Lucknow Mahotsav is an annual event organized by the Department of Tourism, Government Uttar Pradesh with the help and support of various other departments. It must be mandatory for the Lucknow Mahotsav Committee to be active throughout the year. This is essential with the view of pro-active environmental friendly planning and implementation. A survey was conducted to gain insight into the eco-friendly practices followed in the Mahotsav. The attached questionnaire was filled in randomly by participants, local community, stall owners and the organizers. Inferences were drawn and certain suggestions and recommendations were drawn through those results.

As the Lucknow Mahotsav is a highly resource-intensive event, and can have negative environmental consequences for the host city and population, therefore it must be hosted in an environmentally, socially and economically responsible way. The initiative must be taken to make event greening a part of the tender process for the Mahotsav. This would not only reduce the negative environmental impact, but would also leave a positive and lasting legacy for the local community.

Following are a few strategic points which should be considered and adopted by the organizers, participants, service providers and the local community:

- o Positive reputation: An event is a very visible demonstration of commitment to sustainability, and your support of actions against the negative influence of environment degradation and global warming. Thus the Uttar Pradesh government must utilize this annual opportunity to portray a positive image of itself as an eco-friendly destination. Gradually this positivity will not only influence its Tourism sector but other industries as well.

- o Cost savings through conserving energy, reducing waste, purchasing local products, and simply consuming less can save money. This should be the parallel mantra for the organizing committee of the Lucknow Mahotsav. Although some green practices are not cost efficient but planning ways around them could prove to be a worthwhile effort for all concerned parties.
- o Environmental innovation: Greening efforts promote innovative technologies and techniques, which help us to use resources more efficiently. These innovations will not only bring in a lot of fresh ideas for the green planning of the Mahotsav but will also prove to be a basis for encouragement to the stakeholders and their reputation.
- o Creating Awareness: this will bring forth a unique opportunity to raise awareness among the various stakeholders of the Mahotsav, such as, participants, staff, service providers and the local community about the benefits of sustainable living, and enhance pro-environmental practice in the region.
- o Social benefits will be an intrinsic advantage if the Mahotsav is planned and implemented carefully, it will not only benefit the local region through providing jobs, selecting regional suppliers, promoting better working conditions, and acting as a catalyst for social improvement.
- o Return on investment: By establishing green standards, the Mahotsav organizers will not only reduce costs, but also increase strategic opportunities.

Conclusion

Event greening is the need of the hour and therefore cannot be dealt on a superficial basis by event organizers whether the event is high, medium or low budget. The event might be low, medium or high profile but the environmental considerations to make it eco-friendly must be put into place with the same sincerity.

We have been green-washing our events since the last few decades with minimum or no results. Now it is time to put in real effort and make the events green inside out. The seriousness of effort must be evident in the regeneration of the environment. This again requires the entire machinery, consisting of the stakeholders, to be oiled and should run smoothly and efficiently. This is only possible if there is coordination among various parts of the functioning machinery.

Awareness in general and especially amongst the host community can prove to be the most critical of all points. This could either make or break the whole philosophy of executing green events.

Monitoring and evaluation is an essential component of event greening, and should be used to make continuous improvement. A detailed plan needs to be in place to ensure that information is gathered on all aspects of the event - before, during, and also after the event. This ensures that information is available to understand the effects of greening interventions. With large events it is best to ensure an independent report, which complies with international standards. This would give the Lucknow Mahotsav an unbiased, and with time, not only a national rather an international platform.

References

Allen, J. (2005) Time Management for Event Planners. New York: Wiley

Getz, D. (2007) Event Studies: Theory, Research and Policy for Planned Events. Oxford: Butterworth-Heinemann.

Jones, M. (2010) Sustainable Event Management: A Practical guide. New York: Earthscan

Masterman, G. and Wood, E. (2005) Innovative Marketing Communications: Strategies for the Events Industry. Oxford: Butterworth-Heinemann.

Raj, R., Walters, P., Rashid, T. (2008) Events Management: An Integrated and Practical Approach. London: Sage.

www.lucknowmahotsav.com (10 December, 2013, 13:45) Statistics provided by the Tourism Department, Uttar Pradesh.

RURAL TOURISM: AN INNOVATIVE APPROACH FOR SUSTAINABLE DEVELOPMENT

Amit Katoch

Research Scholar (Tourism), Central University of Himachal Pradesh, Dharamsala, Kangra, Himachal Pradesh, M No +91-9418385084, amitkatoch2007@gmail.com

Abstract: The concept of rural tourism is the new buzz word for developing tourism at village level. It is a form of tourism which occurs at rural locations, showcases our rural culture and benefits the rural population socio-economically. The Indian villages are live witnesses of Indian culture and natural beauty along with cordial behaviour of the hosts. But prior to involving the concept of rural tourism, it is very important to understand the culture and social setup of the village in order to propagate the concept. This research article highlights the concept of rural tourism and emphasize on sustainable tourism development. The study has been conducted in Himachal Pradesh and is based on review of tourism policy, related literature and experts' opinion. The paper concludes that the state is having great potential for rural tourism, if planned carefully and promoted strategically.

Keywords: Rural Tourism, Sustainable Tourism.

Introduction

Rural tourism has time and again been well thought-out to be an antidote for rural demur, and as a means for creating employment, economic growth and ultimately to rural development. In a country like India, where 74% of the population resides in its 7 million villages, this concept can be very beneficial. It can be used to improve the socio-economic condition at the level of villages. Tourism in villages will lead to local community development through entrepreneurial prospects, employment opportunities, development of arts and crafts, financial assets for infrastructure development, preservation of the environment and heritage. Rural tourism not only helps in the progress of the rural areas, but also provides an opportunity to the urban population to have interface with its roots.

Rural tourism can also give great impetus to the agriculture at village level. But, at the same time, we should not forget that rural tourism has got great dimensions. It has also got great budding for other sections of tourism such as cultural tourism, nature tourism, ecotourism, geotourism, adventure tourism, religious tourism and farm tourism. The rural tourism studies in Europe have shown that it has made a considerable contribution to individual cultivators as well as to local community. This strategy was adopted primarily to economically restructure the rural economies & attract the domestic population from cities. (Kouli & Kumar, 2012; Williams & Shaw, 1998; Hoggard, Buller, & Black, 1995; The green light: a guide to sustainable tourism,1991). However, if you take case of India, then it can be a new niche for the domestic as well as foreign tourists.

But apart from the affirmative effects, tourism at times also has a negative side such as the imitation of foreign models by the local community, the commercialisation of human interactions, the transformation of regions of exceptional natural beauty into over satiated urban regions, the pollution of the surroundings, the pessimistic cultural changes, etc, (Kokkosis & Tsartas, 2001). Tourism is often criticized for its evil or monstrous effects (Romeril, 1985; Vanhove, 1997) which result in demolition of tourist regions & their cultural fabric.

But, in addition rural tourism is a complicated undertaking as rural areas suffer from problem of depopulation, competition of labour etc. Also, very little practical research in rural tourism has further aggravated the problem & there is no solid base for support to regional and village tourism initiatives. So, the tourism initiatives are not based on knowledge or strategic planning, but are implemented randomly. The rural tourism is standing on the crossroads, where one direction points to a promising future & development, while the short term vision is limiting the concept to unfold its wings. Greater production and integration of knowledge into rural tourism seems to be a good step towards realizing the potential of rural tourism for sustaining rural communities. (Muller, et al., 2012)

We need to understand Indian rurality in its actual form. This means that an Indian village is diverse in many respects such as its culture, traditions, folklore, cuisines, dances, art, craft and surroundings.

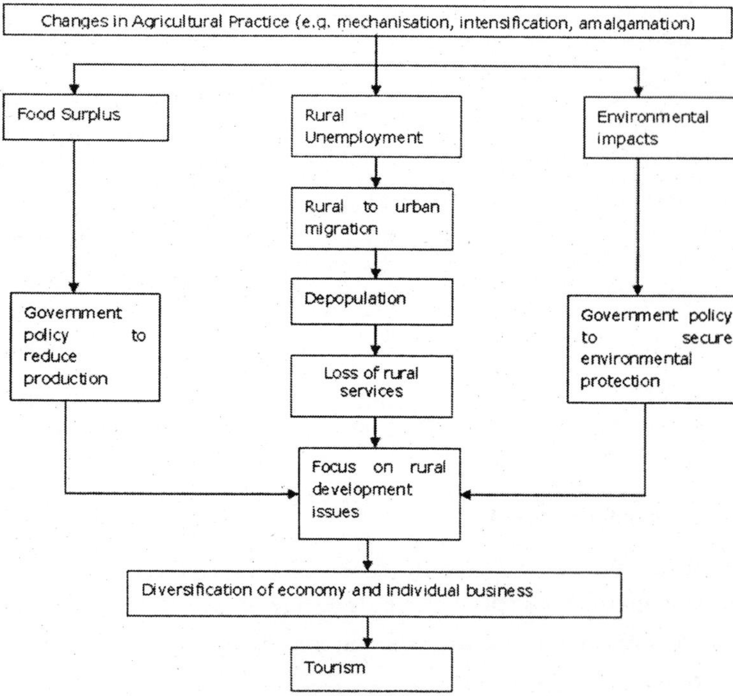

Figure1: The context of rural tourism

Source: Thompson learnıng ((Sharley & Sharpley, 1997)

But, if we see the policies & schemes, they are implemented randomly rather than in a way that can cause significant effect at the grass root level. If we really want to implement the concept for the common good of the local community, then we need to realize that results of tourism in villages cannot be got by simply propagating the concept, but by implementing them in an effective way through involvement of the locals. Also, the review report given by the ministry of India and UNDP (2008) of the Endogenous Tourism Project, Rural Tourism Scheme implemented in 2003 highlights that due thought and attention should be given before expanding rural tourism sites in India as each site needs focused and individual attention. It further recommended establishment of a facilitation centre within the union ministry of tourism for co-ordination of tourism activities with the state boards & ministries; a incentive fund to promote experimentation, duplication and propagation of practices and establishing an innovation register; and setting up of a centre for learning, innovation and practice on rural tourism. And surely this rural tourism centre will not serve as a project management tool rather a resource centre to put together and share learning & best services. (Sustainability in Tourism- A Rural Tourism Model, 2008)

But prior to implementing the concept of rural tourism, the willingness of villagers should be taken prior to such projects. As when villagers, know that huge expenditure would be done in their villages by government, then they are ready to involve rather than by choice (Sustainability in Tourism- A Rural Tourism Model, 2008). Also, the type of rural environment and tourism product should also be clear, according to which model of rural tourism should be adopted.

Objectives of research:

The broad objectives of the study are:

1. To highlight the concept of rural tourism from global perspective.
2. To review the rural tourism policy in Himachal Pradesh.
3. To project rural tourism, an innovative approach for sustainable development.

Research methodology:

The basic motive of the study is to highlight the role of rural tourism, by its implementation in a sustainable way. The study has been done by reviewing the tourism policy, related literature, magazines, journals and presenting opinion of the experts. The example has been taken of the state of Himachal Pradesh which has got the unique rural blend of culture.

Rural Tourism Policy in Himachal Pradesh:

The appearance in which rural tourism is currently taking shape can be traced to an International Conference and Exhibition on Rural Tourism in India organised by Federation of Indian Chambers of Commerce and Industry (FICCI) in association with the Udaipur Chambers of Commerce and Industry in Udaipur (Rajasthan) in 2001 (From Rural Tourism to Sustainable Rural Tourism, 2006). The consequence of this event was that Union Ministry of Tourism and culture; Rural Development; Other nodal Agencies and FICCI mapped a 10 year project for developing Rural tourism in India. Also, A.F.Fergusson was given task of studying this project and estimated that each one million visitors to India can lead to Rs. 4300 crore returns for the Indian Industry. In India rural tourism scheme started in the year 2002 under the National Tourism Policy, with the objective of highlighting rural life, art, culture and heritage at rural locations and in villages which have core competence in art, craft, handloom, textiles and natural environment. Also, it lead to the Endogenous Tourism Project, Rural Tourism Scheme by the Ministry of Tourism and UNDP in 2003 with five core objectives such as capacity building at the local level; involve location specific models of the community tourism enterprise; build community private partnersips; sustain supportive & promising initiatives and provide inputs to the national & state level tourism policies. As, such rural tourism project was also implemented at Himachal Pradesh at Naggar. Though, rural tourism activities were also initiated at other locaions consequently.

The Home stay scheme was also launched in 2008 in Himachal pradesh to augument rural tourism and decongest the urban areas. Also, this scheme has proved to be very popular among locals and over 332 units registered by February 2011. (Tourism in Himachal Pradesh and way ahead, 2012) And this scheme further provided the platform required for rural tourism. Har Gaon Ki Kahani, a tourism initiative was also launched by Himachal Pradesh Government in 2010 to promote the historical villages. As such one village in every twelve Districts were selected and fascinating tales, folklore and anecdotes related to these countrysides are used to entice tourists. This scheme endeavors at developing villages of historic significance as tourism villages by providing basic amenities and provides tourists a sneak to look into rustic living of the mountain state (KMPG, 2012). And a total budget outlay of Rs 20243.92 crore has been declared for this purpose. Through the ground-breaking scheme of 'Har Gaon Ki Kahani', rural infrastructure would be developed in Himachali hamlets for the endorsement of the rural tourism. In this programme there will be contribution of all government departments as well as the local community. This will give a major boost to the development of the rural areas besides promoting the local handicrafts, indigenous products and cultural activities. As per the plan one village from each district was selected such as Shamsher in Kullu, Salasi in Bilaspur, Bela in Hamirpur, Sangrah in Sirmour, Baggi in Mandi, Saho in Chamba, Nerti in Kangra, Udaipur in Lahaul & Spiti, Brua in Kinnaur, Baniya Devi in Solan, Hewan in Shimla and Nari in Una (Katoch & Gautam, 2013). Naggar in Kullu District; Garli Paragpur and Baroh in Kangra are three commissioned rural village sites in Himachal Pradesh. And, surely the potential in Himachal Pradesh is unlimited.

Sl. No.	**Name of the Villages in Himachal Pradesh**	**U.S.P.**
1.	Naggar (Kullu)	Topi & Shawl Weaving
2.	Paragpur (Kangra)	Himachal Heritage
3.	Baroh (Kangra)	Gurukul Culture

Figure 2: Commissioned rural village sites in Himachal Pradesh

In the twelfth five year plan (2012-2017), in order to develop rural tourism, emphasis has been given on cluster approach i.e. Rural Tourism Clusters (RTCs) rather than the single village approach. For a cluster of 6 villages a central financial assistance of 11 crore is recommended for physical infrastructure and capacity building. For each village a amount of Rupees 1.5 crore is allocated, keeping Rupees two crore for common facilities/ activities in each cluster.

Sustainable Rural tourism development in Himachal Pradesh:

Tourism is one of the leading and top growing industries in the world. It provides work for millions of populace and generates 9% of the worldwide GDP. In more than 150 countries, tourism is one of the five pinnacle export earners, and in 60 it is the number one export. It accounts to 6% of the world's exports amounting to US$ 1.3 trillion & generates one in eleven jobs. In India, too tourism has shown an impressive growth. It contributes 6.23 percent to the national GDP (WTTC) and provides 7.9% of the total employment in India (Ministry of Tourism, Government of India). Himachal Pradesh also shows good potential of Tourism. There has been a growth in the total number of tourist (domestic as well as foreign) from 88 lakhs in 2007 to 151 lakhs in 2011. There has been good performance in attracting tourists from the average growth of the number of tourists across India. Though the rank of the state is 13 in terms of tourists visiting the state in India. This further show that still there is a lot of scope to improve this figure.

Himachal offers a diverse tourism product to the tourists & surely it is "A destination for all seasons and all reasons. It offers nature tourism; pilgrimage tourism; ecotourism, adventure tourism, Heritage Tourism & still has space for many other types of tourism like rural tourism, geotourism etc. The 75% of its population lives in villages & so it is a new area, which can also be explored for sustainable development. Rural tourism development throughout the world was based on two fold motives of passing on socio-economic benefits to the local community and preserving the natural environment. The rural tourism can fetch a large number of positive benefits to the rural people in terms of economic, ecology and socio-cultural aspects. But at the same time, the rural tourism concept should be analyzed minutely to avoid the negative impacts caused by tourism.

Negative economic impacts	Negative ecological impacts	Negative Socio-cultural impacts
1. Lead to Commodification of local products	1. Leads to deterioration of biodiversity & life supporting systems.	1. Leads to change of lifestyle affecting the local culture.
2. Tourism may cause inflation in the local economy.	2. Unethical practices such as hunting causes ecological imbalance.	2. Increase the crime such as prostitution, child labour, drug abuse and gambling.
3. Exploitation of rural resources.	3. Leads to pollution -land, air & water.	3. Leads to vandalism of the local architecture.
4. Leakage of money & generate less benefit to the economy.	4. Infrastructure & superstructure leads to disturbance & distortion of landscape & land use.	4. Leads to competition among locals & hosts for local resources.
5. Due to the greater control of non-locals, the host community may search for livelihood options in cities.	5. Leads to pressure on local natural resources.	5. Leads to staged authencity rather than blend of original culture.
6. Rural population may be under paid.		6. Destroy overall culture of the place
7. The rural market may be flooded by urban products & in turn reduce the value of local products.		
8. Generate pressure on local resources.		

Figure 3: Negative impacts of Tourism (Katoch, Rural Tourism Development in India, 2014)

And hence to overcome it, we need sustainable tourism development. The development which looks after the resources, local community and also the guests. Tourism in rural environment is seen as a driving force for rural economic regeneration and as a way for valorizing preservation (Bramwell, 1990) (Brown & Leblanc, 1992) (Jamieson, 1990) (Bramwell B., 2005). Hence, rural tourism is an innovative tool to bring sustainable development at the villages.

The economy of Himachal Pradesh is dependent on farming, horticulture, forests and hydro power. Also, agro aligned industries such as sericulture, cattle farming, wool based industry and herbal based Industry are the main industries of Himachal Pradesh. A wide number of researches in the past have pointed out that scope of tourism is much more than the present scope in Himachal Pradesh. And this can only happen by the wider participation of local communities in tourism policy making can boost the local level democracy which is extensively associated with sustainable tourism development in general and ecotourism in particular. As the residents are the natural and potential custodians of their home area. (Parmar, 2012) Rural Tourism is now the new buzz word in Himachal Pradesh due to the rich culture it houses. Also, the rural areas are going into good tourist destinations due to the decline in traditional industries. Thus, this type of tourism can contribute significantly to the rural people of the state. In the state, both foreign and domestic tourists have shown growth.

But in order to percolate the concept of rural tourism in grassroot level, it should be sustainable and responsible in nature. In order to make villages notified & identified as rural tourism villages, the villages should have some uniqueness such as architecture, heritage & culture and an MOU is signed with Panchayat to maintain it. The villagers can modify their houses internally, but not externally. And, if the location of village is adjacent to some tourist destination then the dispersal of tourists can be easily done to the the rural site as well as marketing of the tourist product also becomes easier. The ministry of tourism also gives funding to create infrastructure like roads, streets, drainage, lighting, parking, bus stand, water supply, sanitation, tourist reception centre, rural museum, open air theatre, parks, nature trails ,crafts bazaar etc. Also, several funding schemes are available for weaker sections of society for renovating the homesteads. In such villages no luxury tax or commercial rates are there up to 5 bedroom homesteads.

Table 1: District wise Tourist inflow in Himachal Pradesh (2008-2010)

Table 1: District wise Tourist inflow in Himachal Pradesh (2008-2010)									
	2008			2009			2010		
District	**Indian**	**Foreigner**	**Total**	**Indian**	**Foreigner**	**Total**	**Indian**	**Foreigner**	**Total**
Bilaspur	683761 (7.30)	190 (.05)	683951	886495 (8.03)	170 (.05)	886665	962061 (7.50)	86 (.02)	962147
Chamba	644309 (6.37)	3853 (1.05)	648262	686136 (6.22)	3353 (0.84)	689489	786163 (6.12)	3253 (0.72)	789416
Hamirpur	279745 (2.98)	53 (0.01)	279798	432433 (3.92)	34 (0.01)	432467	554970 (4.33)	12 (0.003)	554982
Kangra	1275155 (13.61)	70819 (18.80)	1345964	1403963 (12.72)	75549 (18.86)	1479512	1631232 (12.73)	91709 (20.22)	1722941
Kinnaur	147754 (1.58)	20773 (5.51)	168527	271287 (2.46)	13811 (3.45)	285098	384963 (3.00)	18742 (4.13)	403705
Kullu	2001674 (21.36)	112910 (29.97)	2114584	2224649 (20.16)	119514 (29.84)	2344163	2395990 (18.70)	133707 (29.48)	2529697
Lahaul Spiti	172931 (1.85)	41398 (10.99)	214329	251415 (2.28)	65101 (16.25)	316516	362660 (2.83)	59125 (13.03)	421785
Mandi	603086 (6.43)	9154 (2.43)	612248	869904 (7.88)	8070 (2.01)	877974	1006418 (7.86)	10485 (2.31)	1016903
Shimla	2061539 (21.99)	112917 (29.97)	2174456	2175314 (19.71)	108981 (27.21)	2284295	2485564 (19.40)	127737 (28.16)	2613301
Sirmaur	575798 (6.14)	1785 (0.47)	577583	653668 (5.92)	2090 (0.52)	655758	748599 (5.84)	2712 (0.60)	787311
Solan	480125 (5.12)	2693 (0.71)	482818	586388 (5.31)	3811 (0.95)	590199	673932 (5.26)	5780 (1.27)	679712
Una	446820 (4.77)	91 (0.02)	446911	594920 (5.39)	99 (0.03)	595019	819461 (6.40)	268 (0.06)	819729
Total	9372697 (100.00)	376736 (100.00)	9744433	11036572 (100.00)	400583 (100.00)	11437155	12811986 (100.00)	453616 (100.00)	13305602

Source: Directorate of Tourism and Civil Aviation, Government of Himachal Pradesh. (Figures in parentheses denotes percentages to the column totals)

But apart from the government initiatives the villagers should also work in a cohesive & integrated way to implement concepts of tourism and policies of government by having a sound knowledge about these aspects. A rural tourism awareness campaign should be launched prior to rural tourism activity, so that the sustainable development occurs & that negative impacts w.r.t economic, social and ecological could be avoided. (Katoch& Gautam, 2013).

Table-2 Tourist Arrival in Himachal Pradesh(2000-2011) (in lacs)

Year	Domestic	Percentage increase/ decrease	Foreigner	Percentage increase/ decrease	Total	Percentage increase/ decrease
2000	45.70		1.11		46.81	
2001	51.11	11.84	1.33	19.82	52.44	12.03
2002	49.6	-2.95	1.44	8.27	51.04	-02.67
2003	55.44	11.77	1.68	0.17	57.12	11.91
2004	63.45	14.45	2.04	21.43	65.49	14.65
2005	69.28	8.42	2.08	1.96	71.36	08.96
2006	76.72	10.74	2.82	0.36	79.54	11.46
2007	84.82	10.55	3.39	20.21	88.21	10.90
2008	93.72	10.49	3.77	11.21	97.49	10.52
2009	110.37	17.77	4.01	6.37	114.38	17.32
2010	128.12	16.08	4.54	13.22	132.66	15.98
2011	146.04	13.98	4.84	6.60	150.89	13.74
2012	156.46		5.00		161.46	

Source: Directorate of Tourism and Civil Aviation, Government of Himachal Pradesh.

The issues like high joblessness levels, migration of better educated community members to urban areas and loss of public services have endangered the framework and structure of rural areas (OECD, 1993). All this has compelled the policy makers & rural chiefs to actively consider recreation & tourism as an economic development base in rural areas & benefit the local area by local job creation, environmental preservation, low investment cost, active role of women and closer urban rural contact. (OECD, 1994; Sharpley and Sharpley, 1997; Sharpley, 2002). Tourism is a good option in remote & peripheral areas where other development options cannot be worked out easily. (Busby and Rendle, 2000; Kline, 2001). The amount of rural tourism is difficult to compute on a worldwide basis (OECD, 1994), but may possibly cover 10-20% of all tourism activities (Henegan, 2002).

No doubt there are great expectations with regard to influence & potential of tourism throughout the world, but despite it should not be taken as economic & development panacea(Binns and Nel, 2002; Ribeiro and Marques, 2002). This clearly points out that whether we implement any type of Tourism the development strategies should be well researched, well funded and thoughtfully implemented.

Limitations of your research:

The research is simply based on the review of literature of reports, research papers, books, articles and surely can be supported further by conducting a practical research in Himachal Pradesh. The rural tourism as a whole is a complex phenomenon and its context may vary from place to place. Hence the above research is only limited to the state & cannot be generalized in other areas completely, rather selectively.

Conclusion:

Rural tourism is a sustainable development tool by which we can develop the rural backward areas. But, it's very important to first of all bring Tourism awareness in these areas and carry out a study to understand the cultural fabric of that place. Then only, we can implement the rural tourism concept in up righteous form. Government policies cannot alone bring great benefits through rural tourism, but cohesiveness and integration of the local community is equally important.

Rural tourism in itself is a complex phenomenon. Also, the tourism initiatives are not based on knowledge or strategic planning, but are implemented randomly. Hence, rural tourism for sustainable development needs a long term vision rather than a short term vision. Also, greater production and integration of Knowledge can further lead to sustainable tourism development.

References: .

Binns, T., & Nel, E. (2002). Tourism as a local development strategy in South Africa. The geographical journal(168), 235-247. Retrieved January 19, 2014

Bramwell, B. (1990). Shades of Green:Working Towards Green Tourism in the countryside. london: English Tourist Board.

Bramwell, B. (2005, August). Sustainable Tourism Strategies: A R Tool for Development and Conservation. Interamerican Journal of Environment and Tourism, 1(1). Retrieved January 21, 2014

Brown, V., & Leblanc, F. (1992). The Ontario Heritage Regions Projects. Ottawa: Heritage Canada.

Busby, G., & Rendle, S. (2000). The Transition from Tourism on Farms to Farm Tourism. Tourism Management(21), 635-642. Retrieved January 19, 2014 (2006, June). From Rural Tourism to Sustainable Rural Tourism. Bangalore: Equations. Retrieved January 18, 2014

Henegan, M. (2002). Structures and Processes in Rural Tourism. Rural Development Conference. Teagasc, Ireland.

Hoggard, K., Buller, H., & Black, R. (1995). Rural Europe: Identity and change. London: Arnold. Retrieved January 19, 2014

Jamieson, W. (1990). Maintaining and Enhancing the Sense of Place for Small Communities and Regions. University of Calgary.

Katoch, A. (2014). Rural Tourism Development in India. Pacific Hospitality Review.

Katoch, A., & Gautam, P. (2013, November 16). Rural tourism as a medium for local development in Himachal Pradesh: The example of villages around Dharamshala (Kangra). Sanghol, Punjab, India. Retrieved January 5, 2014

Kline, J. D. (2001). Tourism and National Resources Services Management: a General Overview of Research and Issues. Washington DC: USDA Forestry Services.

Kokkosis, H., & Tsartas, P. (2001). Sustainable Development of Tourism and the environment. Kritiki Publishers.

Kouli, R. S., & Kumar, K. (Eds.). (2012, May). Kurukshetra, Vol. 60 No.7, p. 52. Retrieved January 18, 2014, from www.publicationsdivision.nic.in

Muller, D., Halkier, H., Thor, F., Personen, J., Tahvainen, N., Rnusmen, R.,. .. Taatein, T. (2012). Lillehammer. Retrieved January 17, 2014, from http://www.nordregio/Publications/Publication-2013/small-scale-Tourism-in-Rural-Areas/

Parmar, J. S. (2012, may). Tourism an engine to economic growth in the rural economy of Himachal Pradesh. (R. S. Kouli, & K. Kumar, Eds.) Kurukshetra, 60(7), p. 52. Retrieved January 19, 2014, from publicationsdivision.nic.in

Ribeiro, M., & Marques, C. (2002). Rural tourism and the development of less favoured areas - between rhetoric and practice.

International journal of tourism research(4), 211-220. Retrieved January 19, 2014

Romeril, M. (1985). Tourism and the environment: towards a symbiotic relationship. International Journal of Environmental Studies, 25(No. 4), 215-218. Retrieved January 18, 2014

Rural Tourism and Challenge of Tourism Diversification: the case of Cyprus. (2002). Tourism Management(23), 233-244. Retrieved January 19, 2014

Sharley, J., & Sharpley, R. (1997). Rural Tourism: An Introduction. London: International Thompson learning press.

Sharpley, R., & Sharpley, J. (1997). Rural Tourism: an Introduction. Boston: International Thomson Business.

(2008). Sustainability in Tourism- A Rural Tourism Model. Ministry of Tourism, Government of India & UNDP India. Bangalore: Equations. Retrieved january 18, 2014

(1991). The green light: a guide to sustainable tourism. London: European Tourism Board.

(2012). Tourism in Himachal Pradesh and way ahead. KMPG, PHD Chamber of Commerce and Industry, Shimla. Retrieved January 21, 2014, from www.kmpg & www. phdcci.in

(1994). Tourism Policy and International Tourism in OECD Countries. Paris: Organisation for Economic Co-operation and Development.

Vanhove, N. (1997). Mass tourism: Benefits and costs. London: Routledge.

(1993). What future for our countryside? A rural development policy. Paris: Organisation for Economic Co-operation and Development.

Williams, A., & Shaw, G. (1998). Tourism and economic development: European experiences (Eds ed.). Chichester: Wiley.

AN APPROACH FOR SUSTAINABLE TOURISM DEVELOPMENT IN MOUNTAINS: A CASE STUDY OF SHIMLA ENVIRONS

Punit Gautam

Associate Professor Dept. of Tourism & Hotel Management North-Eastern Hill University (NEHU), Shillong, punitgautam@yahoo.co.uk

Pallavi Thakur

Research Scholar- CMT&HS HNB Garhwal University, Srinagar, Uttarakhand pallavithakur.tourism@gmail.com

Abstract: Himachal Pradesh with its spectacular mountains cape is a paradise for tourists. Himachal Pradesh lies in the lap of Himalayas with a topography which varies from foothills of the Shivalik ranges to lofty mountains in the interior of the Himachal Pradesh which separates it from Tibet. It provides ample opportunities for all kind of touristic activities particularly adventure activities such as trekking, ice-skating, day hikes, camping, para-gliding, mountain climbing, heli-sing skiing, white water rafting, kayaking etc

The magnet of mountain tourism in H.P. is the capital city, Shimla, which was India's summer capital during the British occupation and after independence became a popular tourist destination. In recent years, Shimla has developed into an ill-reputed center of environment degradation. The touristic value of Shimla appears to be on the decline because environmental problems have severely inhibited its capacity to attract tourists. Remedial actions have been formulated, but excess stress on carrying capacity and unsustainable development continues to occur, indicating failure of existing policies or their ineffective enforcement. This paper conceives new methods and ideas like identifying satellite tourist destinations, minimizing undesirable environmental and socio-cultural impacts of tourism, generate and retain tourism income in the local economy and diversify tourism products which are needed to reduce overcrowding in such areas and to promote tourism in sustainable manner in new areas.

Keywords: H.P., Shimla, Environment, Sustainable Tourism etc.

Background

The north Indian state of Himachal Pradesh derives its character and identity from the mighty Himalayan Mountains. The word Himachal translates as "the home of eternal snows " these mountains also determine the state's history, culture, heritage, and lifestyles. As a destination Himachal is a place where nature has woven a combination of both the majestic and the tender touristic attractions.

"Queen of Hill Stations", "Star of Hill Resorts" and "Town of Dreams". Shimla, located at a commanding site in the interior of this state and the Himalayas, connected by road, rail and air, it has traditionally been a preferred destination for tourists from all over the world. Thousands of miles away from their mother land, amidst picturesque Himalayan environs, Shimla can be called 'a Wonder of Colonial Era'. The British established many architectural masterpieces such as Vice Regal Lodge, Gorton Castle, Railway Board Building, Gaiety Theatre, Town Hall, Auckland House, Ellerglie, Barnes Court, Bungalows, Churches and Challet Day School.

Shimla, prior to its development as a hill station was described as an "obscure village. The village was named 'Shimla' after the temple of Goddess Shyamala located in the village. In 1817, it was "a middling village", where a fakir used to give water to the travelers. Another legend is that 'Shimla' or 'Simla' is named as is pronounced by the hill people. According to Mr. W.H. Carrey the original Shimla, the Summer Capital of British India, is popularly known as 'Jewel of the Orient'. Amidst the Central Himalayas, it is a charming hill resort for tourists from all over the globe. Ever established by the British on hill top, with unique urban design, it is known as 'Queen of Hill Stations'. Shimla possesses distinct British heritage. During recent decades, after acquiring the status of state capital of Himachal Pradesh, it emerged as a major cultural, educational and institutional centre. Still considered as the star of India's hill resorts, Shimla is dominated by 19th Century colonial buildings.

The 96.5 kilometer section of Kalka-Shimla railway line with 103 tunnels is an engineering feat and provides unique experience to those who travel by this historic route. It is the most spectacular narrow gauge railway line in the world. The city possesses distinct British heritage including institutional buildings, bungalows, churches, socio-cultural spaces, hotels, cemeteries, coffee houses, clubs, theatres, schools, hospitals, street pattern and street furniture, immensely add to grace of the city with their distinct expressions. The facades of buildings, sloping roofs, dormers, windows, doors, entrances and chimneys of numerous types replicated from European buildings leave an ever- lasting impact on one's mind and provide an opportunity to understand the Western saga of art and architecture. Shimla has become a multifunctional city along with dominance of tourism, administration and institutional activities. The Central Shimla, has got congested and crowded and requires meticulous approach to harness its potential, on one hand and to rehabilitate the spill-over functions suitably with public participation, on the other. Inspite of carrying manifold constructions than the family requirements, people are still involved in horizontal and vertical expansion and thereby creation of more and more floor space. Ironically, about 30 to 40 percent floor space is presently lying idle. Shimla's lost glory has to be restored at any cost. This living model of meticulous planning, heritage, environment and development in consonance with ecological imperatives has to be preserved for posterity at any cost.

The British Empire may have ceased to exist but its echo lingers on Shimla (2250m). As the state capital of British in India, Shimla was the country's focus for the better part of every year and now, is the state capital of Himachal Pradesh. Today, it has well developed facilities, easy accessibility and numerous attractions making it one of India's most popular hill resort. Situated in the lower ranges of the Himalayan Mountains, it is surrounded by pine deodar, oak and rhododendron forests. Towards the north lie the snow-covered high-ranges, while the valleys breathe whispering streams and swaying fields. Within the town are host of splendid colonial edifices, quaint cottages and charming walks. Shimla offers a variety of shopping, sport and entertainment activities.

Perceived and established by the British during colonial period in first half of 19th century as their Summer Capital, Shimla acquired global fame by the time they left in the year 1947. At the dawn of independence, Shimla was known as 'Capua of India', the Indian Mount Olympus, the Viceroy's "shooting box" "Home of the heaven born",

The people of Shimla are informally called Shimlaites. With largely cosmopolitan crowds, a variety of festivals are celebrated here. The Shimla Summer Festival, held every year during peak tourist season, and lasting 3-4 days, is celebrated on the ridge. The highlights of this event include performances by popular singers from all over the country. Shimla has a number of places to visit. Local hangouts like the mall road and ridge are in the heart of the city. Most of the heritage buildings in the city are preserved in their original tudorbethan architecture. The Viceregal lodge which houses the Indian Institute of Advanced Study, and Wildflower hall that is now a luxury hotel are some of the famous ones. A collection of paintings, jewellery and textiles of the region can be found at the State Museum (built in 1974). Further out from the city is the Naldehra nine-hole golf course, the oldest of its kind in India. Kufri is a ski resort (winter only) located 19 kilometres (11.8 mi) from the main city. Lakkar Bazaar, a market extending off the ridge, is famous for souvenirs and crafts made of wood. Tatta Pani, 55 kilometres (34.2 mi) from the main city, is the name of hot sulphur springs that are believed to have medicinal value located on the banks of river Satluj. Shimla is also home to Asia's only natural ice skating rink. State and national level competitions are often held at this venue. The Shimla Ice Skating Club, which manages the rink, hosts a carnival every year in January, which includes a fancy dress competition and figure skating events.

Due to effects of global warming and increasing urban development in and around Shimla, the number of sessions on ice every winter have been decreasing in the past few years.

Shimla has many temples and is often visited by devotees from nearby towns and cities. The Kali Bari temple, dedicated to the Hindu goddess Kali is near the mall. Jakhoo Temple, for the Hindu god Hanuman is located at the highest point in Shimla Sankat Mochan, another Hanuman temple, is famous for the numerous monkeys that are always found in its vicinity. It is located on Shimla-Kalka Highway about 10 kilometres (6.2 mi) from the city. The nearby temple of Tara Devi is a place for performing rituals and festivals. Other prominent places of worship include a Gurudwara near the bus terminus and a Church on the ridge.

Natural vegetation caught the attention of some of the visitors. Prominent among these were the thick growths of Acer ablongum Ushan in Valley near Chhota Shimla. At Mt. Jakhoo there are white oaks and rhododendron. The valley commencing at Elysium Hill is thriving with Pinus Excelsa. Several St. Helena weeping willows can be seen growing in and around Shimla. Himalayan Holly (ilax dipyrena) is much commoner in Shimla along the Mall on the northern side of Jakhoo. The elegant pines, stately deodars, large oaks, interspersed with hilly shrubs 'gave an idea of looking over a gaudy carpet of scarlet and green".

Presently as per revenue records, the identified green belts in Shimla Planning Area spread over 414 hectares, out of which 78% area is either under forests or open area. Out of the remaining 22% area, 13% is built up and 9% under roads & paths. About 42% of the total green Green Belt in Chaura Maidan area rest, Green Belt in Bioleauganj area area is under forest cover and 36% is open area occupied by shrubs, bushes and grasslands. Out of this 150 hectares open area, 124 hectares is under Government ownership and just 26 hectares is in private ownership. The green pockets are located either in Core or in Restricted Areas, wherein there is already heavy stress and strain with respect to services infrastructure and transportation, whereby there is inconvenience to already residing population. Thickly built up pockets amidst green areas namely Boileauganj, Tutikandi, Phagli, Lalpani, Himland locality, Dhobighat, Jakhoo, Bothwell Estate, Goodwood, Shankli, Ruldu-ka-Bhatta, Chaura Maidan and Ellesium Hill near Chaura Maidan are highly congested, facing severe infrastructural and environmental problems.

An irreparable loss of green cover has already been caused by providing accessibility to such pockets. The prime green pockets on the higher altitude and on slopes, though form the crown of the town, already carried constructions thereon and in their immediate surroundings, however, look ugly and visually disturbing and some are disliked by the tourists. Adjoining to Green pockets, spread at several locations, on either side of cart road/ National Highway-22, Circular Road and Mall Road or in vicinity thereof, there is already inadequate width of the roads, a heavy traffic load, inadequate parking lots to cater even for present requirements and mixed traffic. The Core wherein many green pockets are situated, comprising of activities in and around green pockets precious coniferous Deodar green cover.

The natural setting of the premier city of Shimla has already been disturbed a lot, due to felling of trees, even by foul means, to give way for constructions. Any more construction in these areas has already caused a lot of damage to will aggravate the threats to green cover. Excessive use of R.C.C. has already most of the Shimla, possess a precious natural and built heritage, requiring preservation at any cost. Cutting and filling damaged the eco-system to a large Expanding Shimla, encroaching green cover extent Indiscriminate tapping of natural resources in terms of wood, and stone, construction of roads, has led to loss of scenic beauty of green cover in the city and its surroundings, which has been acting as a major tourist attraction, throughout the year. As majority of tourists visit Shimla for pleasure and site seeing, it is imperative that areas with predominant green cover are not at all allowed for construction activities. Furthermore green cover is required to be increased for the vital cause of environment and betterment of eco-system of future Shimla, at any cost. Geologically weak areas, identified as highly sinking prone areas, which include the northern slope of the Ridge extending up to Grand Hotel in the west, covering Lakkar Bazaar, Central School, up to Auckland Nursery School, Dhobi Ghat below Idgah electric sub-station and sliding areas, including Ladakhi Mohalla, the spur below the office of the Director areas.

Any further addition of load is likely to be hazardous in these areas. Shimla also falls in seismic Zone-IV, which is also susceptible for earthquakes. and added to traffic problems, besides they look ugly over hill slopes and are hated by the tourists, against the serene natural landscape and green cover., unauthorized constructions, land degradation, mixed land use, lack of integration between place of work and place of living and mismatch between population and surrounding areas of Clark's Hotel are also integral parts of green zone but buildings have led to manifold increase in pressure on land resources ion and urban infrastructure development are the common problems of Shimla, which are required to be tackled by restricting construction activities in central Shimla, including green areas, comprising of even the private ownerships.

Sustainable development: it's relevance

Economic benefits of tourism

Tourism comprises an extensive range of economic activities and can be considered the largest industry in the world. Tourism is now the second largest source of foreign exchange earnings in the least developed countries (LDCs) as a whole. Foreign exchange earnings can, however, vary significantly among these tourism driven economies because of 'leakages' arising from imports of equipment for construction and consumer goods required by tourists, repatriation of profits earned by foreign investors and amortization of foreign debt incurred in tourist development. Besides earnings, tourism also generates an increasingly significant share of government (national and local) tax revenues throughout the world. In addition, the development of tourism as a whole is usually accompanied by considerable investments in infrastructure, such as airports, roads, water and sewerage facilities, telecommunications and other public utilities. Such infrastructural improvements not only generate benefits to tourists but can also contribute to improving the living conditions of local populations. This increase in social overhead capital can also help attract other industries to a disadvantaged area and thus be a stimulus to regional economic development.

The tourism sector is an increasingly important source of employment-including tourism-related sectors, such as construction and agriculture-primarily for unskilled labour, migrants from poor rural areas, people who prefer to work part-time, and notably women. Because the sector is relatively labour-intensive, investments in tourism tend to generate a larger and more rapid increase in employment than equal investment in other economic activities. Furthermore, given that the sector provides a considerable amount of jobs for women and unskilled workers, tourism can significantly contribute to empowering women and alleviating poverty. At the same time, available data suggest that most workers in the tourism sector, notably in hotels and catering, tend to earn less than workers in socially comparable occupations in both developed and developing countries

Interaction between tourism and the environment

While tourism provides considerable economic benefits for many countries, regions and communities, its rapid expansion can also be responsible for adverse environmental, as well as socio-cultural, impact. Natural resource depletion and environmental degradation associated with tourism activities pose severe problems to many tourism-rich regions. The fact that most tourists chose to maintain their relatively high patterns of consumption (and waste generation) when they reach their destinations can be a particularly serious problem for developing countries and regions without the appropriate means for protecting their natural resources and local ecosystems from the pressures of mass tourism. The two main areas of environmental impact of tourism are:

1. Pressure on natural resources
2. Damage to ecosystems

Furthermore, it is now widely recognized not only that uncontrolled tourism expansion is likely to lead to environmental degradation, but also that environmental degradation, in turn, poses a serious threat to tourism activities.

Pressure on natural resources, In addition to pressure on the availability and prices of resources consumed by local residents-such as energy, food and basic raw materials-the main natural resources at risk from tourism development are land, freshwater and marine resources. Without careful land-use planning, for instance, rapid tourism development can intensify competition for land resources with other uses and lead to rising land prices and increased pressure to build on agricultural land. Moreover, intensive tourism development can threaten natural landscapes, notably through deforestation, loss of wetlands and soil erosion.

Without careful land-use planning, for instance, rapid tourism development can intensify competition for land resources with other uses and lead to rising land prices and increased pressure to build on agricultural land. Moreover, intensive tourism development can threaten natural landscapes, notably through deforestation, loss of wetlands and soil erosion.

Environmental threats to tourism in many mountain regions, small islands, coastal areas and other ecologically fragile places visited by tourists, there is an increasing concern that the negative impact of tourism on the natural environment can ultimately hurt the tourism industry itself. In other words, the negative impact of intensive tourism activities on the environmental quality of beaches, mountains, rivers, forests and other ecosystems also compromise the viability of the tourism industry in these places.

There is now plenty of evidence of the 'life-cycle' of a tourist destination, that is, the evolution from its discovery, to development and eventual decline because of over-exploitation and subsequent deterioration its key attractions. In many developing and developed countries alike, tourism destinations are becoming overdeveloped up to the point where the damage caused by environmental degradation-and the eventual loss of revenues arising from a collapse in tourism arrivals-becomes irreversible. Examples of such exploitation of 'non-renewable tourism resources' range from a small fishing village in India's Kerala state-which saw its tourist sector collapse after two decades of fast growth, because inadequate disposal of solid waste-to several places in the industrialized world, such as Italy's Adriatic coast and Germany's Black Forest. It can also be argued that environmental pollution and urban sprawl tend to undermine further tourist development in major urban destinations in developing countries, such as Bangkok, Cairo and Mexico City.

Sustainable tourism development

Countries and regions where the economy is driven by the tourism industry have become increasingly concerned with the environmental, as well as the socio-cultural problems associated with unsustainable tourism. As a result, there is now increasing agreement on the need to promote sustainable tourism development to minimize its environmental impact and to maximize socio-economic overall benefits at tourist destinations.

The concept of sustainable tourism, as developed by the World Tourism Organization (WTO) in the context of the United Nations sustainable development process, refers to tourist activities" leading to management of all resources in such a way that economic, social and aesthetic needs can be fulfilled while maintaining cultural integrity, essential ecological processes, biological diversity and life support systems" (see UN, 2001a). International efforts to promote sustainable tourism development Although tourism was not specifically addressed in Agenda 21-the international action plan on sustainable development agreed on at the 1992 Earth Summit in Rio de Janeiro (Brazil)-its growing economic importance, significant use of natural resources and environmental impact all contributed to its gradual introduction into the international sustainable development agenda over the past ten years.

The International Year of Ecotourism offered an ideal opportunity not only to review ecotourism experiences around the world, but also to promote worldwide recognition of the important role of sustainable tourism in the broader international sustainable development agenda.

There is, however, a crucial distinction between ecotourism and sustainable tourism: while the former can be broadly defined as an alternative, nature-based type of tourism, sustainable tourism calls for adherence to the abovementioned sustainability principles in all types of tourism activities and by all segments of the tourism industry. In this way, ecologically fragile areas can be protected with the financial returns of ecotourism activities. Ecotourism has been particularly successful in attracting private investments for the establishment of privately owned natural parks and nature reserves in an increasing number of developing countries, such as Costa Rica, Ecuador, Malaysia and South Africa.

A primary challenge of local governance, both today and in decades ahead, is to steer increasingly external, global forces on local development so that development achieves the shared vision of the local population. In cities, towns and villages throughout the world, the primary responsibility for this steering process rests with the institution of local government and its diverse local authorities.

As providers of social services, builders of economic infrastructure, regulators of economic activity, and managers of the natural environment, local authorities have many direct instruments at their disposal to influence development. Yet in addition to their direct roles in the development process, perhaps the most important role that local authorities can play in a global economy is that of facilitator among the diverse interests seeking to influence the direction of local development. Only with such a facilitator can a community of diverse interests define a shared vision and act consistent with this vision.

The role of local authorities as facilitators in the development process is reinforced through municipal international cooperation (MIC). With globalisation, the governance challenges facing local authorities in different parts of the world have increased in their similarities, transcending the national political and economic systems upon which different communities rely. These shared challenges of governance have instigated thousands of local authorities to establish municipal international cooperation projects and to join international local government organisations (LGOs) to advocate for local self-governance and control over the development process.

Even prior to the UN Conference on Environment and Development, but particularly since the adoption of Agenda 21, many local authorities and their LGOs have focused on the unique challenges of governance for sustainable development. At the local level, sustainable development is achieved by steering local development activities to simultaneously achieve three objectives:

- o increased local social welfare;
- o greater, and more equitably distributed, local economic wealth; and
- o enhanced integrity of local ecosystems.

Tourism is one of the many external forces influencing the direction and options for local development. The question of whether tourism can be sustainable-that is, whether it can contribute to local sustainable development-is rightfully addressed in the context of the Local Agenda 21 process. The true proof of "sustainable tourism" will be the sustainable development of local communities that serve as tourist destinations. It is time for the sustainable tourism debate to focus on this challenge. Local authorities worldwide welcome the leadership of the UN Commission on Sustainable Development, and the interest of the tourism industry, to reduce tourism's negative impacts and to increase the positive contribution of tourism business and consumption activity to local sustainable development.

Policy analysis

According to the policy of Himachal Pradesh 2005

The Policy Objectives were

(1) to establish Himachal Pradesh as a leading tourist destination in the country and abroad;

(2) to make tourism a prime engine for economic development and prosperity of the State and as a major means for providing employment;

(3) to encourage a strong and sustainable private sector participation in creation of tourism infrastructure especially through public private partnerships;

(4) to promote sustainable tourism, which is not only environmentally compatible but also leads to economic betterment of the rural people.

(5) to attract quality tourist and to increase their stay in the State;

(6) to safeguard the State's natural and manmade heritage ;

(7) to encourage civil societies & non-governmental organizations for promotion & the conducting of tourism related activities;

(8) to position Himachal Pradesh as a one stop destination for adventure tourism;

But according to the current reports given below it can be concluded that state government undertaking has virtually failed to deliver goods in the absence of proper planning policies. Increasing political interference in its affairs has made the matter worse.

The century-old civic centre of Shimla, comprising imperial buildings that were once institutions of power when this hill town was the summer capital of British India, is among four Indian historical monuments that have been included in the endangered list by the World Monuments Fund (WMF).

The list - 2010 World Monument Watch - comprising 93 monuments worldwide has been compiled by the WMF, a non-profit organisation working to identify and preserve the world's endangered cultural landmarks. 'Shimla's civic centre, stretching from the neo-Gothic Christ Church to the Telegraph Office is a monument to the state's apathy. Increased and unplanned development has caused considerable degradation to the town's historic urban fabric,' says a report posted on the WMF website.

According to The Tribune, Tourism which plays a significant role in the economy of the state, is facing rough weather, thanks to the apathy of the state government which had not bothered to develop the tourist attraction places of state in a planned manner.

Haphazard construction of hotels at Manali, Dhalousie, Shimla, Dharmshala, Macleodgunj and other places in the state has given rise to various problems, like disposal of garbage, contamination of drinking water, parking of vehicles, pollution and large scale soil-erosion. Despite the fact there is vast tourism potentials in Himachal Pradesh, it is most unfortunate that little has been done in this field in the absence of political will.

The frequent traffic jams has become a regular feature at Manali, Dhalousie, Palampur, Shimla, Dharmshala and Macleodgunj. Although the state government has time and again announced to come out with a new "Master Plan" for the development of tourism in the state, but all remained confined to the official files and most of the tourists place in the state have turned into slum.

Government has been making tall promises to provide better amenities to tourists visiting the state time and again, but in reality nothing has been done. What welcome the tourists in Himachal Pradesh "corrupt traffic police officials", costly hotels, poor parking facilities and heavy taxes? Besides, bumpy roads with narrow width, poor transport and air service, expensive food and fleecing of tourists by the taxi operators also hurt them. The hotel tariff in Himachal Pradesh is quite heavy as compared to other states.

The rise in the cases of rape, theft and murder has adversely affected the pilgrimage tourism particularly in northern parts of the state. In Chintpurni and Kangra alone one dozen cases of murder and rape were reported in past one year. Police had recovered half dozen dead bodies which remained unidentified till date. The victims were the tourists from outside the state.

Present problems

Encroachment in the forested area

As the tourist industry in Shimla is active all year round it has given way to a lot of environmental and basic amenity crux. Shimla is a small town and as discussed earlier was established by the British to escape the heat of the plains. It was made keeping in mind only a few thousand of people.

But as the population of the area grew and people from outside also came to visit the hill station the town started experiencing problems which are time to time tackled by the government but the solutions are either temporary or at the cost of nature. Shimla is in danger of being buried by huge quantities of garbage, which is left behind by visiting tourists. Mountains of filth and plastics, ranging from plastic mineral water bottles to soft drink cartons can be found in the mountains.

The HP Government's decision to ban the use of polythene bags has not yet been enforced. The Mall in Shimla is not a pedestrian's paradise anymore. The frequent digging up of the road, sometimes by telecom department and at other times by water and electricity departments causes many inconveniences to strollers. The hill station, which was neat and clean, is getting more polluted each day. Increasing air pollution in Shimla is associated with the rapid rise in population.

According to data obtained from air pollution recording station, the pollution level touches the maximum in winters and minimum during the rainy season. The main reason behind a higher pollution level during the winters is the use of heating devices, mainly bukharies that use coal or wood as fuel for cooking and other purposes in many houses and hotels in Shimla. Garbage burning and decay are equally responsible for air pollution which is higher between September and November, the peak tourism and apple harvest season. The number of vehicles coming to Shimla increases tremendously during these days. Vehicles of visiting tourist buses and apple carrying trucks (more than 1,000 trucks a day) along the circular road raise the pollution level in the area by smoke emission.

Water scarcity

Maximum tourist visit Shimla in the summers, to flee from the heat. On an average around 1200 tourists enter Shimla on everyday basis in that season. This entry can be for permanent stay in the town for a stretch or can be a halt for the next destination. In both cases the strain is felt on the resources of Shimla. water shortage in the summers is getting grave year by year, as all factors are interrelated, so due to lack of adequate snowfall in the winters, and drying up of nallas in the summers the authorities find it hard to give a continuous supply of water to its citizens and also fulfil the demands of the many hotels that easily get permission to start construction. When Shimla was made the Britisher's made an tank under the ridge to meet the water demands of the people, it continued to do so for many years but then as population grew it was not adequate enough to cater so alternative sources of water supply were explores. Presently the water demand of Shimla is met by the Ashwani khad and Gumma pumping Station.

Garbage disposal

This is a problem that is haunting the hill side of Shimla presently. As is evident that people are are bound to generate waste and it gets doubled when more is added by people coming from outside.

A lot of organic and inorganic waste is generated everyday in the town by residents and hotels and because of faulty government policies and all can be seen on the hill sides of the main town. Tourists visit the spots and then litter around even if the dustbins are available. At many places you can see hill slopes full of plastic and other material.

A very good step in this regard was the banning of plastic in Shimla, then the government did introduce the "home to home garbage collection scheme" also in 2006 but as no stringent rules were applied the policy and so it has failed to show results as u can see in the above picture.

Lack of Parking Place

According to a report if around 1200 tourist enter Shimla in the summers and around the same no. in winters then it was seen that most of them come by their personal or hired cars.

In this respect the availability of parking is not enough. As it is a hilly state a big continuous parking is not possible. So Shimla has some parking's here and there. The government has to provide parking to the residents and the tourists and in this need to meet the demand the environment is put at stake! Forested area is used and trees are felled to accommodate the growing no. of cars in the town.

So,

1) In popularising tourism the governments are failing nature and are not promoting sustainable tourism. For e.g. The International summer festival that is an annual feature in Shimla is organised on the Ridge which has a water tank under it. In spite of warnings

that the tank is now old and it is not appropriate to have a huge gathering on the ridge the festival every year continues there.

2) The Ridge area has been designated as a sinking zone and the area sinks by half a centimetre each year. Still construction in the area is permitted, and in order to promote tourism and make their stay comfortable a lift was proposed connecting the Lakkar bazaar to the Ridge. But with a PIL and the sinking area tag it has been stopped.
3) Thus it's seen that in order to please the tourist and run the state's economy that is predominantly based on tourism the governments and people flout the environment unendingly.
4) The need of the hour is not pleasing the tourist but sustaining our nature because that is the only thing that is sustaining the tourism industry.

Satellite towns & their development

The following sites were identified that can act as possible satellite destinations that will ease the pressure on Shimla and will also help in the development of these areas.

Khara Pathar (Kupar)

Khara Pathar is located Shimla and Jubbal-Rohroo road at the height of 9000ft and can be developed for trekking. Small treks can be conducted in kharapathar-kupad area and it offers nice walk amid alpine plateaus and dense forests.

The beautiful shrine of Giri Ganga is another attraction to the trekkers. Climbing into the Kupar one can have 360 degrees view all around and can trek down to Sirmaur, Jubbal and Rohroo. Choordhar range is more easily approachable and has an identical view of famous mountains of Japanese alps- "Mount Fiji"

The potential for all kind of mountain related adventure sports is tremendous. Infrastructure is lacking and will have to be given priority if the area is to be developed and investment is to be attracted to the region .at present the activities in the areas will have to be popularised by bringing youth on a low cost basis. Seasonal activities such as skiing could be conducted. Since the area is yet unknown the start point of all activity should be well known place such as Shimla to overcome the initial hesitation of the visitor Pabbar valley the Pabbar river originates from chander nahan area and flows across the picturesque and scenic valley through sandhashu, rohru, hotkoti, and sawara before meeting the tons of tuni in (u.p) the entire valley is rich in with forests, horticulture and agriculture .the region is famous for its apples. Orchid owners inhabit beautiful cottages built from local material .The people have a rich cultural heritage, are friendly and peace loving.

Surprisingly, tourism in these areas is virtually non existing .there are hardly any hotels or resorts. The approach roads are also not of standard that would sustain tourism. The area is rich in scenic beauty and the climate ideal for holidaying. Rohru, which is the centre for all commercial activities, is 120 km from Shimla, a distance which can be covered in 5 hours. The road headed in the Pabbar valley is tikri, which is 23 km further adventure sports potential e.g. angling, trekking, paragliding, water sports, heliskiing, skiing.

The potential for all kind of mountain related adventure sports is tremendous. Infrastructure is lacking and will have to be given priority if the area is to be developed and investment is to be attracted to the region .at present the activities in the areas will have to be popularised by bringing youth on a low cost basis. Seasonal activities such as skiing could be conducted. Since the area is yet unknown the start point of all activity. Should be well known place such as Shimla to overcome the initial hesitation of the visitor

Chail

The former 'summer capital' of Patiala, Chail is 43-km from Shimla and dwelling in the midst of a lush green setting. At 2,250m, it has the world's highest cricket pitch and a polo ground, the old palace, now a hotel and the possibility of some angling are added attractions. Chail is hiker's paradise. The area is very peaceful away from the hustle and bustle of Shimla. It also has the world's highest cricket ground. Close by is a national park, which has limited number of birds and deer's. In 1891, Maharaja Bhupinder Singh of Patiala incurred the wrath of Lord Kitchener, the then commander-in-chief. As a result, he was banned entry into the summer capital of the raj, Shimla. This enraged the maharaja and he vowed to build a new and better summer capital for himself. He looked around and after quite some time realized it had all the while been in his possession.

Chail, a little village close to Shimla, was a 'slice of heaven' surrounded by lush forests with a commanding view of the snow-capped Himalayas. He rebuilt the city according to his requirements and built himself a wonderful palace. The picturesque resort located amidst scented forests of chir pine and gigantic deodars. Chail is built on three hills, the palace is on Rajgarh hill, and the residency snow view once occupied by British resident is on Pandhewa hill and on the third hill Sadh Tiba where Chail is situated overlooking Satluj valley, Shimla and kasauli are also visible at night from here. Chail has also the highest cricket ground in the world. well kept and well maintained the ground is surrounded by huge trees of deodar and pine. On the other side of the town are situated the massive Himalayan ranges spectacularly gleaming in the sun and snow-covered everything under it. This small area can be developed in terms of infrastructure so that the tourist coming to Shimla does not halt there but straight away go to Chail.

Kufri

Some great hiking, some skiing, some beautiful scenes and a cool environment that's what Kufri is all about. It is famous for its trekking and hiking trails. Adventure-seeking travellers throng Kufri in winters to enjoy skiing and tobogganing along its snow-covered slopes. The skiing season spreads between November to February and the tourist inflow is at its peak during winters. Kufri is a tiny hill station located 19-kms from Shimla on the national highway. It has a Himalayan nature park and close by is the Indira tourist park with HPTDC's Cafe Lalit. The region around Shimla including Kufri was once a part of the kingdom of Nepal. This region remained obscure from the rest of the world until the British 'discovered' it in 1819.

Fagu

Sedentary or strenuous, for the expert or beginner, Shimla can have a niche of adventure for everyone. Looking at any tourist map of the state, one wouldn't think of Fagu as any major spot. It is 22kms from Shimla and 6kms from Kufri. Fagu is a vantage point with a panoramic view of ranges and valleys. It serves as a good base for exploring the nearby countryside which is flooded with orchards and forest we can promote this place for village tourism and make use of the resources in a sustainable manner.

Conclusion

Conclusively, as stressed at the beginning of this paper, tourism is expected to resume its rapid growth in the near future. This growth can be harnessed not only for the enjoyment of tourists themselves but, more importantly, for maximizing economic benefits and thus increasing the living standards of host communities and countries. At the same time, unless corrective measures are taken, it is bound to have negative environmental and socio-cultural impact on those communities. Ecotourism and other sustainable tourism strategies have gone a long way towards minimizing this negative impact and ensuring that the economic benefits of tourism can contribute to environmental protection and the sustainable use of natural resources.

References

Affairs, D. O. (2007). Report on Sustainable Development: A developing Countries View. London, Warwick: Oxford Report Series.

Callicott, J.B. and Mumford, K. (1997), Ecological Sustainability as a Conservation Concept. Conservation Biology, 11, 32-40.

Cater, E. (1993), 'Ecotourism in the Third World: Problems for Sustainable Tourism Development' Tourism Management April, pp. 85-90

E, D. (1992). Making the Alternative Sustainable Development for Tourism. Philadelphia: Univrsity of Pennsylvania Press.

Fayos-Sola Eduardo (1996), Tourism Policy; A Mid-summer night's dream. Tourism Management 17(6).

Gaston, A. J. and Garson, P.J. (1992), A Re-Appraisal of the Great Himalayan National Park, Himachal Wildlife Project III. Himachal Pradesh Department of Forest Farming & Conservation, International Trust for Nature Conservation, World Wide Fund for Nature India, Oriental Bird Club, 1-80.

Gaston, A.J. (1998), Report on Monitoring and Evaluation, Consultancy Report, FREEP-GHNP Research Project, Wildlife Institute of India, Dehra Dun.

Gaston, A.J., Hunter, M.L. and Garson, P.J. (1981), The Wildlife of Himachal Pradesh, Western Himalayas. Report of the Himachal Wildlife Project. The Notes No. 82, School of Forest Resources. University of Maine, Orono.

Gunn Clare A. 1988 B Vacation Scope : Designing Tourist Regions second edition.

Guru, Lal Prasad 1989, Socio-Cultural, economic & Physical impacts of tourism in the southern part of Annapurna region, Nepal.

Hass H. (1984), A Decade of Alternative Tourism in Sri Lanka. Alternative Tourism with a focus on Asia. Ecumenical Coalition on Third World Tourism, Bangkok.

Kabia, S.K. (2005), Tourism Industry: Reference Press, New Delhi

Kumar, H., Mathur, P.K., Lehmkuhl, J.F., Khati, D.V.S., De. R., and Longwah. W, (2002), Management of Forests in India for Biological Diversity and Forest Productivity, Vol VI, Tarai Conservation Area (TCA), WII-USDA Forest service Collobrative Project Report, Wildlife Institute of India, DehraDun, 1-158.

Kumar, P., Rathore, B.M.S. and Nangia, S. (1999), Social Monitoring of Conservation of Biodiversity Project in GHNP. Final Report, FREEP-GHNP Research Project, Wildlife Institute of India, Dehra Dun.

Kurien, A. (2005), Response of Tiger (Panthera tigris), Prey Species and Their Habitat in Relation to Human Disturbance in and Around Chilla Range of Rajaji National Park, Uttaranchal. M.Sc. Dissertation, Sau

M, M. (2003). Tourism & Sutainability. New York: Routledge.

Mian Goverdhan Singh. (1994). Himachal Pradesh: History, Culture and Economy. Minerva Book House.

Olson, S.F. (1975), 'A longing for Wilderness'. In Olson, S.F. (ed.) Wilderness: USA. Washington DC: National Geographic Society.

Orams, M. (1995), Towards a More Desirable Form of Ecotourism. Tourism Management 16 (1), 3-8

Singh, G. (2002). Evaluation of Tourism Policy of Himachal Pradesh. Shimla: HPU.

Wildlife Institute of India (1999 a), An Ecological Study of the Conservation of Biodiversity and Biotic Pressures in the Great Himalayan National Park Conservation Area - An Eco-development Approach. Forestry Research Education and Extension Project - Great Himalayan National Park (FREEPGHNP), Final Project Report, Wildlife Institute of India, Dehra Dun, Vol. 1 to 6.

Wildlife Institute of India (1999 b.), Ecological and Socio Economic Studies on the Kalakad Mundanthurai Tiger Reserve - An eco-development approach. Forestry Research Education and Extension Project - Kalakad Mundanthurai Tiger Reserve (FREEP-KMTR), Final Project Report, Wildlife Institute of India, Dehra Dun.

SUSTAINABLE ECO-TOURISM & ITS IMPACT IN INDIA

Rajesh kumar Jhamb

Lecturer, Govt. Polytechnic for Women Sector-10, Chandigarh. jhamb.rajesh@gmail.com

Anu Jhamb

Assistant Professor, Deptt. of Management. UIET, Panjab University, Chandigarh. anujhamb2000@gmail.com

Abstract: Eco-tourism involving travel to areas of natural or ecological interest, typically under the guidance of a naturalist, for the purpose of observing wildlife and learning about the environment. Eco-tourism is consecrated for preserving and sustaining the diversity of the world's natural and cultural environment. It accommodates and entertains visitors in a way that is minimum intrusive or destructive to the environment, it sustains & supports the native cultures in the location in which it is operating upon.

Ecotourism, is low-impact tourism with an eye toward protecting the environment and culture of an area. Eco-tourism can cover a wide range of standards and conditions, from fully compliant to less stressful on the environment than standard tourism. Eco-tourism doesn't necessarily mean a vacation spent roughing it with little or no comforts. Many people believe that it can be a wonderful adventure. Ecotourism resorts and eco lodges exist in almost every style and taste. From recycling and gray water systems to tents on tree house-like platforms with a rain forest canopy, there are numerous vacationing options, such as keeping & designating pathways, Eating where locally grown cuisine is served and visiting cultural areas instead of typical tourist attractions, can go a long way toward "greening up" a standard vacation. The number of tourists traveling in the India has been increasing, which makes ecotourism not only preferable but a necessity in some areas. It might seem wiser to some people to protect natural habitats and pristine, fragile environments by banning visitors completely to these areas, but many areas depend on the income from tourism to support the local economy. Sustainable Eco-Tourism is considered offer the best of both worlds, protecting the ecology of an area.

The country abounds in attractive and well- preserved historical sites and ancient monuments of architectural grandeur. There is a vast variety of building styles, which chronicle the cultural and historical diversity of their creators. India offers enormous diversity in topography, natural resources and climate. There are land-locked mountainous regions, lush valleys and plains, arid desert regions, white sandy beaches and islands. Central India has numerous wildlife sanctuaries with countless varieties of flora and fauna. The country has unparallel cultural diversity, a kaleidoscope of races, languages, religions, customs and traditions. Indians have embraced almost all the major religions of the world and the country has given rise to various religions.

This article explored the benefits of environmental management practices and sustainable eco-tourism at a major Indian Ecotourism destination. To achieve this purpose the article investigated changes in tourists' environmental sustainability, awareness, attitudes and its impact in India.

Keywords: Sustainability/Ecotourism/Environment.

Introduction

India, a country situated in south Asia is of subcontinental dimension with a population of over 120 crore people. India is primarily an agricultural economy with a vast range of crops. The livelihood of over 70 percent of the population continues to be based on agriculture. There has been a growing trends of urbanization and diversification away from agriculture. The industrial sector is now playing a larger role in the economy.

India has spectacularly attractive natural and cultural tourist attractions. It has a rich, over 5000-year-old, cultural heritage and thousands of monuments and archaeological sites for tourists to visit and enjoy. The remains of one of the most ancient river valley civilizations of the world (the Indus Valley civilization) are found in India. The Taj Mahal and 16 other World Heritage Properties and several national heritage sites are in India

The geographical diversity of India provides opportunities for a wealth of outdoor and adventure sports activities. Travel plays a significant role in global environmental issues, especially climate change. Considering and tinkering with just a as making use of public transport and employing local people for local needs as guides can contribute to leaving a more sustain leave you with a very experience rich journey. Over 430 languages are spoken in India, and there are hundreds of indigenous cultural traditions.

India is fortunate to have several charismatic wildlife species like elephant, rhino and tiger and has several well managed protected areas where the potential for eco-tourism is high. However, constraints like small park area, improperly tourist activities and excessive tourist operations The major adventure tourism activities are trekking and skiing in the Himalayas, river running in the Ganges, water sports in Goa, trout fishing in Himachal Pradesh, heli-skiing in Himachal Pradesh, wind surfing, scuba diving and yachting in Andamans and Lakshadweep islands. India has some of the best beaches in the world, many of which are still unexplored, as in the Andamans and Lakshadweep Islands.Hospitality to visitors is an ancient Indian tradition. The peoples' lifestyles are varied. Life is full of culture, fairs and festivals, colour and spectacle. India is a land of folk fairs and festivals, some say that there is a fair each day of the year. Some of the important fairs and festivals are the Pushkar fair in Rajasthan, the Crafts Mela at Surajkund, Holi and Diwali in North India, Pongal in Tamilnadu, Onam in Kerala, Baisakhi in Punjab, Bihu in Assam, dance festivals at Khajuraho and Mamallapuram. Each region has its culinary specialty but the best part is to sample the exotic fare in the thousands of restaurants. There is something for all tastes and interests, from the "soft" adventures to fast-paced thrills, and there is something for every level of experience. Ecotourism more than any other form of tourism depends on the environment of a destination. Of course the growth of all forms of tourism leads to modifications of the environment. Ecotourism strives to keep these modifications to a minimum. In order to do this it is important to take account of these modifications and assess what their impacts on the environment are.

Meaning of Eco Tourism

Eco-tourism endeavours to encourage and support the diversity of local economies for which the tourism. The international eco-tourism society defines eco-tourism as "Responsible travel to natural areas that conserves the environment and improves the well-being of local people." This means that those who implement and participate in eco-tourism activities should follow the following principles.

Eco-tourism is a relatively new concept in tourism. Eco-tourism is primarily meant to create awareness about conservation, generate revenue for protected area development and help in development of local communities.

Eco-tourism has been suggested as a key to sustainable development of protected areas. It presents a mix of threats and opportunities for protected areas. Success depends on careful planning and management. Carelessly planned or poorly implemented Eco-tourism projects can easily become conventional tourism projects with all the associated negative impacts.

Eco Tourism consist of nature and off-beat destination tours. India enjoys unique geographical features, making it one of the most sought-after destinations in Asia. The country has fascinating Himalayan landscapes, snow-capped peaks, dense forests, holy rivers, a long shoreline with serene beaches, tranquil backwaters, sprawling plantations and green fields, exotic wildlife, historic cultural monuments, Ayurveda retreats, diverse culture, magical festivals and a divine cuisine - all of which offer a unique experience.

Significance of Ecotourism

Environmental Conservation

The entire concept behind ecological tourism is for people to visit exotic landscapes and aid the protection and conservation of nature -- hence ecotourism offers an incentive for local people to help preserve and protect their environment and wildlife as it can provide them with a 'sustainable' income from tourism. This, as opposed to the exploitation of their surrounding environment for its natural resources to make a quick singular unsustainable gain with negative environmental impacts.

Benefits to Local Small Business and People

With the industry of tourism, comes an increase in the demand for local jobs and hence correspondingly an increase in employment for locals -- that are often provided through merchandise retailers, restaurants, tour guides, hotels etc. This then contributes towards boosting the local economy -- by meeting local people's economic needs as well as teaching them life-long commercial skills with the provision of experience and assistance helps in the welfare of local people and businesses.

Cultural Awareness

The pros and cons of ecotourism lies around the environmental and economical aspects, it is also important to consider the cultural and social impacts also. As tourists visit local indigenous people and exotic landscapes and wildlife, there is a cultural education to be found. By showing tourists a wider and broader perspective of nature and differing cultures, they are perhaps instilled with a greater conservation ethic -- to act more 'green'.

'Greener' Tourism

As tourism is, and probably always will be, a huge industry within modern day living, ecological tourism can at the very least -- despite its mismanaged -- be considered a step in the right direction towards resolving and mitigating the potential outcomes of global climate change, which leads to green tourism Although ecotourism, can be judged to be better than that of traditional tourism in India.

Increase in Monetary Value

It increases the monetary value of standing (vs. logged, degraded, extinct) biological systems and thereby hopefully encourages the preservation of biological diversity. The problem is that some kinds of "eco-tourism" do not contribute much to the local economy, meaning that they can enrich a few people while leaving others left out of the loop. In this case, for those left out, there is still little incentive to engage in conservation. So the fulfillment of the promise depends on the details of how an eco-tourism business is established -- whether it's community-owned or owned by just a few individuals.

It is supposed to bring people closer to nature and thus instill a greater desire to protect it. It is very difficult to define eco-tourism, however, so not all "eco-tourist" activities do this equally well. For example, is off-roading eco-tourism? Is swimming with captive dolphins in an artificial lagoon eco-tourism? Is trekking through a rainforest in a small group eco-tourism? They may all be, but they probably impart different impressions of nature and the desire to preserve it.

Advantages of Eco-Tourism:-

- o Less impact on the environment
- o Builds awareness and respect for the local Culture and environment
- o Positive experiences for all the concern stakeholder
- o Employment of local people
- o Educates visitors about Social, legal and Environmental issues.
- o Resources from the tourists can be used for the conservation of the area.
- o Protection of wildlife habitat.
- o Visitors carry new ideas backs to influence their own environment.

Resources extraction

It is mainly water and fuel wood to meet the tourism needs are degrading the habitat equality of the region and most of all excess eco tourism is becoming a threat to wildlife- there is insufficient attention being paid to the tourist carrying capacity of each Protected Area (PA) and there is no limit on the number of vehicles or number of tourist entering a Protected Area per day. Several ecotourism projects opened up in Himalayas in the past have proven to be unsustainable. Places like Nanda Devi Biosphere reserve had to be closed because of high environment degradation caused by ecotourism activities.

Eco tourism activities carried over by the tour operators are generally not overseen by government and turning largely commercial. There are around fifty resorts operating on the reserve forests of Masinagudi region in Nilgiris Biosphere reserve. Sometimes the resorts do not follow operation guidelines. Or serve the purpose of increasing awareness about conservation. With no obligation of tour operators to involve local people, much of the ecotourism projects here are becoming purely commercial. This leads to economic leakages- significantly reducing the funds available for local people and the protected area.

Eco Tourism supports sustainable tourism that protects the local environment and culture as well as provides livelihood for the locals. The effort is to care for and conserve nature and to provide an authentic cultural and nature experience by of collaboration between the government, non-governmental bodies, the local business community, community members and the media.

Since all these stakeholders are direct participants in enhancing the success of the project, there is need for effective communication and networking in order to enhance coordination.

Problems of Ecotourism:-

Local People

In some circumstances, ecotourism is severely mismanaged, local people do not always benefit economically or socially as a result of ecotourism. When assuming an influx of tourism, many often overlook the type of employment that local people get into, where they are usually low paid service jobs that are based on temporary contracts.

Unable to Meet the 'Eco' Standard

As ecotourism is essentially a commercial industry, there is evidence of certain companies simply "green-washing" -- which is the process of simply making the holiday appear eco-friendly when it is in fact not. There is not much substance needed for a company to term a holiday 'ecotourism' and they often fail to get scrutinized by consumers. Hence, leading a holiday through false pretences.

Wildlife Disturbance

The promotion of ecotourism and environmental friendliness -- it is still inevitable on some levels that 'tourism' will cause a negative impact on wildlife through consumer pressures (e.g. Polar bears are meant to conserve energy through the winter months, however as a result of ecotourism, this causes them to be constantly aware -- causing them to burn much of the needed energy -- 43 metres is the suggested distance not to disturb them. However is this good enough for the demands of consumers who want close up photos.

Environmental Degradation

It is almost certain that as a result of tourism, there will be some negative impacts on the environment whether it be through littering (accidental or otherwise) through to the unplanned destructive infrastructure. Even tourists, who claim to be environmentally sophisticated and aware, usually fail to realize the damage them simply travelling to their destination through means of non-renewable energy

Disadvantages of Eco-Tourism

- It leads to overcrowding constructions
- It creates pollution of the habitat
- No control or unlimited numbers of tourists
- It leads to traffic congestion
- There are chances of erosion, footpath erosion, soil loss, etc.
- Lack of vision among tourists
- They don't understand or care what eco-tourism really is?

Greenwash: It's the dissemination of misleading information by an organization to conceal its abuse of the environment in order to present a positive public image, a term that is used to describe the actions of a company, government, or other organization which advertises positive environmental practices while acting in the opposite way.

They destroy forestland to build a hotel in middle of a jungle and say "ecotourism". Criticism as "greenwashing" where the environment is used as a bait to attract tourists

- Establishing a huge energy intensive hotel in a splendid jungle setting with no understanding of sustainable development or the correct provision for the disposal of waste and sewage etc.
- Establishing a tourist resort which displaces the local people and illegally keeps endangered animals in cages to attract visitors.

Sustainability of Ecotourism

Ecotourism has been developing as strongest and fastest developing industry in the world it was expected that 'the green' would start implementing eco rules there. Ecotourism has its benefits not only to our environment but also to the economy of the areas with ecotourism. Ecotourism is a form of tourism visiting fragile, pristine, and usually protected areas, intended as a low impact and often small scale alternative to standard commercial tourism. Its purpose may be to educate the traveler, to provide funds for ecological conservation, to directly benefit the economic development and political empowerment of local communities, or to foster respect for different cultures and for human rights. Ecotourism is not merely an alternative to mass tourism, nor is it the only alternative. Tourism is now the world's largest industry and it has an increasing impact on protected areas. Our understanding of these mechanisms, their ecological impacts and our capacity to manage tourism in protected areas lags behind the growth of tourism to protected areas. A rapid growth in nature tourism and tourism to protected areas has coincided with a shift in protected area management strategies towards integrated development. Tourism is one means available to protected area managers seeking to increase the economic value of a protected area and to offer sustainable opportunities for economic development to local people.

Ecotourism is the fastest-growing sector of the tourism industry offers tourism companies and Third World destinations alike the prospect of capitalizing on the comparative advantage of these nations in terms of unspoiled natural environments. By definition, such development should benefit destinations more in terms of small-scale, local involvement with fewer adverse impacts. The opportunity for these countries to enhance their development potential by harnessing their natural resources without, at the same time, destroying them cannot be denied. What is essential, however, is the recognition that, without adequate understanding of underlying factors and careful planning and management, ecotourism may include unsustainable aspects.

Ecotourism claims to combine environmental responsibility with the generation of local economic benefits that will have both a development impact and serve as conservation incentives. Economic incentives are imperative for nature conservation, particularly in remote and ill-monitored regions where a weak presence of the state hinders the use of alternative tools of environmental regulation. It is concluded that in the whole study area, tourism has actually provided significant additional income. Counter to common belief, the mode of participation is less decisive for local income generation than the tourist attraction of the natural site, the degree of tourism specialization and the level of local organization. However, as a conservation incentive, the effectiveness of tourism income depends on the incentive structure inherent in the mode of participation, and on the substitution versus complementarities of other productive activities: only if tourism changes labour and land allocation decisions, will it have a local conservation impact. It is discussed under which circumstances the conjectured link between tourism, local incomes and conservation is likely to be effective.

Process of Sustainable Ecotourism

Ecotourism can be sustainable only if it will planned guiding principles. The process of sustainable ecotourism is as follows:

a. Selection of Suitable Site : The selection of tourist zones can be based on number of factors like areas rich in wildlife or that have charismatic species that can attract tourist, logistics requirement like access to nearest road and rail. Once tourist zones are identified, it is necessary to conduct a study on environmental impacts of operating eco tourism facilities in that area. Early investigation of sociological and ecological features is needed in site selection. But most of times small projects are never evaluated for their impact and contribution on wildlife in India.

b. Evaluation of Site: The next step is site evaluation to ensure suitability of the site for the project. Carrying capacity of the region in terms of number of resorts that can be built or the number of visitors and vehicles that can be present at a given time needs to be worked out.

The likely impacts on wildlife and local community's needs should be also assessed. The site design should ensure that the tourism zone does not fall onto critical habitat like waterholes or breeding grounds.

c. Assessing the Alternatives: The next step is to assess the alternatives and to make sure that the selected site is the best available for the project. The land acquisition aspects need to be considered as well prior to site. The assessment of site should take into account and the local condition also.

d. Design and Implementation: The last step is comprehensive design and implementation plan. Competent agencies plan and design ecotourism projects. With Geographic Information System (GIS) becoming a useful and reliable planning tool, it has become easy for decision makers and planners to evaluate the resources and make designs and plans in a sustainable manner. Ecotourism planning has helped in site selection and assessing site suitability. Further GIS based carrying capacity analysis for many protected areas in India as part of design of sustainable ecotourism plans.

Planning at landscape level is necessary and the entire planning process should involve Administration authorities, Members of Forest department, Tourist department and there stakeholder and should be based on full consultation with the local people of the region.

e. Feedback: Tourist's feedback is very important. It helps in knowing the success of ecotourism and also help in improvement of eco-tourism if requires. Feedback helps in guiding the policy framework for the sustainable tourism.

Impact of Ecotourism

Eco-tourism or ecological tourism is as much about responsibility as it is about the joys of being in the midst of nature. Today, international tourism earns more than automotive products. Man is an inveterate traveler. His desire to reach across to foreign shores and understand a culture different from his own gave birth to travel. Tourism is the commercial offshoot of that cultural activity.

With that definition in mind, eco-tourism can be thought of as a slightly distinct activity. Eco-tourism is defined by The International Eco-tourism Society (TIES) as "Responsible travel to natural areas that conserves the environment and improves the well-being of local people." Eco-tourism is not only about enjoyingthe natural heritage of an indigenous locale but also creating a sustainable relationship with it. Eco-tourism seek not only to create a congenial atmosphere for the visitor but also two other important touch points -

1. Provide sensitivity to the local environment.
2. Helps in the sustainable use of biodiversity by involving the local population in environmentally friendly activities.

A well planned ecotourism plan seeks to minimize the environmental impact of tourist footfalls while seeking to raise the socio-economic profile of an area. Probably, this is why ecotourism has climbed the agenda of every country as they seek to reap the benefits of this latest standard. In some countries, especially of Africa, ecotourism garners a significant portion of the GDP. Eco-Tourism has entered the mind space because of greater environmental awareness. While this is a positive development, what remains to be examined are the fallouts of this trend on the society and the environment around us.

Socio-Cultural Impact of Eco-Tourism

Eco-tourism is the melting pot of cultures and people. National and/or local pride is a direct manifestation of how appreciative a foreign culture is of one's own. Income generated through eco-tourism benefits the locals and keeps migration for jobs at bay. Local knowledge also stays within the community and is passed on. A successful example can be found in a developed country - Canada. Nunavut in Northern Canada chose eco-tourism as a viable industry.

On the other hand, there is a very high probability of a culture clash. Outside influences can wreck havoc with the ethnic way of living. Local culture and heritage should be showcased but often it is 'packaged' to conform to Western expectations. Eco-tourism often forms the single source of revenue for a community. Any cyclical changes in the economy affect it as a whole. Today, corruption and environmental degradation has left its industry in shambles.

The architectural program for ecotourism centres should include controlled access points, roads, self-guided nature trails, transportation options, interpretation centres, signs, observation towers and adequate but unpretentious lodging and dining facilities, docks, garbage disposal facilities and other utilities as needed. If required, suitable living quarters and facilities for project personnel should be provided. Box 7 is a list of actions for the development of ecotourism, where the responsibility is with the government.

Economic Impact of Eco-Tourism

Eco-tourism has amply demonstrated its potential to be a huge resources earner. The resources earned should be ploughed back into the local society. This can go to create a better life for the local population though schools, better roads and hospitals. Through taxes and consumer spending the whole country stands to benefit the fruits of eco-tourism. Again, the funds generated through eco-tourism can be used for the preservation of the fount itself, the natural resource. But two stumbling blocks directly emerge from an ill managed eco-tourism plan. The first is 'enclave tourism'. The very little currency gets into the hands of the local community. 'Import Leakage' is another difficulty.

To meet the luxury demands of particular tourists, locals must import other goods from outside.For e.g. beverages and food. This essentially means that wealth leaves the community to pay for outside imports. Eco-tourism at the cost of the environment puts a load on the local resources. Scarce resources have to compete with volume of tourist traffic.

Environmental Impact Of Eco-Tourism

The most valuable contribution of eco-tourism is the preservation of biodiversity. Biodiversity is increasingly looked upon as a sustainable asset and eco-tourism forms a vital cog of it. The world's largest wetlands in Brazil's Pantanal's are also a large grazing ground for the beef industry. Mostly populated by private ranches, a sustainable development plan as an eco-tourism destination made it a success story.

But on the other hand, Eco-tourism improperly managed means a walkthrough by droves of tourists through virgin lands. This invasion rapidly spirals into an orgy of opportunism as everybody attempts to cash in. Environmental degradation follows. The popularity of an eco-tourism destination could be directly proportional to its rate of destruction.

Ecotourism In India

The thousands of species of flora and fauna find its natural abode in 89 of national parks and approximate 430 of wildlife sanctuaries set in different naturally rich locations of the country. Besides, many of the dense forests, mountains and its hills, and rivers offer an immense range of adventurous Eco activities like Mountaineering, Rock Climbing, Trekking, Mountain Biking, Nature Walking, Wildlife Viewing and River Rafting.

The Monasteries and Himalayan glaciers of Ladakh in Northern part or roaming through rich Coffee plantation and world famous Kerala Backwater in South or enjoying the arduous trekking in Kanchenjunga in North-East or taking a desert camel safari tour in That desert in Western part of the country, the Eco tourism spots are pervaded everywhere. Many of them lying still in the pristine lap of mother lap guarantee its visitors to fetch them a unique view of their natural richness. Some of the great potentials of Sustainable Ecotourism in India are as follows:-

Himalayas: Himalaya with its many of highest peaks and rivers is one of the most favourite destinations for Eco tourists. Extending over 2500 Km in East to West, and 250 Km to 400 Km from North to South direction,

Garhwal: Snow capped mountains, beautiful meadows, serene lakes and dense forests offering amazing wildlife view are some of the embedded geographical features of this Northern region of country.

Goa: The beaches are the biggest fascination attracting tourists. Besides, many of the wildlife parks and birding spots are hoarded by thousands of Eco tourists.

Kodaikanal: The small place is assembled in its beauty of untouched serene and virgin lakes and caves, which are full of offering diverse range of Eco adventure.

Kerala: It is a combination of beauty of untouched serene and virgin lakes and caves, which are full of offering diverse range of Eco adventure.

Ladakh: The colorful monasteries pervaded everywhere and abundance of snow peaks and glaciers of Ladakh make it not only a popular cultural hub but also one of the most popular trekking spots.

Manali: This is a beautiful place is full of snow capped peaks and rich greenery - both making it a popular hill station and sought after Eco adventurous place in Kullu valley.

Munnar: One of the most famous hill resort in south India, Munnar lets visitors indulge into many of recreational and eco activities like nature walk in cardamom and coffee plantation, boating, para-gliding, trekking and wildlife viewing.

Rishikesh: The natural splendour of Himalaya and Ganga, Rishikesh along with being itself one of the most revered Hindu cities is the entry point to the most important Hindu pilgrimage, Char Dham.

Sikkim: The Trekking in the second highest peak of the world, Kanchenjunga, and exploring the Rhododendron trek and beautiful land of orchid, Sikkim is unmatched anywhere else in the world.

Shimla: Fine opportunity to enjoy excursion like Oak and Rhododendron forest exploration, skiing and ice-skating, and Himalayan sightseeing make this small hill station one of the most favorite vacationing spots for the tourists.

Thenmala: This first planned Eco tourism destination in India has its charm lying in its culture zone, leisure zone and adventure zone, besides in its two famous attraction Shenduruney Wildlife Sanctuary and Deer Rehabilitation Park.

Is Ecotourism Bad?

1. The idea of yours is to spend a vacation in the wilderness, or a place with natural wonders, such as the Grand Canyon. You are not alone in this, because more and more people like the idea of spending time in an environment free from cars, traffic, and tall buildings. However, while ecotourism was initially invented to help preserve the environment, there are actually a number of reasons why ecotourism is bad.
2. In the woodland areas and areas where animals live, is the element of surprise to the animals. Animals that have lived their entire lives in the forest are not tame, and pose a problem to humans, especially if those humans are carrying food. The presence of humans alternately causes stress to wild animals.
3. A visit to National Park, you have seen at least a few pieces of litter in different places. No matter how diligent the park rangers can be, sometimes the forest is too big to find every single piece of litter. Not only does litter make the environment look messy, but it also can be hazardous to the animals in the environment. Plastic especially is very hard to destroy and is not biodegradable.
4. Another prevalent reasons for bad ecotourism is to do with the structures that are built for various ecotourism events. For example, if a park decides to have a nature walk aspect to it, paths will be cleared and some trees cut down to make way for the paths. Also, in parks, lookout towers are sometimes built in trees. While these structures have a purpose, they cannot help but damage the delicate environment.

Recommendations For Sustainable Ecotourism

Even after careful planning and implementation much of ecotourism can become unsustainable- the main reason being lack of operational guidelines. To make ecotourism sustainable in the long run careful planning, implementation and monitoring is required.

- o The declaration of tourist zone and operation guidelines should form a distinct section of the 'Protected Area Management Plan' which should be prepared by the PA manager in collaboration with local people, resort owners, ecologists and conservationists. Such plans should aim at long term benefits and not be short sighted.

- The Tourism plan must also be revised and updated periodically.
- The state wildlife board should over see all ecotourism related operations near protected areas. This should include grant of permits to private tour operators, establishment of interpretation centers, and involvement of local people in ecotourism activities. The board should also oversee the operation of tourist activities in the park areas with the help of park managers.
- There should be an advocacy centre in each protected area where ecotourism is being promoted to educate and create awareness about conservation of wildlife.
- Resorts should be given the environmental management system plans and also trained requisitely to implement these plans. Solid waste management has become a major issue in tourist sites. Plastics and wastes left over by tourists are not only degrading the environment but are harmful to wildlife- tones of solid wastes are left in the Himalayas because of ecotourism activities. The environment management or suitable way to transport to other disposal sites.
- Impact of ecotourism need to be closely monitored by competent agencies and the operation guidelines should be modified as and when necessary. The carrying capacity should not be exceeded, irrespective of potential economic or social gains.
- The tourist operators must be brought to operate under the guidelines and must work in a way that benefits local people than as pure commercial business. Steps that serve to attract population increase in these sensitive areas should be thoroughly discouraged as these are not in the long-term interest of Ecotourism plans.
- Changes in vegetation, biomass and biodiversity value need to be monitored in tourist zones. The human wildlife conflict in tourism zones needs to be recorded.
- The findings should help in shaping recommendations on mitigating the adverse impacts of tourism and help in creating better tourism plans.

- o Ecotourism has high potential in India, and with ecologically sensitive areas in North east India, Himalayas and islands of Andaman and Nicobar becoming open as eco-destinations, it is important to conduct ecotourism in a planned and sustainable manner to reap the economic gains without affecting the Environment.

Conclusion

All the ecotourism can be judged the same, place has its own unique set of strengths and weaknesses regarding its environmental friendliness. There is still a lack of 'regulation and accreditation' regarding exactly what constitutes ecotourism, so although there is tourism activities that are in fact environmentally friendly, there are also 'wildlife theme parks' and 'eco-helicopter rides' and mismanaged 'ecotourism' programmes that get away with being dubbed as 'ecotourism' -- despite little regard for its true principles. However, on the whole ecotourism as a concept is obviously a good thing -- the promotion and protection of nature -- despite some issues of mismanagement it is certainly a step in the right direction.

This article found, significant effects of Visitor awareness among visitors Involvement in, the environmental management practices, Participation in Nature activities on environmental attitudes and behaviours. It is suggested that awareness of in-resort environmental practices and satisfying experiences in ecotourism accommodation may lead to reinforcing visitors' favourable environmental attitudes, thus increasing their interest in further ecotourism experiences. Through these cumulative effects, ecotourism accommodation could achieve its educative goal. Eco-tourism remains a story of triumphs and failures. In the end, we as preservers must realize that eco-tourism must not be only about plants and animals but also a little about the people who are born around it. It is about sustainability or its converse and its ripple effects. Ecotourism is very much a fledgling industry in India but could be a boon for the country. Currently every part of the country "out of bounds" areas) by twisting the right arms-even the reserve parks are not spared.

To preserve the natural areas, boundaries so as not to disturb the integrity of the ecosystem and ensure that the cultural and natural history of the environment a travel destination sustainably for centuries to come. One of the key roles of ecotourism is to support the local people and provide opportunities for them to benefit from tourism industry i.e job opportunities as guides, porters and also providing them the opportunity to sell their locally-produce nature-based, sustainable ecological concept where education gaining is imparted to local people as well to travelers to develop un-management of resources and not affect the surroundings in the course of generating revenue from tourism.

References

Mowforth, M & Munt, I (1998) - Tourism and sustainability: new tourism in the Third World, Routledge, London.

Murphy, PE (1994) - Tourism and Sustainable Development, in Global Tourism: The Next Decade (1994), edited by W.F.Theobald, Butterworth-Heinemann, London .

Pat, W (2001) -Ministry of Tourism and Youth Publication, Belmopan, Belize .

Pearce, PL (1994) - Tourist-resident Impacts: Examples, Explanations and Emerging Solutions, in Global Tourism: The Next Decade (1994), edited by W.F.Theobald, Butterworth-Heinemann, London Prosser, R (1994) - Societal Change and Growth in Alternative Tourism, in Ecotourism: A Sustainable Option? (1994), edited by E.Cater & G.Lowman, Wiley, UK.

Scheyvens, R (1999) - Ecotourism and the Empowerment of Local Communities, Tourism Management 20, p.245-249.

Sherman PB & Dixon JA (1991) - The Economics of Nature Tourism: Determining if it Pays, in Nature Tourism (1991) edited by T.Whelan, Island Press, Washington.

Bird, C (1997) - Communal Lands, Communal Problems, in Sustainable Tourism (1997) edited by L.France, Earthscan ,

UK .Boo, E (1991) - Making Ecotourism Sustainable: Recommendations for Planning, Development and Management, in Nature Tourism (1991) edited by T.Whelan, Island Press, Washington.

Duffy, R (2002) - A Trip too Far: Ecotourism, Politics and Exploitation, Earthscan, UK .Farrell, BH & Runyan D, (1991) - Ecology and Tourism, Annals of Tourism Research 18, p.26-40.

Gunn, C (1994) - Tourism Planning: Basics, Concepts, Cases, 3 rd edition, Taylor & Francis, Washington .Hardin, G (1968) - The Tragedy of the Commons, Science 162, p.1243-1248.

Harrison, D (1992) - Tourism to the Less Developed Countries: the Social Consequences, in Tourism and the Less Developed Countries, edited by D.Harrison, Wiley, Chicester.

"Travel & Tourism 2013". World Travel and Tourism Council. Retrieved 8 November 2013.

"India Tourism Statistics at a Glance". Market Research Division, Ministry of Tourism, Government of India. 23 July 2012. Retrieved 30 December 2012.

Websources

www.asenjournal.com

tourism.gov.in

www.ecoindia.com

kerala.gov.in

books.google.co.in

dste.puducerry.gov.in

ecoclub.com

dspace.iimk.ac.in

ECO TOURISM AND HOSPITALITY INDUSTRY: TRENDS AND ISSUES

Rajpreet Kaur

Research Scholar, Department of Management, SLIET,Longowal, Punjab, India.

Pardeep Jain

Professor,Department of Management,SLIET,Longowal, Punjab, India.

Abstract: This article gives a brief summary of green tourism and hospitality in the industry and introduces the information related to sustainability that may be helpful for use in hospitality and tourism education. Specifically, the focus of this paper is: What are the issues & problems in the hospitality and tourism field? Themes in sustainability education in the lodging, meetings and events, and food and beverage sectors are identified, applications of sustainability practices in hospitality and tourism operations are introduced, and views about the future direction of sustainability education in this field are provided. After reading this article, the reader should be able identify themes in positive and negative impact in a variety of hospitality related sectors. Next, attention is given to trends in the hospitality and tourism areas of lodging, meetings and events, and foodservice segments of the industry.

Keywords: Tourism, Hospitality, Sustainability, Green tourism, Trends

Introduction

This article provides a brief overview of eco tourism in general in the hospitality industry and introduces content information about sustainability that may be of useful in hospitality and tourism education.

In the continuum of tourism activities that stretch from conventional tourism to ecotourism proper, there has been a lot of contention to the limit at which biodiversity preservation, local social-economic benefits, and environmental impact can be considered "ecotourism". For this reason, environmentalists, special interest groups, and governments define ecotourism differently. Environmental organizations have generally insisted that ecotourism is nature-based, sustainably managed, conservation supporting, and environmentally educated. The tourist industry and governments, however, focus more on the product aspect, treating ecotourism as equivalent to any sort of tourism based in nature. As a further complication, many terms are used under the rubric of ecotourism. Nature tourism, low impact tourism, green tourism, bio-tourism, ecologically responsible tourism, and others have been used in literature and marketing, although they are not necessary synonymous with ecotourism.

Green Tourism

Green tourism is a form of sustainable tourism which calls for a clean healthy environment to put the tourism and hospitality industry on the path to sustainability. The following aspects need to be taken into consideration:

Sustainable development involves meeting the needs of the present without compromising the ability of future generations to meet their own needs.

The principles for environmental management comprise:

- o Corporate priority, highest corporate concern.
- o Employee education to be environmentally conscious.
- o Prior assessment, EIAs before development and after decommissioning of a project.
- o Researches on waste, pollution, emissions, etc

Positive Impact of Tourism

Tourism can bring many economic and social benefits, particularly in rural areas and developing countries, but mass tourism is also associated with negative effects. Tourism can only be sustainable if it is carefully managed so that potential negative effects on the host community and the environment are not permitted to outweigh the financial benefits.

Economic Effects

- o Creation of employment both through direct employment within the tourism industry and indirectly in sectors such as retail and transportation
- o Provides opportunities for small-scale business enterprises, which is especially important in rural communities, and generates extra tax revenues, such as airport and hotel taxes, which can be used for schools, housing and hospitals.

Social Effects

The improvements to infrastructure and new leisure amenities that result from tourism also benefit the local community. Tourism encourages the preservation of traditional customs, handicrafts and festivals that might otherwise have been allowed to wane, and it creates civic pride. Interchanges between hosts and guests create a better cultural understanding and can also help raise global awareness of issues such as poverty and human rights abuses.

Environmental Effects -- Positive

Tourism -- particularly nature and ecotourism -- helps promote conservation of wildlife and natural resources such as rain forests, as these are now regarded as tourism assets. It also helps generate funding for maintaining animal preserves and marine parks through entrance charges and guide fees. By creating alternative sources of employment, tourism reduces problems such as over-fishing and deforestation in developing nations.

Negative Impact of Tourism

- o Overcrowding
- o Decline of traditional activities such as farming
- o Regions become over-dependent on tourism
- o Demonstration effect

Local people aspire to the material standard and sex openness of the tourists

- o Acculturation

  Local culture gradually give way to foreign culture

  McDonaldization, Coca-colaization

Environmental Effects -- Negative

Tourism poses a threat to a region's natural and cultural resources, such as water supply, beaches, coral reefs and heritage sites, through overuse. It also causes increased pollution through traffic emissions, littering, increased sewage production and noise.

Ecotourism has become one of the fastest-growing sectors of the tourism industry, growing annually by 10-15% worldwide (Miller, 2007). One definition of ecotourism is "the practice of low-impact, educational, ecologically and culturally sensitive travel that benefits local communities and host countries" (Honey, 1999). Many of the ecotourism projects are not meeting these standards. Even if some of the guidelines are being executed, the local communities are still facing other negative impacts. South Africa is one of the countries that are reaping significant economic benefits from ecotourism, but negative effects-including forcing people to leave their homes, gross violations of fundamental rights, and environmental hazards-far outweigh the medium-term economic benefits (Miller, 2007). A tremendous amount of money is being spent and human resources continue to be used for ecotourism despite unsuccessful outcomes, and even more money is put into public relation campaigns to dilute the effects of criticism. Ecotourism channels resources away from other projects that could contribute more sustainable and realistic solutions to pressing social and environmental problems. But there is a tension in this relationship because ecotourism often causes conflict and changes in land-use rights, fails to deliver promises of community-level benefits, damages environments, and has plenty of other social impacts. Indeed many argue repeatedly that ecotourism is neither ecologically nor socially beneficial, As stated, the ecotourism structure must be improved to direct more money into host communities by reducing leakages for the industry to be successful in alleviating poverty in developing regions, but it provides a promising opportunity.

Environmental Hazards

The industrialization, urbanization, and unsustainable agriculture practices of human society are considered to be having a serious effect on the environment. Ecotourism is now also considered to be playing a role in this depletion. While the term ecotourism may sound relatively benign, one of its most serious impacts is its consumption of virgin territories (Kamuaro, 2007). These invasions often include deforestation, disruption of ecological life systems and various forms of pollution, all of which contribute to environmental degradation. The number of motor vehicles crossing the park increases as tour drivers search for rare species. The number of roads has disrupted the grass cover which has serious effects on plant and animal species. These areas also have a higher rate of disturbances and invasive species because of all the traffic moving off the beaten path into new undiscovered areas (Kamuaro, 2007) Kamuaro brings up a relatively obvious contradiction, any commercial venture into unspoiled, pristine land with or without the "eco" prefix as a contradiction in terms. To generate revenue you have to have a high number of traffic, tourists, which inevitably means a higher pressure on the environment.

Issues & Problems

Tourism and Hospitality industry impacts that cause concern

Hospitality is dogged by five major problem areas:

Energy consumption - Hospitality sector is a huge energy consumer for heating, cooling, electricity, transportation and imports over long distances Chlorofluorocarbons (CFCs) Refrigeration, and air conditioning equipment, are ozone depleting substances.

Water use - tourists are high consumers of water, for baths, showers, swimming pools, laundry, maintaining green and garden areas and sports facilities. Water quality and supply are therefore affected.

Solid waste disposal - large amounts of liquid and solid waste are produced mainly through boating and transportation and sometimes left to flow into rivers and lakes.

Environment commitment to protecting the Fragile nature - for example, accommodation in fragile or sensitive environments such as safari lodges can cause serious damage to the flora and fauna.

Employee education and Community Development, affect the willingness of the local population to accept the impacts and influences of the visitors.

Trends Shaping Tourism and Hospitality Development

- Lifestyles
- Branding
- Food production and supply
- Technology
- Legislation and regulations

Hospitality Trends

- Location: restaurants and bars will be available everywhere, plus a few exceptional places being 'destination' restaurants
  - Bars in Dublin, Ireland
  - Meson de Candido, Spain
  - Hospitality products are designed for market segments based on lifestyle
  - Family restaurants, sports bars and boutique hotels
- Branding
  - It is a key factor for companies to stand out from the competitors
- Trends in hospitality process design
  - Production lining: services are organized on a production-line basis
  - Decoupling: separating back-of-house from front-of-house activity in place and time

  - Customer participation: customers help themselves for service
- o Sustainability
  - Concerned about the environment
- o Security and assets
  - Customers expect that hotels are safe places for the guests and their property

  Implications

  - As new lifestyle groups emerge, hospitality products will be developed to meet the tastes of different groups.
- o More boutique hotels providing unique experiences
  - The baby boomer market is important in terms of size, their propensity to travel and the willingness to spend.

Code of Conduct for Tourists

A code of conduct can be developed for tourists and hosts alike that encourages use of renewable energies and reduced negative impacts on the environment through inclusion of the following:

1) Be energy conscious, turn off lights when you leave your hotel room, if necessary adjust thermostats;
2) Enjoy the National Parks, wildlife and monuments but leave them intact;
3) Use trash bins and if there isn't one carry your litter until you can dispose of it properly;
4) Use maps to plan routes before venturing out in a rental car. Use energy efficient transportation; and
5) Conserve water; ensure that all taps are not running before you leave. This will go a long way in conserving energy.

Conclusion

In addition to content about sustainability, an important part of sustainability education in hospitality and tourism is getting students to ask questions of operators and others about their practices related to sustainability. Educating students to become leaders and managers in the hospitality and tourism industry is not easy in an industry with high labor costs and frequently low profit margins, but ultimately the sustainability of the industry itself hinges on not only adapting to changes that necessitate sustainability, but becoming proactive innovators in the practice of sustainability. Hospitality and tourism professionals need to practice sustainability in financial operations; employee experiences; community action; facilities management; purchasing; food production, preparation, and service; planning and staging events and meetings; and as part of overall business plans and processes. Further policies on educating stakeholders on the benefits of using renewable energy sources via the internet, through a website and the development of a code of conduct to ensure best practices for tourists and hosts have been proposed.

References

Cooper, D.R. and Schindler, P.S. (2003), Business Research Methods, New Delhi, TataMcGraw-Hill.

Gunn, C.A. (1994), Tourism planning: Basics, concepts, cases, (3 ed.), Washington, D.C, Taylor & Francis.

Holden, A. (2000), Environment and Tourism, Routledge, London.

Honey, M. and Gilpin, R. (2009), Tourism in the Developing World: Promoting Peace and Reducing Poverty, United States Institute for Peace, Washington.

International Union for the conservation of Nature and Natural Resources (1980), World Conservation

Strategy. Living Resource Conservation for Sustainable Development, IUCN, Gland.

Kamauro, O. (1996). Ecotourism: Suicide or Development? Voices from Africa #6: Sustainable Development, UN Non-Governmental Liaison Service. United Nations News Service.

Leiper, N. (1990), Tourism systems: an interdisciplinary perspective, Palmerston North, N.Z, Massey University

Marunda, E., Sai, J.P. and Muchenje, B. (2013), "Challenges facing use of energy in the tourism and hospitality industry in Zimbabwe and policies that can promote the sustainable use of renewable energy and tourism development", International Journal of Development and Sustainability, Vol. 2 No. 2, pp. 472-484.

Mellgren, Doug (2007-05-16). "Travel Experts See Worrisome Downside to Ecotourism". Associated Press. Retrieved 2007-05-21.

Tuohino, A., and A. Hynonen (2001). Ecotourism-imagery and reality. Reflections on concepts and practices in Finnish rural tourism. Nordia Geographical Publications. pp. 30(4):21-34.

UN-WTO (1999), United Nations - World Tourism Organization, Marketing Tourism Destinations On-line:

Strategies for the Information Age, Madrid: UN-WTO.

UN-WTO (2011), World Tourism Organisation, Yearbook of Tourism Statistics, Compendium of Tourism

Statistics and data files, Madrid: UN-WTO.

http://www.jsedimensions.org/wordpress/content/sustainability-education-focusing-on-hospitality-tourism-and-travel_2013_02/

http://en.wikipedia.org/wiki/Ecotourism

http://www.jsedimensions.org/wordpress/content/sustainability-education-focusing-on-hospitality-tourism-and-travel_2013_02/

http://traveltips.usatoday.com/positive-negative-effects-tourism-63336.html

ECOTOURISM - WAY TO GO GREEN

Ram Mehar

Assistant Professor, Department of Education, USOL, Panjab University Chandigarh, India.

Abstract: The present paper highlights the green tourism, ecotourism and role of ecotourism in developing a sustainable green economy. Ecotourism is nature based tourism that involves education and interpretation of the natural environment and is managed to be ecologically sustainable. The various principles of ecotourism are to minimize the negative impacts on nature and culture that can damage a destination, to educate the traveler on the importance of conservation, to stress the importance of responsible business, which works cooperatively with local authorities and people to meet local needs and deliver conservation benefits, to direct revenues to the conservation and management of natural and protected areas, to emphasize use of environmental and social base-line studies, as well as long-term monitoring programs, to assess and minimize impacts, strive to maximize economic benefit for the host country, local business and communities, particularly peoples living in and adjacent to natural and protected areas and to rely on infrastructure that has been developed in harmony with the environment, minimizing use of fossil fuels, conserving local plants and wildlife, and blending with the natural and cultural environment. This paper also highlights the role of ecotourism in developing a sustainable green economy.

Introduction

The emergence of tourism as a major industry is one of the most remarkable changes that have taken place in the global economic activity (Sinclair, 1998). Tourism is the third largest economic activity in the world (after oil and automobiles), and it is one of the fastest-growing activities (Batta, 2009). The World Tourism Organization (WTO, 2008) projects that by the year 2010, international tourist arrivals will have increased to 1.018 billion and a direct receipt is expected to US$1.55 trillion. Receipts from tourism make an important contribution to the economies of the developing countries in terms of income, employment, and balance of payments effects. Because of this, many developing countries have begun to actively pursue tourism as a means to create jobs, diversify their economies, and earn foreign currency.

Among the three major impacts of tourism-economic, socio-cultural and environmental-the economic impact played a dominant role in policy-making (Sinclair, 1998). Based on the economic benefits, tourism development was prescribed as a panacea for many social and economic problems. This led to the indiscriminate and unplanned growth of tourism infrastructure in many countries, and soon the negative effects in the form of social and environmental degradation began to emerge. Due to enhanced awareness of the negative impact of tourism on the environment, efforts have been made to develop approaches for making tourism sustainable. The last two decades have witnessed a growing interest in the relationship between tourism development and environmental quality (Erdogan and Tosun, 2009), with the emergence of special interest tourism including green tourism.

Green tourism

The concept of a green product is one that is easier to use than to define. Green tourism is used to indicate environmentally friendly tourism but have different focuses and meanings. Often such claims use terms which lack of accepted or standard definitions, or utilize extravagant language to wash the emptiness of the claim being made (NCC, 1996). These terms are used for two purposes: first, to tell customers that the holiday destination they are going to is beautiful. Green tourism or another term related to environmental concern is mostly used to label nature holidays to exotic destinations (Wight, 1994). Second, green tourism claims can be used to signal that tourism operations taking place in that area do not harm the environment (Font and Tribe, 2001). In other terms, a product or service can be said to be green when it is beneficial to the producer and consumer without harming the environment. The difficulty starts when a stakeholder attempts to measure the negative effects of their activities on the environment. Even in cases where measurement seems possible, the next difficulty arises at agreeing the criteria to be considered and the threshold levels of unacceptable effects. Tourism traditionally has been considered a relatively green industry, with the exception of its transport and land development implications, and for this reason it has only recently become an area of concern (Font and Tribe, 2001).

Green tourism, which is an important component of sustainable tourism, is defined as ? travel to destinations where the flora, fauna, and cultural heritage are the primary attractions. This definition is further expanded to include environmentally sustainable travel to destinations where climate impacts are minimized with the aim of respecting and preserving natural resources and adapting programs to fit the context of fragile resources (NCC, 1996; Graci and Dodds, 2008). Green tourism is important to encourage travel that would help support natural and cultural aspects, while encouraging respect for and conservation of urban resources and cultural diversity.

Green tourism is defined as environmentally friendly tourism activities with various focuses and meanings. In a broad term, green tourism is about being an environmentally friendly tourist or providing environmentally friendly tourist services. The green tourism concept would be highly appealing to tourism enterprises and operators owing to increasing governmental pressure to improve environmental performance by adopting effective and tangible environmental management techniques. According to Dodds and Joppe (2001), the green tourism concept can be broken down into four components:

i. Environmental responsibility-protecting, conserving, and enhancing nature and the physical environment to ensure the long-term health of the life-sustaining eco-system.

ii. Local economic vitality-supporting local economies, businesses and communities to ensure economic vitality and sustainability.

iii. Cultural diversity-respecting and appreciating cultures and cultural diversity so as to ensure the continued well-being of local or host cultures.

iv. Experiential richness-providing enriching and satisfying experiences through active, personal and meaningful participation in, and involvement with, nature, people, places and cultures.

Ecotourism

Ecotourism was coined by Hector Ceballos-Lascurain in Mexico City in 1983. He defined it as "travelling to relatively undisturbed or uncontaminated areas with the specific object of studying, admiring, and enjoying the scenery, its wild plants and animals, as well as any existing cultural manifestations found in these areas". Ecotourism is also known as ecologically based tourism or nature based tourism. Ecotourism goes beyond sightseeing to enhancing visitors' understanding of the scientific and ecological features of our natural attractions. This means that ecotourism must:

- recognise the intrinsic value of nature and accept that National Parks are primarily for conservation of fauna, flora and landscapes
- promote and develop ecologically and culturally sustainable travel and tourism
- promote and foster the conservation of and investment in the natural and cultural resources used for tourism
- develop ethics and standards for ecotourism
- educate and inspire tourists through participation to enjoy and appreciate the importance of natural and cultural assets

In other words, ecotourism is based upon ecologically sustainable visitation to natural areas that fosters environmental and cultural understanding, appreciation and conservation.

The National Ecotourism Strategy (1994) defines ecotourism as: "Ecotourism is nature based tourism that involves education and interpretation of the natural environment and is managed to be ecologically sustainable."

Principles of ecotourism

- o Minimize the negative impacts on nature and culture that can damage a destination.
- o Educate the traveler on the importance of conservation.
- o Stress the importance of responsible business, which works cooperatively with local authorities and people to meet local needs and deliver conservation benefits.
- o Direct revenues to the conservation and management of natural and protected areas.
- o Emphasize the need for regional tourism zoning and for visitor management plans designed for either regions or natural areas that are slated to become ego-destinations.
- o Emphasize use of environmental and social base-line studies, as well as long-term monitoring programs, to assess and minimize impacts.
- o Strive to maximize economic benefit for the host country, local business and communities, particularly peoples living in and adjacent to natural and protected areas.
- o Seek to ensure that tourism development does not exceed the social and environmental limits of acceptable change as determined by researchers in cooperation with local residents.
- o Rely on infrastructure that has been developed in harmony with the environment, minimizing use of fossil fuels, conserving local plants and wildlife, and blending with the natural and cultural environment.

Green economy

The Green Economy can be considered synonymous to a 'sustainable' economy that ensures economic systems conserve natural resources through balancing growth and equity. This conservation and management of ecosystems provides a long-term benefit for people while allowing for sustainable growth. The Green Economy balances natural resource values with other values, and takes into account the loss in value of ecosystem services due to environmental impacts. These requirements for the need for greater valuation of ecosystem services fit well with other aspirations of the Green Economy in respect of clean, renewable energy. The Green Economy provides a chance to "get the balance sheet right" by accounting for both the current and future value of the benefit ecosystems provide to people. The essence of the Green Economy is that it recognizes the sum total of all ecosystems services and how they collectively provide the complete life system support we need.

Role of ecosystems in developing a sustainable 'green economy'

Ecosystems mitigate Climate Change

Planet Earth is a dynamic geological and biological system. It produces and absorbs carbon and other green house gases through a range of natural cycles and across a wide variety of ecosystems, which has resulted in the past climate patterns. However, human activity has intervened in these natural carbon cycles by:

i. creating major new sources of carbon emissions from the use of fossil fuels;

ii. releasing carbon through deforestation, forest degradation, agricultural practices, and other land use change; and

iii. destroying or transforming natural ecosystems that capture and store carbon. Put crudely, humans activities are now releasing more carbon to the atmosphere than natural systems can absorb.

Ecosystems currently absorb about half of anthropogenic carbon dioxide emissions. But ecosystem absorption capacity is declining by about 1% per decade and is likely to decline more rapidly due to global warming and human impacts. At the present time emissions due to human activity are increasing. The net effect is that there is an increasing imbalance between carbon emissions and absorption capacity of the Earth. Therefore, to achieve climate stabilisation there is a need to manage all three components of the global carbon cycle, not just those resulting from fossil fuel emissions and other human activities. This means managing the carbon sinks, too: the world's oceans, forests, grasslands, soils, and other ecosystems which can uptake and store carbon and in so doing, decreasing another source of emissions. Well managed and adequately protected ecosystems can help mitigate climate change impacts by both reducing emission levels while increasing carbon uptake and storage. Inadequate ecosystem protection has lead to degradation and therefore a decline in various ecosystem services whilst reducing the ability of ecosystems to regulate our climate.

Ecosystems provide valuable adaptation mechanisms

Ecosystems and the benefits they provide (e.g. climate regulation, food security, freshwater supply, disaster risk reduction) are fundamental to supporting people's livelihoods and other life on Earth. Ecosystems play an important role in both ecosystem-based mitigation (carbon sequestration and storage), as described previously and ecosystem-based adaptation (i.e. nature-based societal adaptation to climate change impacts). For example:

- o Naturally connected floodplains and riparian ecosystems can provide flood protection for millions of people who are likely to experience increased flood risk
- o Forest protection and reforestation can provide clean water and reduced flood risk.
- o Deep-rooted, nitrogen fixing plants can naturally replenish soil nutrients in agricultural systems helping maintain access to food supplies. These same plants can help filter sediments and nutrients keeping our waters clean and available for human consumption while enhancing carbon sinks.
- o Mangrove forests provide protection services from coastal erosion and protect human lives in the face of severe storms while providing nurseries for fish which can feed coastal populations of people
- o Coral and Shellfish reefs provide protection from storm surges and are a source of food and economic resources.
- o Well managed and conserved grasslands provide forage for livestock while storing carbon in above and below ground biomass.

Ecosystems support people's well-being and can alleviate poverty

Maintaining a healthy natural resource base is critical for the benefit of all people, especially the rural poor. Over 2 billion (usually rural) people live on less than $2 per day, many of whom depend on natural resources for their well-being. Conserving natural resources can, therefore, have significant positive gains for these peoples' well-being. For example:

- Those who fish or farm for subsistence requires natural resources to survive. Sustainable harvest and production practices can help ensure longer-term access to these products.
- The poor have the least ability to change if and when their way of life is threatened - i.e. least ability to relocate, change land use, alter income source, etc. Conservation or sustainable use of natural ecosystems can help buffer potential climate impacts through helping ensure provision of key services such as water purification or soil stabilization making people less likely to have to relocate.
- The poor are the most likely to lack basic shelter and sanitation needs and therefore those most impacted by weather and changing weather patterns. Maintaining and protecting particular ecosystems can provide protection services, as mentioned previously, for vulnerable populations. As demonstrated in these examples, ecosystems can play a pivotal role in climate adaptation through service provision. Ecosystem services are often beneficial at a local level and/or a small scale so conservation and restoring natural ecosystems can help the poor who directly depend on such benefit and buffer them from impacts due to climate and weather changes.

Hence, ecosystem recognizes that 'natural environment' included cultural components and that 'ecologically sustainable' involves an appropriate return to the local community and long term conservation of the resource. It notes that ecotourism, like any other tourism type, should be sustainable, provide visitor satisfaction, local benefits, and be 'appropriate' to its environment and cultural setting. A five-fold solution is proposed:

- Decrease fossil fuel based and other greenhouse gas emissions.
- Reduce deforestation and degradation of forests and other ecosystems to expand natural carbon sinks.

- o Promote ecosystem-based adaptation across all sectors.
- o Develop strategies to extract growth and employment from the ecosystem restoration based activities (social forestry, coastal zone management).
- o Centralize nature based solutions within all areas of economic policy development.

References

Batta, R. N. (2009). Green tourism certification manual. Tokyo: Asian Productivity Organization. Retrieved from http://www.apo-tokyo.org/00e-books/GP-18_GreenTourism.htm#contents

Dodds, R., & Joppe, M. (2001). Promoting urban green tourism: The development of the other map of Toronto. Journal of Vacation Marketing, 7(3), 261-267.

Erdogan, N., & Tosun, C. (2009). Environmental performance of tourism accommodations in the protected areas: Case of Goreme historical National Park. International Journal of Hospitality Management, 28(3), 406-414.

Font, X., & Tribe, J. (2001). Promoting green tourism: The future of environmental awards. International Journal of Tourism Research, 3(1), 9-21.

Graci, S., & Dodds, R. (2008). Why go green? The business case for environmental commitment in the Canadian hotel industry, Anatolia: An International Journal of Tourism and Hospitality Research, 19(2), 251-270.

Knight, J. (1996). Competing hospitalities in Japanese rural tourism. Annals of Tourism Research, 23(1), 165-180.

NCC (1996). Green claims: A consumer investigation into marketing claims about the environment. London: National Consumer Council.

Sinclair, M. T. (1998). Tourism and economic development: A survey. The Journal of Development Studies, 34(5), 1-51.

Wight, P. (1994). Environmentally responsible marketing of tourism. In E. Cater, & G. Lowman (Eds.), Ecotourism: A sustainable option, 39-52. Wiley: Chichester.

A STUDY OF TOURIST SATISFACTION IN KURUKSHETRA PANORAMA & SCIENCE CENTRE

Ravi Bhushan Kumar

Professor, Department of Tourism & Hotel Management, Kurukshetra University, Kurukehetra. ravibhushankumar1999@rediffmail.com

Lakhvinder Singh

Research Scholar, Department of Tourism & Hotel Management, Kurukshetra University, Kurukehetra. lakhvindersingh.kuk@gmail.com

Abstract: Museums/science centers are increasing becoming the important attractions of many destinations. Many times such museums/science centers become so popular that they are integral part of tourist itinerary. So, the measurement of tourist satisfaction has become the key factor to survival in competitive tourism business. The present study is based on Science centre situated at the religious destination of Kurukshetra. The present paper discusses the visitor satisfaction towards Kurukshetra Panorama & Science Centre and their intention to revisit and willingness to recommend it to others. The data for the study were primarily collected through a well structured questionnaire however some secondary sources such as journals, books, and several reports related to research area were also used to provide a theoretical framework for the study. The result of the study revealed that tourists were satisfied to a large extent with their visit to the Panorama and positive attitude their intention to revisit and willingness to recommend. The study will contribute in the improvement of the services in the similar establishments of tourism industry.

Keywords: Tourist's satisfaction, Panorama & Science Centre Tourist loyalty, Service sector.

Introduction

Science museums/ centers provide a good range of educational, social, cultural and economic benefits to societies. In every sense they enhance the quality of lives of the people and can play a significant role in develop a sense of identity (Ecsite, 2001). By the turn of the last millennium, there were about 1200 science centers all over the world attracting some 184 million visitors and with a turnover of USD 1.4 billion (Beetlestone et al, 1998; Persson, 1999; Persson, 2005). Along with its contribution in enhancement of employment of local revenue it also plays a significant role in the development of local, regional and international tourism.

The Indian Science Centers at present are carefully studying and assessing the impact of their activities at the individual, societal and economic levels for increasing efficiency and higher impact. This, of course, is a very important aspect of the Science Centre movement in a country like India where diversities in language, customs, local issues and scientific illiteracy are major social issues (Mukhopadyay, 2005). Museums are frequently visited by the tourists as they serve the tourist with physical, socio- cultural and psychological entertainment.

Museum is a place, building or institute for gathering and collecting things which have significant historical, cultural and scientific importance with great value of information and knowledge. It disseminates information, on an enduring basis, through exhibits and displays presented in an entertaining framework to a visiting public. The Longman Dictionary of Contemporary English defines a museum as 'a museum is a building where important cultural or scientific objects are kept and shown to the public (www.dictionary.msn.com).

The development of the science museum net in India started in 1956, when the government of that country created the Industry and Technology Museum in Calcutta. Later on the Government of

India decided to incorporate an autonomous society titled 'National Council of Science Museums' on 4th April 1978 to work for the expansion and formulation of science museums/centres in India (Mukhopadyay, 2005). The existing Science Museums at Kolkata, Bangalore, Mumbai, Kapurthala, Science centre at Hyderabad, Digha, Dharampur, Panaji, Ahemadabad, Bhubhneshwar, Bhopal, Lucknow, Calicut, Patna, Kurukshetra and many more were subsequently serving to the society.

These sites were visited by numbers of tourists as they they provide the visitors with reasonable and reliable explanations about all kinds of phenomena related to science in simple and complex way. Hence, it is necessary to study the visitor based studies on science centers in order to bring together expansion of museums and tourism industry.

Panda & Mohanty (2010) after recognizing the touristic importance of museums some of them were established near picnic spots and historic cities so that visitors enjoy both of the places. For example the Kurukshetra Panorama & Science Centre is situated at the destination of Kurukshetra which is world famous land of historical and mythological importance famous for its great battle of Mahabharata and origin of great epic Gita by Lord Krishna. There are several places of tourist interest in the entire city of Kurukshetra. But the Science museum / science centre situated there is a type of museum with specific characteristics, special ways of presentation, exhibition, and interpretation.

This paper is an attempt to find out the satisfaction level of the tourists visiting Kurukshetra Panorama & Science Centre. So, the researcher is interested to discuss only science museums/centre in this paper.

Kurukshetra panorama & science centre

The Kurukshetra Panorama and Science Centre are a beautiful cylindrical building that is used for exhibitions and working models for visitor's activities. It has two different types of exhibits in the ground floor and in the first floor with cylindrical walls. A few scientific objects also are displayed in the centre.

In the ground floor, an exhibition called 'India-A Heritage in Science, Technology and Culture, consisting of working and interactive exhibits on ancient Indian concept of properties of matter, structure of atom, geometry, arithmetical rules, astronomy medicine and surgery. Housed in a tall and cylindrical building, with its elegant architecture and ambience, the main attraction of the Centre is a life-like Panorama of the epic battle of Kurukshetra. Standing at the centre of the cylindrical hall, one can feel the towering 34 feet high paintings of the episodes from the 18-day confrontation between the Pandavas and the Kauravas come alive before his eyes. Merged with this is the diorama of the battleground that epitomizes the carnage realistically. The chanting of Gita and distant war crimes mingled with lighting illusions create the perfect ambience. A Science Park has also been set up outside the four walls of the centre's building.The centre is located is within the town centre of Kurukshetra which offers many local hotels and dharmshalas having deluxe and economy accommodation. A guest house of Haryana Tourism Corporation is also situated near Panorama. The centre is located about 1.5 kms from railway station. Taxis / cabs are available in abundance to take the tourists to the attraction. Buses, both private and HSRTC operated also run within the city.

Objective of the study

The present research work based on Kurukshetra Panorama & Science Centre with following objectives has been considered.

1. To study tourist' satisfaction with selected attributes of Kurukshetra Panorama & Science Centre.
2. To study the tourists' intention to revisit and willingness to recommend the museum to others.

Literature review

Millions of tourists visit number of destinations in search of education with entertainment to informal learning facilities such as zoos, aquariums, botanical gardens, and science centers. These purposes may appear to be inconsistent, entertainment and education placing different demands on such facilities in relation to the nature of exhibits, context in which they are displayed. In particular, as numerous researchers have noted (Lucas, 1983; Rennie & McClafferty, 1996; Tunnicliffe, 1996), that an exhibit is no guarantee that an individual has engaged intellectually or perceives the experience as one from which learning about a scientific concept or principle could result.

Science education movements have enhanced from the last few decade which created the need to promote a better understanding of science and technology, to develop applicable knowledge on fundamental science concepts, on the methodological nature of science and on its relations with other domains of the society, science museums and science centers, aimed at accelerating the pace of change through the sharing of knowledge about science, technology and ancient history & culture. Science museums/centers provide an opportunity for visitors to learn about the phenomena of nature and substance of science. As open-ended, unstructured environments, science museums allow for freedom of learning.

However, there now exists a growing body of research centered on the learning-associated behaviors of nonschool visitors: families, couples, and peer groups (Dierking et al, 1994 and Macmanus, 1987). The present study got guidelines from this body for research by investigating satisfaction of such visitors at an interactive Kurukshetra Panorama & Science Centre

The level of interaction with exhibits depends on a number of variables. Several studies have focused on visitor characteristics and on the relation between these characteristics and learning data. Gender is among the aspects studied most often. Some investigators noted differences between interactions with exhibits on the basis of the gender of the visitor (Kubota & Olstad, 1991; Tully & Lucas, 1990).Science museums and science centers can generate a sense of wonder, interest, enthusiasm and motivation to learn that should be explored (Pedrett, 2002; Ramney et al, 1994). Moreover, science centers can & address aspects of science education that might be missing in more formal, class-based learning, like the promotion of an awareness of the relevance of science to society (Jarvis & Pell, 2002). A network of science centers, distributed throughout the country, intended to be interactive spaces of science and technology, are now visited by hundreds of students every year, assuming an important role in science & technology dissemination. Kurukshetra Panorama & Science Centre one amongst the science centers of the country which are frequently visited by the tourists as well as learners. Visits to interactive science and technology centers, museums, aquariums, and zoos provide valuable motivational opportunities for students to learn science and they affect students' learning. Overall, the research suggests that students usually find visits enjoyable but both the amount and nature of their cognitive and affective learning vary (Rennie & McClafferty (1995).

Visitors are not necessarily coming to museums to learn, and that visitors want to have a variety of experiences available. "Visitor needs must be met by providing what will have been perceived to have been an enjoyable, enriching, satisfying and beneficial experience (Beehu & Prentice, 1995). There are a number of studies that consider other ways of researching and Conceptualizing visitor experience in museums & science centers.

In a study to measure visitor satisfaction by comparing their expectations and experiences with three museums of Port Elizabeth. The author stated that museums play a significant role in becoming the fastest growing segments of the tourism industry. So, it is becoming more important for museum managers to identify the variables that will enhance the attraction and retention of museum visitors. The author presented a brief overview of the museum experience, and visitors' satisfaction with different museum attributes and functions that might impact customer satisfaction. The study is based on eight factors, namely, human interaction, physical evidence, facilities, facility quality, exhibition, edutainment, escape and aestheticism. It was found that the satisfaction mean scores were consistently higher than the expectation mean scores. This implies that museum visitors were satisfied with their experience of the three heritage museums in Port Elizabeth (Huo, 2009).

The study on customer satisfaction and the relationships between customer satisfaction and demographics of visitors to history museum stores in New Mexico revealed that three variables: age of participant, place of residence, and those experiencing their first visit to the museum had low positive relationships with customer satisfaction. However, the findings revealed strong positive relationships between satisfaction with the museum, general life satisfaction, and satisfaction with the museum store (Rogers, 1998).

Study on the National Museum of Prehistory was designed to understand the service quality and tourist satisfaction of the Museum of Prehistory through the visitors' experiences. The research was carried out by focusing six factors related to museums i.e. educational entertainment, responsiveness and assurance, reliability, tangibility, convenience, and care. The findings indicated that the tourists were most satisfied with the first three items in survey form which are the overall environmental cleanliness, ticketing process, and air conditioning. All the six factors were directly correlated with most of the overall satisfaction of the Museum of Prehistory (Ying & Chien, 2008).

With the purpose to determine the relative importance of the Robert Louis Stevenson (RLS) museum in Samoa in the measurement of tourist satisfaction was conducted. A correlation model was performed to determine the relationship of the satisfaction and attributes of the museum and visitors' intention to recommend the museum. The results show that the visitor who has a high satisfaction intends to recommend the RLS museum to others (Huo & Miller, 2007).

The relationships among destination image, tourist satisfaction and destination loyalty of tourists was investigated in Sirind horn Museum of Thailand (Yasamorn & Phokla, 2012). The results indicate that destination image relates positively to tourist satisfaction. Moreover, tourist satisfaction relates positively destination loyalty as well. Additionally, the potential discussion with the results, theoretical and managerial contributions are described as well. Interactive exhibits in museums have become commonplace they have been found to be effective teaching tools; they can increase the attracting power of the exhibit and can help create mindfulness in visitors (Fino, 2008). However, interactive are considered primarily the domain of science and technology museums and there is lack of research regarding interactive in living history museums.

As mentioned earlier, museums play very important role in tourist's itinerary. Several destinations are known for their world famous museums and their unique collections. They are essential part of tourists' itinerary, particularly among the students, families or educated group. In India, several museums including science centers are very popular. These science museums are encouraging the development of science and technology in interesting manner. Hence, it is essential to understand how visitors behave in science centre and how much they were satisfied with their visit so that the science museums or science centers can be designed as per visitors' expectation. A satisfied visitor brings word of mouth publicity to the science centers and ensures their repeat visitation.

From the above studies it can be revealed that there is lack of studies on Science Centre in India mainly in study area. The present paper is an attempt to fill the existing gap in this scenario by focusing on tourist satisfaction towards Kurukshetra Panorama Science Centre.

Research methodology

The study has used both; the primary data collected in the form of survey audit from tourists as well as the secondary sources of information in terms of reports, data, literature related with museums and science museums. The study area was Kurukshetra Panorama & Science Centre. The duration of this study was about six months, to reduce any type of seasonal biasness. The data was collected through a well structured questionnaire, both closed ended and open ended by adopting convenient sampling technique. The questionnaire was distributed to 350 visitors and out of which 250 visitors completely filled up the questionnaire. The questionnaires were filled over a long span of period to reduce biasness of seasonality of tourism. Normally the questionnaires were asked from the leader of groups or family. After collecting the data it has been analyzed and presented with the help of tables & figures in an understandable form. The statistical tools used in this paper are percentage, frequency distribution and mean/average. On the basis of extensive review of literature the researcher explored that it is essential to study the tourist satisfaction towards Kurukshetra Panorama & Science Centre by focusing each & every attributes/elements of the destination. The present study based on several attributes of Kurukshetra Panorama & Science Centre viz. accessibility & location of the Panorama, parking space, entrance fee structure, convenience of visiting Hours, building of the panorama, outside environment of Panorama, toilets & drinking water Facility, clear sign posting and directions, exhibition of items, multimedia presentations, behavior of guides & attendants in Panorama, new learning from Panorama, educational value of the exhibits, scientific & technological value, cultural & heritage value, entertainment value of the exhibits as the variables contributing in the tourist satisfaction. All the above attributes contribute emphatically towards the destination loyalty in terms of Intention to return as well as indicate his willingness to recommend the destination to others.

Result of the study

Result of the study is discussed in three parts namely: demographic profile of the respondents, visitors' satisfaction towards several attributes of the Kurukshetra Panorama & Science Centre and thirdly visitors' intention to revisit the Panorama and their willingness to recommend this to others.

Demographic Profile of the Respondents

Table

S.N.	Tourist Characteristics	Percentage of the respondents
1.	Gender	Male: 72.4%, Female: 27.6%
2.	Age	Up to 20:38.8%, 21-40: 46.8%, 41-60: 12.4%, Above 60: 2%
3.	State of Domicile	Haryana: 60.4%, Other than Haryana: 29.6%.
4.	Education	Up to matric:10.8%, Intermediate:23.6%, Graduate: 46%, Post Graduate: 10%, Above Post Graduate:5.6%
5.	Occupation	Students: 55.6%, Servicemen: 20.4%, Businessman:16.8%, Others: 7.2%
6.	Annual Income	Up to 2 Lakh: 50.4%, 2-5 Lakh: 32.8, 5-10 Lakh: 13.6%, Above 10 Lakh: 3.2%

7.	Frequency of Visit	First Visit: 72.4%, Repeat Visit: 27.6%
8.	Purpose of Visit	Education: 42%, Entertainment: 44%, Unique Experience:14%

Out of 250 respondents 72.4 percent were male where as 27.6 percent were female. 38.8 percent respondents were up to 20 years of age, near about half of the respondents 46.8 percents were between 21-40 years, 12.4 percent were in the age group of 41-60 years and remaining 2 percent were either of 60 or above 60 years. More than half of the respondents 60.4 percent from the home state Haryana instead of 29.6 percent those who were from outside Haryana. Only 10.8 percent were educated up to matric, 23.6 percent intermediate, largest portion of respondents 46 percent graduate, 10 percent were post graduate and only 5.6 percent above post graduate level. Major portion of the respondents were students 55.6 percent, 20.4 percent respondents were serviceperson, 16.8 percent were businessperson and only 7.2 percent were involved in some other occupations. A total of 50.4 percent respondents were hold income level up to 2 lakh, 32.8 percent were among those who were in income group of 2-5 lakh, 13.6 were among 5-10 lakh and only 3.2 percent respondents were above 10 lakh. On asking about frequency of visit to the Panorama researcher found 72.4 percent were repeat visitors in comparison of 27.6 percent who were first time visitor. Out of total 42 percent respondents visited the Panorama for the purpose of education, 44 percent were visited for entertainment and only 14 percent were those who visited for some unique experience.

Tourist satisfaction with attributes of kurukshetra panorama & science centre (in percentage)

Table: I

Attribute	Highly Satisfied	Satisfied	Neutral	Dissatisfied	Highly Dissatisfied
Accessibility & Location of the Panorama	55.6	33.2	11.2	0	0
Parking Space	22	58	17.6	2.4	0

Entrance fee Structure	28.4	52.4	18	0.4	0.8
Convenience of visiting Hours	28	54	17.6	0.4	0
Building of the Panorama	36.8	50.4	12.4	0.4	0
Outside Environment of Panorama	27.6	55.2	14.4	2.8	0
Toilets & Drinking Water Facility	20	62	14.8	2.8	0.4
Clear sign posting and directions	30	50.4	16	3.6	0
Exhibition of items	29.6	54.4	13.2	2.8	0
Multimedia Presentations	28.8	53.2	12	5.2	0.8
Behavior of Guides & Attendants in Panorama	28	50.8	11.6	9.6	0
New Learning from Panorama	30.8	53.2	15.2	0.4	0.4
Educational value of the Exhibits	30.8	57.2	11.2	0.4	0.4
Scientific & Technological Value	29.2	58.4	12.4	0	0
Cultural & Heritage Value	30.8	57.2	12	0	0
Entertainment value of the Exhibits	29.2	58.8	12	0	0

Tourists were questioned to express their satisfaction level towards the different attributes of Kurukshetra Panorama & Science Centre. First of all tourists were questioned about accessibility & location of the Panorama and more than half of respondents i.e. 55.6 percent were highly satisfied followed by 33.2 percent satisfied and 11.2 percent were neutral on this question whereas no respondents is dissatisfied with accessibility & location of the Panorama. Regarding parking space available almost one fifth i.e. 22 percent of respondents were highly satisfied, more than half of the respondents 58 percent were satisfied. 17.6 percent respondents were showed their neutrality whereas only 2.4 percent respondents were dissatisfied. In respect of entrance fee structure 28.4 percent respondents were highly satisfied, 52.54 percent were satisfied followed by 18 percent who were neither satisfied nor dissatisfied whereas only 1.2 percent respondents were dissatisfied and highly dissatisfied jointly.

28 percent respondents were highly satisfied with the convenient visiting hours, 54 percent were satisfied, 17.6 percent were neutral in their response where only 0.4 percent were dissatisfied. Almost one third 36.8 percent were highly satisfied with the building of the panorama, 50.4 percent respondents were satisfied, 12.4 percent neither satisfied nor dissatisfied only 0.4 percent respondents showed

dissatisfaction. Regarding outside environment of the Panorama almost one fourth 27.6 percent respondents were highly satisfied, more than half of the respondents 55.2 percent were satisfied. 14.4 percent respondents were showed their neutrality whereas only 2.8 percent respondents were dissatisfied. While responding about drinking water and toilets facilities one fifth 20 percent respondents were highly satisfied and 62 percent were satisfied where as only 14.8 percent were neither satisfied nor dissatisfied. A total of 3.2 respondents were dissatisfied and dissatisfied collectively.

In respect of signs posting and directions inside the panorama 30 percent respondents were highly satisfied, almost half of the respondents i.e. 50.4 percent were satisfied and 16 percents respondents were neither satisfied nor dissatisfied whereas only 3.6 respondents were dissatisfied. 29.6 percent respondents were highly satisfied with exhibition of items inside the Panorama and more than half 54.4 percent were satisfied. A total of 13.2 percent respondents were showed neutral response and only 2.8 percent respondents were dissatisfied with the exhibition of items of the Panorama. In response to multimedia presentations 28.8 percent respondents were highly satisfied, 53.2 percent satisfied, 12 percent were neither satisfied nor dissatisfied. A total of 5.2 percent respondents were dissatisfied whereas only 0.8 percents were highly dissatisfied.

A total of 28 percent respondents were highly satisfied with the behavior of the guides and attendants of the panorama and almost half 50.8 percent respondents were satisfied with the same. 11.6 percents respondents were neutral on this question where as 9.6 percent respondents were not satisfied with the staff of the panorama.

Respondents were also questioned about learning value of the panorama 30.8 percent respondents were highly satisfied and 53.2 percent were satisfied. Only 15.2 percent were neither satisfied nor dissatisfied where as only 0.8 percent respondents were dissatisfied and highly dissatisfied collectively. 30.8 percent respondents were highly satisfied with educational importance of the exhibits of Panorama, more than half 57.2 percent were satisfied where as 11.2

respondents showed neutral response on this question and only 0.4 respondents each were dissatisfied and dissatisfied respectively. In respect of scientific & technological value of the panorama 29.2 percent respondents were highly satisfied and 58.2 percent were satisfied. 12.4 percent respondents were neither satisfied nor dissatisfied. In response to cultural & heritage value of the panorama 30.8 percent respondents were highly satisfied, 57.2 percent were satisfied, 12 percent were neither satisfied nor dissatisfied. 29.2 respondents were highly satisfied regarding entertainment value of the panorama. 58.8 percent were satisfied where as 12 percent were neither satisfied nor dissatisfied.

Overall satisfaction of the visitors with kuruskhetra panorama & science centre

Table: II

N: 250

Overall Satisfaction Level	**Point Scale (x)**	**Frequency (f)**	**fx**	**Percentage**
Highly Satisfied	5	65	325	26
Satisfied	4	137	548	54.8
Neutral	3	33	99	13.2
Dissatisfied	2	9	18	3.6
Highly Dissatisfied	1	6	6	2.4
Total	996			

Overall satisfaction Mean: fx/n= 996/225=3.984

Note: Overall satisfaction scale ranges from 1 (extremely dissatisfied) to 5 (extremely satisfied)

The results are summarized in Exhibit IV indicated that combined together, 26% respondents were highly satisfied, 54.8 were % were satisfied; 13.2% respondents were neutral in their responses and 3.6% & 2.4% respondents were dissatisfied and highly dissatisfied respectively. The mean value of respondents' overall level of satisfaction was 3.98 which tended more toward the high end of the overall satisfaction scale (a five point scale). This suggests that the visitors were moderately satisfied with Kurukshetra Panorama & Science Centre.

Tourists loyalty indicators at kurukshetra panorama & science centre

Table: III

Indicators	Yes	No
Do you intend to visit Kurukshetra Panorama & Science Centre in Future?	69.6%	30.4%
Would you recommend Kurukshetra Panorama & Science Centre to others?	60.8%	39.2%

From the analysis it has been found that majority of respondents 69.6 percent respondents show their willingness to revisit the Kurukshetra Panorama & Science Centre. It shows that tourists were highly satisfied from their visit to the panorama. On the other hand there are only 30.4 percent respondents who were shown negative response regarding revisiting the panorama. 60.8 percent of the respondents showed their willingness to recommend the destination to others where as only 39.2 percent showed unwillingness in recommending destination to others. The majoring of respondents spread positive word of mouth and increases the number of potential visitors to panorama in future.

Conclusion

Kurukshetra Panorama & Science Centre has practiced so many innovative objects, exhibitions and multimedia presentations which have been proved successful in attracting tourists and contributing to the tourism development. Tourism is considered as a very important sector and the Panorama's stakeholders continuously working towards the full exploitation of its tourism potential. If we look at the tourist' satisfaction level towards Kurukshetra Panorama & Science Centre it is high severely satisfactory. Thus, it can be concluded that, Kurukshetra Panorama & Science Centre has immense possibility of growth in the tourism sector with its varied attractions such as repositories and multimedia presentations. The effort is being made to create congenial environment to attract more and more tourists to this magnificent science museum.

References

Beetlestone, J.H., Johnson. C.H., Quinn, M. and White, H. (1998).Science Centre Movement:Context, Practice, Next Challenges, Public Understanding of Science,7, pp.5-26.

Beeho, A. J., & Prentice, R. C. (1995). Evaluating the experiences and benefits gained by tourists visiting a socio-industrial heritage museum: An application of ASEB grid analysis to blists hill open-air museum, the ironbridge gorge museum, United Kingdom. Museum Management and Curatorship, 14 (3), pp. 229-251.

Dierking, L.D. & Falk, J.H. (1994). Family behavior and learning in informal science setting: A review of the research. Science Education, 78 (1), pp. 57-72.

Ecsite, UK., (2001). The Impact of Science and Discovery Centers: A Review of Worldwide Studies.

Fino, J.R. (2008). The Effects of Human/Object Interaction on Museum Visit Experience Satisfaction. A Thesis submitted to the Graduate School of Clemson University.

Huo, Y. and Miller, D.(2007). Satisfaction Measurement of Small Tourism Sector (Museum): Samoa, Asia Pacific Journal of Tourism Research, Vol. 12, No. 2,pp.103-117.

Huo, Y. (2009), An Investigation into Visitors' Satisfaction with Port Elizabeth's Heritage Museums. Master Degree Thesis submitted to Nelson Mandela Metropolitan University.

Jarvis, T., & Pell, A., (2002). Effect of the Challenger Experience on Elementary Children's attitude to Science. Journal of Research in Science Teaching, 39 (10), pp. 979-1000.

Kubota,C.A.,&lstad,R.G.(1991).Effects of novelty-reducing preparation on exploratory behavior and cognitive learning in a science museum setting. Journal of Research in Science Teaching, 28(3), pp. 225-234.

Lucas, A.M. (1983), Scientific Literacy and Information Learning. Studies in Science Education, 10, pp.1-36.

McManus, P.M. (1987). It's the company you keep : The social determination of learning-related behavior in a science museum.

International Journal of Museum Management and Curatorship, 6, pp. 263-270.

Mukhopadyay, I.K., (2005). The science centre movement in Índia: a conspectus, História, Ciências, Saúde - Manguinhos, v. 12 (supplement), pp. 281-307.

Panda, J. and Mohanty, B. (2010). Exhbit Depicting India's great Scientific Heritage at the Heritage Gallery at National Science Centre, New Delhi, Science Reporter, pp.8-13.

Pedrett, E., (2002). T. Kuhn meets T.Rex: Critical Conversations and new Directions in Science Centres and Science Museums. Studies in Science Education, 37, pp. 1-42.

Persson, P.E. (1999). Science Centre: A Motivational Asset, Paper presented in World Conference on Science at Budapest.

Prsson, P.E. (2005).Success and Growth of Science Centers; Available online at http://www.candiansciencecentres.ca/2005conference/Persson_CASC_2005.Pdf.

Ramey-Gassert, L., H. J. Walberg III, et al. (1994). Reexamining connections: Museums as science learning environments. Science Education 78(4): pp. 345-363.

Rennie, L. J. and T. P. McClafferty (1995). Using visits to interactive science and technology centers, museums, aquaria, and zoos to promote learning science. Journal of Science Teacher Education: pp. 175-185.

Rogers, M.L. (1998). An Exploration of Factors Affecting Customer Satisfaction with Selected History Museum Stores. A Doctoral Thesis submitted to Texas Tech University

Tully, A., & Lucas, A.M. (1990). Interacting with a science museum: Vicarious and direct experience and subsequent understanding. International Journal of Science Education, 13, pp. 533-542.

Tunnicliffe, S. D. (1996). The relationship between pupils' age and the content of conversations generated at three types of animal exhibits. Research in Science Education, 26(4), pp.461-480.

Yasamorn, N. and Phokha,A.(2012).The Antecedent and Consequence of Tourist Satisfaction: An Empirical Study of tourists in Sirindhorn Museum Thailand. A paper presente at The 2012 International and National Conference For The Sustainable Community Development of "Local Community : The Foundation of Development in the ASEAN Economic Community (AEC)" pp. 16-19.

Ying, S.H. and Chien, C.C.(2008). A Study of Service Quality and Satisfaction for Museums - Taking the National Museum of Prehistory as an Example. The Journal of Human Resource and Adult Learning Vol. 4, Num. 1,pp.159-170.

Websites

www. icom.museum/the-vision/museum-definition. retrieved on 25.08.2013 at 14:20.

www.dictionary.msn.com/find/entry.asp?search=museum. retrieved on 25.08.2013 at 15:30.

VISITING THE ROOTS OF GREEN TOURISM AND TOURISTS: AN ANALYTICAL APPROACH

Syed Ahmad Rizwan
Assistant Professor, UIHMT, Panjab University
syedahmadrizwan@gmail.com
Lipika Guliani
Assistant Professor, UIHMT, Panjab University

Abstract: The paper treats green tourism as an overall philosophy. It attempts to define green tourists and green tourism in terms of the origin of this term's evolvement. The paper converges to establish its relationship with alternative tourism and as well further differentiates the green tourism from its similar terms. The paper also attempts to seek an alignment of green tourist typology with Plog's typology of tourists. The paper helps to relate green tourists with quality of life and seek out the western perception of green tourism.

Keywords: Green Tourism, Green Tourist, Plog's Typology, Sustainable tourism, Rural tourism,

Introduction

It all started with a single photograph of our Earth interpreted as a blue marble in the vast emptiness of space all black darkness of space. This cleared two things First natural resources are not infinite, secondly if resources are exhausted we have nowhere to go (Kane 2010). Often we discuss environment as abstract comparing it with 'arts', 'heritage', 'traditions' etc. It is not so as environment is very real and survival without it is impossible. The mother earth is in crisis due to environmental concerns; the hole in the ozone layer, acid rain, accumulation of toxins in the food chain, loss of biodiversity, loss of topsoil, pollution of seas, lakes and rivers and the unsustainable exploitation of renewable, but depletable resources such as forests, fish stocks and fresh water. This gave rise to mother concept of Green Tourists Movement known as alternative tourism which later culminated into ecotourism.

Methodology

The current study is analytical in nature. It involves a discourse centred approach. Discourse centric approach is more prevalent in anthropology and lingual studies but here it has been used for a movement known as green. We engage in conversations with our informants/consultants, shift to an internal dialogue when trying to analyze what it all means and read and talk with teachers/colleagues in the discipline. In this particular study green as a concept was discussed with tourists both international and domestic. People involved in tourism businesses (travel agents, tour operators, hoteliers, car/coach service providers and airlines professionals, Teachers and colleagues from tourism businesses, environmental sciences and geography were consulted and talked to. Relevant literature on the subject was thoroughly read and typology of green tourists was devised after analysis. While talking to the tourist and stakeholders theoretical jargons related to the field were not used initially until the respondent himself used it. This helped in the discovery of confusing terms in "green" philosophy which has been cleared in this paper.

Meaning of green tourism and green tourists

The Alternative tourism of 70's and 80's was a result of industry's saturation with the word mass tourism. It was an attempt where tourism and sustainability could co-exist and detrimental ill practices were replaced by more worthy and workable solutions which were environmentally sound. It is rejection of ideas which are deemed inadequate, obsolete and out of time. The term alternative encompasses integrated, adapted, controlled, endogenous, responsible, authentic, equitable, convivial and participative and similar semantic forms. It searches for new aims in diverse fields but converging in their desire to stop an uncontrollable development of tourism (Jafari 2000).

Green tourist: the blurring boundary

Green tourism is a form of alternative tourism; green tourism is generally related to rural tourism. It denotes a nature tourism seen to be environmentally compatible and with little or no ecological impact on the destination area. Like many other alternative tourism terms of the 80's it was merged with ecotourism (Oppermann 2000). Green Tourism (used interchangeably here), has been identified as "tourism that consists of traveling to relatively undisturbed or uncontaminated natural areas with the specific objective of studying, admiring, and enjoying the scenery and its wild plants and animals, as well as any existing cultural manifestation found in these areas" (Boo 1990, p. 3).

Green tourists

Tourists practicing green tourism and green tourism ideology are known as 'Green Tourists'. It is not just a label, tag, fashion or fad rather a complete philosophy which encompass the traveler, host, society, organization, thought process and the suppliers and stakeholders.

Differentiation between green tourists, sustainable tourists and rural tourists

Despite definitions of Rural tourist, Sustainable tourist and Green tourist overlap yet there is a fine line drawing a difference between the three confusing categories.

Table 1: Differentiation between Rural, Sustainable and Green Tourists

Rural tourist	Sustainable Tourist	Green Tourist
Is defined as _ The travel of tourist who does valuation and appreciation of the of rural spaces, natural resources, cultural	Designates every form of travel by a tourist to a tourist development, creation or activity, respecting and preserving in the long	Green Tourist is a tourist who practice a form of sustainable, rural tourism (providing natural and cultural resources, traditions,

heritage, rural buildings, village traditions and local products;	term the natural, cultural and social resources.	products all in line with the local identity), but with a sounder aim to respect and preserve the natural resources and adapted to fit the context of fragile landscapes.
They are illustrative of the regional identities also covering their need for accommodation, food, leisure activities, and various services.	They and contribute in a positive and fair way to the economic development and those of the individuals who live, work, and stay in the protected spaces.	The main aim is to find a way of using and appreciating these areas of natural beauty without damaging them.

Source: Author

Studies have funneled on one single choice, the destination choice (Decrop 1999) but now vacation choices are a mixture of many different choices, for example travel mode, activity, and accommodation, which interact and depend on each other (Woodside & MacDonald, 1994).Tourism motivators can be 1) educational and cultural, 2) relaxation, adventure, and pleasure, 3) health and recreation, 4) ethnic and family, and 5) social and "competitive" (i.e. to be able to show that one can afford a certain vacation) (Moutinho 1987; Swarbrooke & Horner 2007). Other reasons might be connected to escaping from every day routines (Murphy 1985). It is important to also recognize the negative consequences tourism has on our environment. As a response to this, green tourism alternatives have been developed by the tourism industry (Butler 1991; Dowling & Fennell 2003).

Psychological parameters seem to define the demographics and especially the vacation choice structure it is important to see to factors which have an impact on vacation choices. Individuals' values have previously been shown to influence both vacation choices as such (Swarbrooke & Horner, 2007) but also green attitudes and green choices in particular (Karp, 1996; Stern & Dietz, 1994). This green tourists will be born out of the conflict between self-enhancement values (motivating individuals to enhance personal interest) and self-transcendent values (motivating individuals to support the welfare of others and the nature) when trying to explain the vacation choice structure and the conflict between individual and collective interests in green choices.

Lindberg (1991) has identified four basic types of nature tourists:

- o hard core: scientific researchers or members of tours specifically designed for education, removal of litter, and so on
- o dedicated: people who take trips specifically to see protected areas and who want to understand local natural and cultural history
- o mainstream: people who travel to destinations such as the Amazon, or the Rwandan gorilla park, primarily to take an unusual trip

Age Group	Attributes	Typology	Travel Participation	Disposable Income
between 44 and 66 years of age	wealthy, healthy, older people	Allocentric	who have previously traveled extensively and exhausted traditional destinations	High
between 33 and 40 years of age	Younger, liberal, middle-class travelers	Mid-centric	who tend to participate in packaged, lower cost ecotours	Average
20 years of age or younger	who seek a travel experience	Psycho-centric	sensitive to environmental issues but one that also reflects an alternative lifestyle (Mundt 1994).	Low-Average

TABLE 2 : Demographics and Disposable Income of Green Tourists and their Comparison with Plog's Typology

Source: Modified from 1995 World Conference on Sustainable Tourism and Plog 1974

o casual: people who partake of nature incidentally as part of a broader trip.

Keeping this in mind the following demographics and disposable Income factors can be modified from study of ecotourism which is equally fitting for Green Tourists too.

TABLE 3: Typologies of Green Consumers based on Quality of Life

Translators	Exceptors	Selectors
For this group, awareness usually translates into action: • They feel very guilty about not doing it before • They gradually include more and more activities • Their concern is often at the level of products rather than companies or industries • They are prepared to make some sacrifices and are open to change if they can see the impact of their actions • Their information seeking is largely passive • Word of mouth and opinion leaders are important to this group • They are uncritical of information sources	Sustainability is a priority. This group have a complex understanding of a wide range of interdependent sustainability ideas: • They are change-seeking • Their information seeking is active, company level and very critical • They are comfortable with non-mainstream outlets, products and information sources BUT: There is one exception to their green lifestyle: • This is usually a conscious exception • It is usually a 'small' exception • During the purchase process for this item they will completely ignore their usual green and/or ethical criteria • They will have a specific justification for this purchase which allows them to be happy with their decision	This group are green or ethical in one aspect of sustainability only - Greenpeace OR recycling OR green energy OR organic: • Probably the most common group • This would explain why green marketing fails and green marketing research can give conflicting results • Support for Peattie's notion of a context dependent portfolio of (possibly inconsistent) purchases • Could be a starting point for the other groups • Information seeking is selective, ad hoc and can be active, depending on the issue

Source: Swarbrooke and Horner, 2007; McDonald, Oates, Alevizou, Young & Hwang, 2006

Why does west is looking forward to green tourism and green tourists

1. Develop Green Jobs and Skills Training: As the world shifts to a progressive carbon reduction regime - a fundamental target of the Green Economy-Tourism can be a lead change agent to encourage and provide employment in sustainable activities. The key will be to identify Green programs and new associated jobs, as well as to provide the appropriate training. Particular consideration should be given to how this goal can be extended to developing countries in an affordable and viable way. Vocational training, 'voluntourism' and alignment with overall tourism green training programs are also important.

2. Respond Effectively to Climate Change: The tourism community should continue to champion carbon neutrality and confront commitments agreed by parties to the UNFCCC to respond to climate change. This should include incentives for adaptation, substantial financial support and low cost technology transfer for the poorest economies. All strategies and the associated financing should help drive sectoral low carbon transport and accommodation, as well as the use of green technology.

3. Profile Tourism in all Green Economy Strategies: Tourism should be integrated into national, regional and international legislation/regulations that encompass and encourage Green Economy strategies. It should also be profiled high in Green employment strategies. Green investment, planning, procurement, fuel efficiency, renewable energy programs must also cover Tourism.

4. Encourage Green Tourism Infrastructure Investment: Transport and buildings are primary green policy and investment targets. Transport infrastructure- e.g. expressways, high speed trains, airports, ports and air traffic management systems- is mostly geared to tourism needs without explicit recognition. The linkages should be made explicit. Climate proofing and sustainable design is often targeted at government buildings but could and should apply equally to hotels, attractions and other tourism facilities.

5. Promote a Green Tourism Culture in Suppliers, Consumers and Communities: Given the massive impact of consumption in modern society, the ultimate challenge will be to increase public awareness on sustainable tourism and stimulate the transformation towards the production and consumption patterns of a Green Economy. Adjustments in public expectations and a widespread industry participation in credible environmental certification programs are both necessary. Tourism must not only be in the change leadership of products/services, but be a beacon for that change through its intensive communications activities. This can be built into internal and external messaging (Summary of Recommendations, United Nations Framework Convention on Climate Change (nd)).

Conclusion

Thus green is not a recent phenomenon but is an extension of rural and sustainable tourism phenomenon and tourist typology. To develop this concept further this has to be related to existing theory as attempted in this paper. Various tourist typology models and tourism types' needs to be brought into picture with the green fad to reap its benefit in its fullness. The western concept has been explained but a comparative with eastern philosophy especially with Indian pilgrimages could be a nice research offshoot of this attempt.

References

Boo, E. (1990). Ecotourism: The Potentials and Pitfalls Vol. 1. Washington,DC: World Wildlife Fund.

Butler, R. W. (1991). Tourism, environment, and sustainable development. Environmental Conservation, 18(3), 201-209.

Decrop, A. (1999). Tourists' decision-making and behavioural processes. In A. Pizam, & Y. Mansfeld (Eds.), Consumer behavior in travel and tourism (pp. 103-133). Binghampton: The Haworth Hospitality Press.

Dowling, R. K., & Fennell, D. A. (2003). The context of ecotourism policy and planning. In D. A. Fennell, & R. K. Dowling (Eds.), Ecotourism Policy and Planning (pp.1-20). Wallingford: CABI.

Jafari,J. (2000). Encyclopedia of Tourism. London. Routledge.

McDonald, S., Oates, C., Young, W. & Hwang K. (2006), 'Towards Sustainable Consumption: Researching Beginner Voluntary Simplifiers', Psychology and Marketing, 23 (6): 515-534.

Moutinho, L. (1987). Consumer behavior in tourism. European Journal of Marketing, 21(10), 1-44.

Murphy, P. E. (1985). Tourism: A community approach. New York: Routledge.

Oppermann, M. (2000). In Jafar, J. (Ed.) Encyclopedia of Tourism. London. Routledge.

Plog, S. (1974) Why destination areas rise and fall in popularity? Cornell Hotel and Restaurant Administration Quarterly, 14(4), 55-58.

Swarbrooke, J., & Horner, S. (2007). Consumer behaviour in tourism (2nd edition). Oxford: Elsevier.

United Nations Framework Convention on Climate Change (nd). Summary of Recommendations. United Nations.

Woodside, A. G., & MacDonald, R. (1994). General system framework of customer choice processes of tourism services. In R. V. Gasser, & K. Weiermair (Eds.), Spoilt for choice. Decision making processes and preference changes of tourists: Intertemporal and intercountry perspectives (pp. 30-59). Thaur-Wien-München: Kulturverlag.

PROMOTIONAL STRATEGIES IN TOURISM: A STUDY OF HIMACHAL

R K Gupta

Director, University Institute of Hotel Management and Tourism, Panjab University, Chandigarh.

Arun Singh Thakur

Assistant Professor, University Institute of Hotel Management and Tourism, Panjab University, Chandigarh.

Jaswinder Singh

Assistant Professor, University Institute of Hotel Management and Tourism, Panjab University, Chandigarh. jaswinder_chef@yahoo.co.in

Abstract: Present study is an outcome of the survey conducted on tourists as well as service providers. This study has undertaken a survey across various tourist destinations in Himachal Pradesh. Study analyses the opinion of service providers and tourists to get insight into the promotional strategies adopted by the service providers in Himachal Pradesh. State government tourism department should lead the private sector for marketing Himachal at national and international level through sponsoring participating in travel trade fairs. Although the tourists and service providers felt that tourism promotion is going in right direction but more needs to be done.

Keywords: Promotional Strategies, Service Providers, Himachal.

Introduction

Competition among tourism destinations continues to intensify. With substitution among destinations being pervasive, competitive advantage requires the ability to effectively manage all components of the tourism system to ensure success is achieved. A tourism destination has two primary roles and a number of important supporting roles. First and foremost, it must seek to enhance the social and economic well-being of the residents who live within its boundaries. Secondly, to be classified as a tourism destination, it must provide this enhancement of resident wellbeing by offering a range of activities and experiences of the kind that we identify as "tourism" experiences. The provision of this range of activities and experiences, when enjoyed by the visitor at a price which he/she is willing to pay, and which enables the destination to operate in a sustainable manner (economic, environmental, social, and cultural) to the benefit of residents might generally be regarded as success in tourism.

'Sustainable tourism' signifies a condition of tourism based on the principles of sustainable development, taking "full account of its current and future economic, social and environmental impacts" (UNEP/WTO, 2005: 11e12) and addressing the needs of stakeholders. The role of stakeholders in the implementation of Sustainable tourism is becoming more prominent in both academia and industry. Given the 'multi-stakeholder nature' of both sustainable development and tourism, the stakeholder concept was an appropriate lens through which to explore stakeholder issues. Stakeholder perspectives of Sustainable tourism and subsequent actions have an overall effect on sustainability initiatives, hence the need for stakeholder analysis.

As stakeholders are instrumental to achieving sustainability objectives, stakeholder views are pivotal for the development of effective stakeholder involvement strategies. Key factors influencing stakeholder involvement in Sustainable tourism were identified as leadership quality, information quality and accessibility, stakeholder mindsets, stakeholder involvement capacity, stakeholder relationships and implementation priorities. These are underpinned by the complexity of Sustainable tourism, contextual circumstances and the diversity of stakeholders.

Review of Literature

As the tourism system context becomes increasingly fragmented and volatile its stakeholders are pressured to adapt collaboration principles to everyday practice, particularly in the planning and marketing areas. Bramwell and Sharman (1999) identify three potential benefits deriving from consensus-based collaboration. First, it may avoid the costs of solving conflicts among stakeholders (Healey, 1996). Second, it may legitimate collective actions if stakeholders are involved in the decision-making processes which affect their activities (Benveniste, 1989). Third, the willingness to collaborate may enhance the coordination of policies and related activities. Their argument is underpinned by stakeholder theory pioneered by Freeman, who defined a stakeholder as "any group or individual who can affect or is affected by the achievement of the organization's objectives" (Freeman, 1984: 46).

Once a community becomes a tourist destination, the lives of residents in that community become affected by tourism activities (Jurowski, Uysal, & Williams, 1997). Over the past several decades, interest in tourism as a tool for regional economic development has grown dramatically. Community leaders and economic development specialists have increasingly treated tourism as an important industry that can enhance local employment opportunities, tax revenues, and economic diversity.

The question remains: Is tourism impact (economic, social, cultural, and environmental) perceived by community residents? If so, do these perceptions of tourism impact influence their sense of well-being in various life domains (e.g., material life, community life, emotional life, and health and well-being) become influenced too? Answers to these questions are very important to both community leaders and tourism officials because these answers can guide successful planning policies in tourism development. For example, if residents' perception of tourism environmental impact is found to be a positive predictor of residents' sense of health and safety well-being, which in turn is found to be a positive predictor of life satisfaction, then environmental policies and programs should be formulated to encourage tourism development in ways that influence residents' positive perception of tourism impact on their sense of health and safety well-being. Similar implications can be deduced in relation to economic, cultural, and social policies and programs. While tourism research continues to expand, there are on-going debates about definitional boundaries and overlaps within the tourism industry. While various subsets of tourism (e.g., wildlife tourism, ecotourism, adventure tourism, nature tourism) have developed definitions specific to their activities, there is considerable overlap between each niche. That being said, it is still difficult to apply conclusions from research on one tourism niche to all niches found within the industry. While at present there is no systematic effort to gather data worldwide on distinct categories of tourism, greater efforts need be placed on understanding the various subsets of tourism in order to ensure effective planning that maximizes tourism benefits and minimizes its impacts, thus ensuring the sustainability of the industry.

"Unfortunately, tourism grows faster than tourism research which creates a questionable gap for sustainable tourism development. Meaningful impact research in various environments (ecology, economy and culture) is very much needed for community based development involving active participation of the indigenous population." Finally there is a need for better understanding of the social and economic opportunities, tourism may provide in previously marginal mountain environments that are now developing the ability to promote tourism activities in their environs.

Community-based Tourism Marketing is used to describe a variety of activities that encourage, support and promote a wide range of objectives in economic and social development and conservation.

Tourism and Sustainable Development

Tourism is in a special position in the contribution it can make to sustainable development and the challenges it presents. Firstly, this is because of the dynamism and growth of the sector, and the major contribution that it makes to the economies of many countries and local destinations. Secondly, it is because tourism is an activity which involves a special relationship between consumers (visitors), the industry, the environment and local communities.

This special relationship arises because, unlike most other sectors, the consumer of tourism (the tourist) travels to the producer and the product. This leads to three important and unique aspects of the relationship between tourism and sustainable development:

- o Interaction: The nature of tourism, as a service industry that is based on delivering an experience of new places, means that it involves a considerable amount of interaction, both direct and indirect, between visitors, host communities and their local environments.
- o Awareness: Tourism makes people (visitors and hosts) become far more conscious of environmental issues and di?erences between nations and cultures. This can a?ect a titudes and concerns for sustainability issues not only while travelling but throughout people's lives.
- o Dependency: Much of tourism is based on visitors seeking to experience intact and clean environments, attractive natural areas, authentic historic and cultural traditions, and welcoming hosts with whom they have a good relationship. The industry depends on these attributes being in place.

This close and direct relationship creates a sensitive situation, whereby tourism can be both very damaging but also very positive for sustainable development.

On the positive note, tourism can:

- o Provide a growing source of opportunities for enterprise development and employment creation as well as stimulating investment and support for local services, even in quite remote communities.
- o Bring tangible economic value to natural and cultural resources. This can result in direct income from visitor spending for their conservation, and an increase in support for conservation from local communities.
- o Be a force for inter-cultural understanding and peace.

Tourist boards, destination management bodies and individual enterprises often declare themselves as innovative in an attempt to identify with a new segment of customers or redirect existing messages and strengthen brands. This may be misuse of the term innovation. However, new marketing concepts can develop into imperative innovations in their own right, when such approaches change the way that overall communication to, and with, customers is undertaken, and how relationships between the service provider and customer are built and withheld. A prominent and early example within the tourism sector is the elaboration and introduction of loyalty programs, which are now widespread and come in numerous versions. These programs basically change the relationships between tourism providers and the customer from a single and simple purchase procedure to an exchange of loyalty and intangible supplements, and transform the interaction to a long-term affair with a bounded and complex rationality.

G. G. Martina, et al., (2002) argued that tourism marketing is important for the growth and development of a destination but, despite its relevance it faces many difficulties. One is the tourism product's characteristics such as its complexity (Smith 1994) and multidimensionality (Gartner 1989). Another is that destination marketing involves the consumer physically moving to the behaviour scenario. There is also great subjectivity in providing a tourism service: images are mixed with impressions about residents, retailers, other tourists, and/or employees. But most of all, the intangibility of tourism service hinders image assessment as it depends on invisible elements of pre-visit selection and a pre-taste of the destination (Fakeye and Crompton 1991). Consequently, in tourism research, "...images are more important than tangible resources", all because "perceptions, rather than reality are what motivate consumers to act or not act".

About the Study

Present study is an outcome of the survey conducted on tourists as well as service providers. This study has undertaken a survey across various tourist destinations in Himachal Pradesh. A sample of 600 respondents, out of the total 600 respondents, 150 were tourism service providers and 450 were tourists. Study analyses the opinion of service providers and tourists to get insight into the promotional strategies adopted by the service providers in Himachal Pradesh.

Need of the Study

Prideaux and Cooper (2002) argue that while marketing is imperative for a destination's survival, the organisation of marketing in destinations is not well understood. Whilst numerous studies have evaluated visitor data, no studies have considered analysing the promotional strategies adopted by tourism service providers. The central theme of the study was to get idea of the sustainable promotional strategies and evaluate them in terms of their effectiveness. This study will provide an insight into the aspirations of the tourists from the marketing campaigns and so as the service providers can reorganise their marketing campaigns.

Analysis of the Results

After applying the appropriate statistical techniques like; one sample test, KMO and chi-square test on the set of the primary data the analysis and presentation of the results are here as under;

Profile of Travel Agents

Table 1: Profile of Travel Agents

		Number	Percentage
Years in travel trade	Under 2 years	40	26.7
	2-5 years	52	34.7
	5-10 years	38	25.3
	More than 10 years	20	13.3
Core area of business	Adventure tours	88	58.7
	Religious tours	13	8.7
	Leisure tours	49	32.7
Main aspect of the state on which you stress while interacting with tourists	Adventure opportunities	27	18.0
	Good climate	59	39.3
	Nature	27	18.0
	Scenic beauty	37	24.7

Do you have direct links with foreign agents	Yes	39	26.0
	No	73	48.7
	No comments	38	25.3
What kind of package you sell	Group	18	12.0
	Individuals	16	10.7
	Both	116	77.3
How do you market your products	Internet/email	89	59.3
	Printed material by post	23	15.3
	Telephonic mode	24	16.0
	In person	14	9.3

Source: Data collected with the help of questionnaires

Table 1 represents the profile of travel agents, which were surveyed during the study. Analysis of the responses tried to find out the promotional strategies adopted by the service providers. While asking about the number of years in travel trade especially in tourism; it was evident that service providers are quite young in the tourism industry as 40% of total travel agents surveyed, has more than 5 years but they seems to be enough experienced. About 82% of the service providers are either graduate or having higher degree of education.

On the issue of interaction with tourists, it was found that 18% of the service providers focus on various adventure opportunities for the tourists in the state, maximum of 39% of the service providers focus on good and pleasant climate in the state, 18% of the service providers focus on nature and natural beauty in the state and remaining 25% of the service providers focus on scenic in the state. All these factors are the supporting features for the tourism and we can say that service providers focus the various strengths of Himachal's tourism product to build the positive image in the mind of tourist which is a symbol of long term approach of marketing.

From the analysis of data it is evident that 26% of the service providers were having links with foreign agents and they are getting business directly from those, 49% of the service providers do not have any links with foreign agents and 25% choose not to comment on this question. This reflects that only one fourth of the travel agents could able to market their products directly to foreign agents and there is dire need to focus on international level marketing individually by the service providers of Himachal Pradesh.

Also 12% of the service providers were only into selling group packages to the tourists, 11% of the service providers were only into selling individual tour packages or FIT's to the tourists and maximum of the service providers i.e. remaining 77% of the service providers sell both group as well as individual tourism services to the tourists. So the travel agents operating business for the particular type of clientele need to adopt differentiated marketing strategy. While asking the service providers about how do they market their products to the customers and outstation travel agents, it was found that highest number of service providers out of total i.e. 60% said that they utilise internet or email for this purpose, 15% said that they uses printed material and send that through post to potential markets, 16% replied that telephonic mode is main tool for marketing their products and only 9% answered in person or one to one marketing of their tour packages to customers and outstation travel agents is done. It can be further concluded that service providers in Himachal have adopted different type of marketing strategy according to their product and clientele requirement.

Opinion of Tourists Regarding the Promotional Strategies

This part of the chapter is focused on finding out the opinion of tourists regarding the promotion of tourism in Himachal Pradesh. Table 2 presents the aggregate responses of tourists regarding the purchase of tourism services. It is found that 46.4% of total tourists purchase such services at destination only while 39.6% purchased from their travel agents. This means that around 86% respondents purchased services from private service providers. Although sufficiently large number of tourists decided about purchasing on the spot. This indicates that this category of tourist is unaware about the services available at destination, which led to the conclusion that there is requirement of ample information regarding the tourism services at various destinations of Himachal Pradesh. Further it can be concluded that maximum number of travel agents in Himachal could not able to market their products to the existing target market.

Table 2: Purchase of Tourism Services

	Frequency	Percent
Through your travel agent	178	39.6
From service provider at destination	209	46.4
Through govt. agencies	63	14.0
Total	450	100.0

Graph 1: Opinion regarding promotion of tourism in Himachal Pradesh

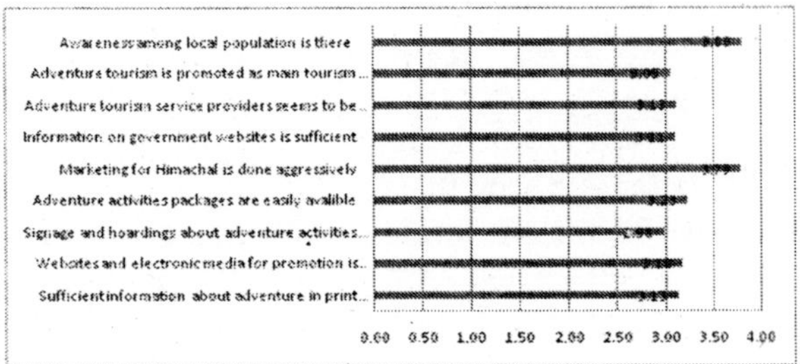

Factor Analysis (Tourists)

Table 3 KMO and Bartlett's Test

Kaiser-Meyer-Olkin Measure of Sampling Adequacy.		.918
Bartlett's Test of Sphericity	Approx. Chi-Square	9.859E3
	df	36
	Sig.	.000

Table 4 Component Matrixa

	Component 1
Sufficient information about adventure in print media	.968
Websites and electronic media for promotion is sufficient	.965
Signage and hoardings about adventure activities are sufficient	.943

Adventure activities packages are easily available	.974
Marketing for Himachal is done aggressively	.930
Information on government websites is sufficient	.966
Adventure tourism service providers seems to be well trained	.974
Adventure tourism is promoted as main tourism product	.973
Awareness among local population is there	.905

Extraction Method: Principal Component Analysis.

a. 1 components extracted.

Here we analysed the responses of the tourist to get more insight into the promotional strategies adopted by the service providers. Graph 1 has already highlighted the top 4 responses of tourists. Further to get more polished; factor analytic approach has been undertaken in the present study. The purpose of this analysis was to find out the top responses but before applying factor analysis KMO test was applied. The value of KMO measure of sampling adequacy comes out to be 0.918 (table 3) which is very close to the perfect value of '1', which give researcher a strong reason for going for factor analysis. For factorizing Hotellings (1935) principal axes method was applied which is also known as the method of principal components. In factor analysis only one component was extracted and which represented 91.33% of variance.

Analysis of data collected form tourist reveals that marketing strategies adopted by the tourism department as well as private sector did not approach the tourist visiting Himachal for tourism. Further it can be concluded that present marketing efforts should not be considered sufficient and more efforts need to be put in. The results also found that 58.4% of the respondents are not package tourists that means marketers could not be able to reach to the target market. It is interesting to know that besides many shortcoming and constraints on the part of tourism industry in Himachal, about 75% of the respondents are willing to come back to Himachal again and are also ready to recommend Himachal to others. With these results in hand one can say that image of Himachal is good in the market and the main thing to do is to approach, inform and persuade the targeted clientele.

Summary

The study focused on analysing the promotional strategy adopted by tourism service providers in Himachal Pradesh. The results also found that 58.4% of the respondents are not package tourists. It is interesting to know that besides many shortcoming and constraints on the part of tourism industry in Himachal, about 75% of the respondents are willing to come back to Himachal again and are also ready to recommend Himachal to others. These very results strongly recommend adopting strategies to focus this target market segment of tourists to make them permanent user of tourism product of Himachal.

Data of service providers reveals that about 70% of the service providers in Himachal have experience less than five years and maximum of them are either graduate of post graduated. Internet technology has proved to be the boon for cheap and effective marketing as 60% of marketing by service providers is done through internet. It was also noted that the service provider's economic status does not match with the requirement of international marketing so a collaborative approach must be adopted by the government agencies for marketing tourism product of Himachal.

As discussed above sufficiently large number of tourists for Himachal purchased their services on the spot and which indicates that the tourists are unaware about the services available at destination, which led to the conclusion that there is requirement of ample information regarding the tourism services at various destinations of Himachal Pradesh. It was also felt that information should also be provided to the target market through appropriate marketing strategy, because merely putting information on the website is not job done completely. State government tourism department should lead the private sector for marketing Himachal at national and international level through sponsoring participating in travel trade fairs. Although the tourists and service providers felt that tourism promotion is going in right direction but more needs to be done.

References

Benveniste, G. (1989). Mastering the politics of planning: Crafting credible plans and policies that make a difference. San Francisco: Jossey-Bass.

Bramwell, B., & Sharman, A. (1999). Collaboration in local tourism policymaking. Annals of Tourism Research, 26(2), 392-415.

Buhalis, D. (2000). Tourism and information technologies: past, present and future. Tourism Recreation Research, 25(1), 41-58.

Fakeye, P. C., & Crompton, J. L. (1991). Images differences between prospective, first-time and repeat visitors to the Lower Rio Grande valley. Journal of Travel Research, 30(2), 10-16.

Freeman, R. (1984). Strategic management: A stakeholder approach. Boston: Pitman.

G. G. Martina, G. Saura, and C. G. Hayde´ (2002). Destination Image-Towards a Conceptual Frame work. Annals of Tourism Research. Vol. 29, No. 1, pp. 56-78, 2002

Gartner, W. C. (1989) Tourism Image: Attribute Measurement of State Tourism Products using Multidimensional Scaling Techniques. Journal of Travel Research 28(2):16-20.

Haahti, A. (1986). Finland's competitive position as a destination. Annals of Tourism Research, 13(1), 11-35.

Healey, P. (1996). Consensus-building across difficult divisions: new approaches to collaborative strategy making. Planning Practice and Research, 11(2), 207-216.

Jurowski, C., Uysal, M., & Williams, D. R. (1997). A theoretical analysis of host community resident reactions to tourism. Journal of Tourism Research, 36, 3e11.

Pollock, A. (1995). The impact of information technology on destination marketing. EIU Travel and Tourism Analyst, 3, 66-83.

Poon, A. (1993). Tourism, Technology and Competitive Strategies. CAB International.

Prideaux, B., & Cooper, C. (2002). Marketing and destination growth: a symbiotic relationship or simple coincidence? Journal of Vacation Marketing, 9(1), 35-51.

Ritchie, J. R. B., & Crouch, G. I. (2003). The competitive destination: a sustainable tourism perspective. Oxon, UK: CABI Publishing.

Sheldon, P. J. (1997). Tourism information technology. Oxon, UK: CAB International.

Smith, S. L. J. (1994). The tourism product. Annals of Tourism Research, 21(3), 582-595.

Thakur, A. S. (2013). Adventure Tourism Market Segments and Promotional Policies Therein: A case study of Himachal Pradesh; India. Unpublished Ph. D. Thesis submitted to Himachal Pradesh University, Shimla.

United Nations Environment Programme (UNEP) and World Tourism Organisation (WTO). (2005). Making tourism more sustainable: A guide for policymakers [online] Available from http://www.unep.org/publications/search/pub_details_s.asp?ID¼3566 Accessed 07.01.14.

ROLE OF GREEN TOURISM IN SUSTAINABLE GROWTH OF INDIA

Rohit Garg

Professor and Director, Hindu Institute of Management, Sonepat-131001, rohit.teacher@gmail.com

Abstract: The objective of sustainable tourism is to retain the economic and social advantages of tourism development while reducing or mitigating any undesirable impacts on the natural, historic, cultural, or social environment. This is achieved by balancing the needs of tourists with those of the destination.

Tourism industry contributes about 10 percent of the total GDP of the world. All Southeast Asian countries have noticed the rising potentials of tourism sector for years.

But, at the present stage, all development issues are urged to consider its approaches within the framework of sustainable development. Sustainable tourism or alternative tourism has become part of sustainable development within the sector of tourism. But the mass tourism will consistently predominate in the world tourism. Pursuing ecotourism and other alternative tourism programs are necessary in upgrading the variety of tourism sector and tapping of its potentials. But the combination or ecotourism/alternative tourism - mass tourism synergy will be the main direction.

Green tourism is defined as environmentally friendly tourism activities with various focuses and meanings. In a broad term, green tourism is about being an environmentally friendly tourist or providing environmentally friendly tourist services. The green tourism concept would be highly appealing to tourism enterprises and operators owing to increasing governmental pressure to improve environmental performance by adopting effective and tangible environmental management techniques. Furthermore, achievement and promotion of internationally recognized environmental awards would be instrumental to the tourism enterprises in marketing their services. As a result, many concerned and responsible parties put forward recommendations for green tourism products to regulate tourism's negative impacts. This conceptual paper attempts to discuss green tourism concept, green tourism certification and its processes as well explain the comparative approaches of green tourism in a few countries. Towards the end, by this green labeling, the industry can legitimately open up new areas for the more discriminating and wider range of the market, and tourists or visitors can enjoy the holiday they want with a clear conscience.

Keywords: Tourism, Green Certification, Sustainability, Eco Tourism, Employment Opportunities

Introduction

Tourism has emerged as one of the world's largest service industries with sizeable economic benefits and immense opportunities. With the emergence of technological advancement, and competitiveness in service-based industries the tourism sector is playing a vital role in contributing to improve gross domestic product (GDP) and creation of employment across the world economy. This accelerating tourism industry is proved to be one of the important drivers of growth and prosperity, employment generation, raises national income and improvement in balance of payments of Indian economy. Indian tourism sector is one of the most vibrating sectors of the economy. It is not only a significant contributor to GDP and foreign exchange reserve of the country, but also it provides widespread of employment.

Tourism is the third largest economic activity in the world (after oil and automobiles), and it is one of the fastest-growing activities. The World Tourism Organization (WTO, 2008) projects that by the year 2014, international tourist arrivals will have increased to 1.518 billion and a direct receipt is expected to US$1.85 trillion. Receipts from tourism make an important contribution to the economies of the developing countries in terms of income, employment, and balance of payments effects. Because of this, many developing countries have begun to actively pursue tourism as a means to create jobs, diversify their economies, and earn foreign currency. Among the three major impacts of tourism-economic, socio-cultural and environmental-the economic impact played a dominant role in policy-making. With the focus on the economic benefits that accompanied the development of tourism, the adverse socio-cultural and environmental impacts of tourism were relatively ignored. Based on the economic benefits, tourism development was prescribed as a panacea for many social and economic problems. This led to the indiscriminate and unplanned growth of tourism infrastructure in many countries, and soon the negative effects in the form of social and environmental degradation began to emerge. Due to enhanced awareness of the negative impact of tourism on the environment, efforts have been made to develop approaches for making tourism sustainable.

The last two decades have witnessed a growing interest in the relationship between tourism development and environmental quality, with the emergence of special interest tourism including green tourism. Tourism sector can also be considered the backbone for allied sectors, like hospitality, civil aviation, and transport. Sensing the importance and worth of the sector, Indian Government has invested abundantly for the development in this sector. It has been partially successful with increase in foreign tourist arrivals over the last decade, courtesy "Incredible India Campaign".

Green tourism concept

The concept of a green product is one that is easier to use than to define. Green tourism is used to indicate environmentally friendly tourism but have different focuses and meanings. Often such claims use terms which lack of accepted or standard definitions, or utilize extravagant language to wash the emptiness of the claim being made. These terms are used for two purposes: first, to tell customers that the holiday destination they are going to is beautiful and un spoilt.

Green tourism or another term related to environmental concern is mostly used to label nature holidays to exotic destinations. Second, green tourism claims can be used to signal that tourism operations taking place in that area do not harm the environment.

In loose terms, a product or service can be said to be green when it is beneficial to the producer and consumer without harming the environment. The difficulty starts when a stakeholder attempts to measure the negative effects of their activities on the environment. Even in cases where measurement seems possible, the next difficulty arises at agreeing the criteria to be considered and the threshold levels of unacceptable effects. Tourism traditionally has been considered a relatively green industry, with the exception of its transport and land development implications, and for this reason it has only recently become an area of concern.

In this paper, green tourism, which is an important component of sustainable tourism, is defined as ?travel to destinations where the flora, fauna, and cultural heritage are the primary attractions. This definition is further expanded to include environmentally sustainable travel to destinations where climate impacts are minimized with the aim of respecting and preserving natural resources and adapting programs to fit the context of fragile resources. Green tourism is important to encourage travel that would help support natural and cultural aspects, while encouraging respect for and conservation of urban resources and cultural diversity. According to Dodds and Joppe (2001), the green tourism concept can be broken down into four components.

- o Environmental responsibility-protecting, conserving, and enhancing nature and the physical environment to ensure the long-term health of the life-sustaining eco-system.
- o Local economic vitality-supporting local economies, businesses and communities to ensure economic vitality and sustainability.
- o Cultural diversity-respecting and appreciating cultures and cultural diversity so as to ensure the continued well-being of local or host cultures.

- o Experiential richness-providing enriching and satisfying experiences through active, personal and meaningful participation in, and involvement with, nature, people, places and cultures.

The emergence and growth of green tourism

In today's interconnected world, passports are stamped with ever-increasing frequency. By 2020, an estimated 1.6 billion tourists will travel the globe annually-twice as many as in 2009. Whether trekking through rainforests, wandering around ancient ruins or scuba diving near coral reefs, travelers gain matchless experiences and helps boost local economies. However, tourism comes at a price, its impact on the earth. Too much traffic can trample a pristine environment, pollute the air, deplete precious resources, and emit gases that contribute to global warming. As awareness about the threat of climate change grows, there is an increasing demand for "green" destinations-those that make an active effort to improve their environmental sustainability by addressing such issues as carbon emissions, biodiversity conservation, waste management, and water supply. Tourism and environmental sustainability are fast becoming natural partners. In 2007, at the second International Conference on Climate Change and Tourism in Davos, global policymakers declared that "the tourism sector must rapidly respond to climate change…and progressively reduce its greenhouse gas (GHG) contribution if it is to grow in a sustainable manner."

Environmentally savvy tourists-especially those in key source markets such as western Europe-increasingly desire green destinations. A 2005 survey by the U.K.'s Devon County Council found that 54 percent of respondents consider environmental issues when booking a trip, 82 percent are willing to pay more for green services and products, and 72 percent think a green business is more likely to be quality conscious.

In response, in an effort to remain both environmentally sustainable and competitive, leading tour operators like TUIAG and Thomas Cook have been demanding higher standards from hotels and giving marketing and booking preference to environmentally sustainable destinations. Thomas Cook recently partnered with the

U.K.-based Federation of Tour Operators (FTO) in order to launch the Travel life awards, which recognize hotels and other business partners that attain high standards of environmental management. In addition, major global travel societies like National Geographic are more often using environmental sustainability as a key measure in their rankings of international travel destinations.

Tourism destinations are realizing that in order to stay competitive, becoming green must be a principal element of their branding and marketing policies. Failing to adopt such an approach may mean losing a loyal customer base.

In addition, as stringent carbon regulations are being implemented across the globe, and investment in green tourism begins to present economic benefits for hosting countries, destina-tions have another goal to keep in mind: the financial rewards of adopting sustainable policies. Under the Kyoto Protocol, an investment scheme known as the clean development mechanism (CDM) allows industrialized countries to invest in emissions-reducing projects in developing countries as an alternative to more expensive ones at homes. Financing schemes like the CDM may become tipping points, motivating destinations to rethink business as usual in favor of sustainable strategies.

Green tourism and its long lasting effects

Although some tourist destinations have embarked on serious sustainability efforts, too many others are lagging behind. These destinations under invest in the preservation of their natural assets and trade their long-term health in areas like biodiversity conservation and waste man-agement for short-term gain. Others use environmental initiatives simply as a public relations and marketing tool, ignoring the fact that tourists are sophisticated enough to know a green façade when they see it.

Yet there is currently both urgent need and tremendous incentive to focus on environmental sustainability and pursue a meaningful, substantive green strategy-and tourist destinations are increasingly interested in doing so.

The recent experience with green tourism initiatives is to believe that the path to success as a green tourist destination lies in a holistic approach to an environmental strategy. We've identified the components required for any destination to call itself green, as well as the "enabling" structures that will ensure the success of green policy. Taken together, they allow a destination to create comprehensive transformation and long-term success.

Destinations that aspire to be sustainable should consider the following four components:

1. Carbon Emissions

The tourism industry is currently responsible for around 5 percent of global carbon emissions, largely a result of air travel and accommodations. A recent global study from the World Economic Forum and Booz & Company estimates that these emissions will double by 2035 if left unchecked. Carbon mitigation efforts, therefore, are key to green policy. These efforts should include eliminating and reducing emissions, substituting environmentally harmful practices with more sustainable ones, and offsetting remaining emissions. Destinations can also reduce their carbon footprints by choosing sustainably sourced goods and materials.

By implementing green technologies and policies such as solar panels, compact fluorescent lighting, energy-efficient appliances, building insulation, renewable fuels, and carbon sequestration from trees, destinations can dramatically reduce their carbon emissions. Slovakia's popular Aqua City resort, which was recently named "World's Leading Green Resort" by World Travel Awards, prevents an estimated 27 tons of CO2 from entering the atmosphere every day by using geothermal water and solar energy-policies that have saved the resort millions of Euros each year. Mitigation options like these increase the "double bottom line" by providing both economic and environmental benefits, and they have a relatively short investment payoff period.

Destinations should also invest in and encourage guests to choose energy-efficient transport and activities. Depending on the location, visitors can be steered toward smart mass transit options such as electrical trains and hybrid buses or individual options like hybrid cars, bicycles, and sailboats instead of SUVs and motorboats.

In addition, destinations can incentivize tourists to offset their remaining emissions through local programs that invest in renewable technologies such as wind power.

2. Biodiversity Conservation:

A location's unique natural assets-its beaches, rivers, forests, mountains, coral reefs, deserts, and wildlife-are key to its value as a tourist destination. Preservation of these assets is therefore a critical component of sustainable tourism. Over the past two decades, tourism in biodiversity hot spots has increased more than 100 percent, making conservation all the more urgent.

Without proper conservation efforts, tourism can contribute to the damage and destruction of flora and fauna. Unregulated wildlife viewing has scared away animals and disrupted their feeding and nesting sites. Coral reefs across the globe have been damaged by cruise ships, divers, and other human activity. Highly trafficked trekking sites, such as the Annapurna Circuit in Nepal, experience serious soil erosion and plant damage. Without biodiversity conservation, destinations leave their most precious assets unprotected. Shielding these assets is a high-yielding investment in the future.

Policymakers should develop national parks and wildlife corridors, regulate access to potentially fragile areas, protect indigenous species, and control pests. Biodiversity conservation efforts should be tailored to specific regional and local needs. After all, a policy that works in the rainforest may not work in the desert, and vice versa.

3. Waste Management:

Effective liquid and solid waste management is key to the "clean perception" of a destination. As a major pollutant, waste affects the entire ecosystem, including land degradation, water quality, and health and hygiene. Reducing potential waste streams, minimizing the amount of solid waste that ends up in landfills and incinerators, and recycling whenever possible are all critical components of an environmentally sustainable tourism policy.

Global best practices for solid waste management dictate that waste should be collected in closed bags or bins, transported in closed trucks, sorted and recycled as much as possible, and then disposed of in sanitary landfills as a last resort. In addition, waste ideally should be used to generate energy.

Best practices for liquid waste begin with reducing the amount created and then better managing it with aerobic treatment and filtration, followed by disinfection to destroy bacteria and viruses. The waste is then treated to remove metals and small biodegradable pollutants. Cutting-edge waste management methods such as waste-to-energy conversion can enhance a destination's reputation in the green playing field.

4. Water Supply:

Water is an increasingly scarce resource, with many countries facing severe shortages. An adequate and healthy water supply is crucial to a destination's long-term environmental sustainability. Because water provision and desalination are typically significant sources of energy usage and emissions, conservative water policy is doubly important. Water consumption should be measured and reduced to the minimum level necessary for adequate operation.

Reusing wastewater increases the availability of potable water and reduces a destination's sewage and clean-up fees. In addition, proper wastewater management reduces aquatic pollution and minimizes the risk of disease.

o Enabling Support Structures:

Clearly, none of these elements exists in a vacuum. On the contrary, they are all interconnected and interdependent. Poor waste management can cause harmful gases to be emitted and the water supply to be contaminated, which in turn may harm biodiversity. A sustainable water supply and waste management program may require additional energy, thereby increasing a destination's carbon footprint. For this reason, a holistic approach to sustainability is essential.

None of these components can be properly addressed and managed without key support structures in place that enable and facilitate greening efforts. Each enabler should be applied to each of the components we've described. And just like the green components themselves, these enablers must be viewed through a holistic lens.

o Regulations and Governance:

A destination cannot successfully embark on a green strategy without the right laws and regulations in place, or the right governance structure to oversee them. Legislation should protect the environment, limit potentially harmful development, control detrimental practices, and encourage healthy behavior.

The Maldives, which has an economy that depends heavily on tourism, has begun implementing strict environmental regulations. Tourism is contained to selected zones and uninhabited islands out of fear of spoiling the nation's fragile ecosystem. Norway's Fjords region, British Columbia's Kootenay and Yoho national parks, and Quebec's Gaspé Peninsula received the highest ratings in the National Geographic Center for Sustainable Destinations' "Places Rated" Destination Stewardship 2009 survey for their environmental stewardship.

A successful sustainability program should be sponsored by the highest levels of government, with appropriate governing bodies at the national, regional, or local level that are responsible for spearheading the program and facilitating its implementation. These entities, which should be adequately staffed, should include representatives from all involved ministries, including tourism, transport, the environment, and aviation as well as the local government and representatives from the private sector.

o Stakeholder Participation:

A truly holistic green transformation program requires the participation of many different players. It is absolutely vital that government, the private sector, and civil society collaborate to create and implement sustainable policy. At the government level, the ministry of tourism should collaborate with ministries responsible for the environ ment, energy, agriculture, transport, health, finance, security, and other relevant areas, as well as with local municipalities. By steering the direction of policy and spearheading environmental sustainability efforts, the ministry can motivate and influence other stakeholders-both public and private-to engage in behavior that bolsters a destination's environmental sustainability. For example, policymakers can provide incentives, such as tax rebates and preferential marketing agreements, to green businesses operating in the tourism sector. The ministry of tourism can also establish an accreditation service that recognizes sustainable accommodations and services.

At the private-sector level, hotel owners, tour operators, and transport services can play a key role in protecting the environment and influencing tourists to make sustainable choices. Hotel owners can offer accommodations with a smaller carbon footprint and sustainable waste, energy, and water policies. Tour guides, who know the destination intimately, are perfect ambassadors for environmental awareness. They can also influence tourists to choose transport options and activities with lower carbon footprints, rotate clients to different ecological sites in an effort to limit human impact on biodiversity, and teach tourists to treat environmental assets with care while they are visiting.

At the civil society level, NGOs and universities can provide critical research and advocacy, educating locals and visitors alike. Destinations embarking on a green transformation must actively engage stakeholders across all sectors.

o Funding and Financing:

Destinations contemplating a green initiative may be concerned about the prospect of financing it. However, destinations should consider not only the costs associated with undertaking a green transformation, but the socioeconomic effects of lost tourism revenue; if destinations do not protect assets such as marine life, rainforests, and desert landscapes, they may irrevocably degrade these tourist attractions. Additionally, destinations can often generate revenue by leveraging their own resources, such as charging tourists a fee to visit protected sites. Many green programs, such as the implementation of energy-efficient technology, have strong financial returns and can be easily and successfully affected as private for-profit invest-ments. Many initiatives that require private funds pay off quickly through savings in operating costs. These savings can then be recycled into other green investment projects. Exhibit 2 shows how one destination was able to recover its investments.

However, not all green initiatives are financially profitable for the parties undertaking them, and destinations are not always able to generate revenue through their own resources. When these resources are insufficient, securing sources of external funding can ensure the long-term sustainability of these efforts.

Global financing schemes like CDM are one option. For instance, Costa Rica sold 200,000 tons of carbon at US$10 per ton to Norway in 1996- a transaction that formed the basis of CDM projects in the Kyoto Protocol. The $2 million Costa Rica received financed reforestation programs. In addition to CDM, there are public-private partnership financing models, biodiversity conservation funds (such as the World Wildlife Fund), and international tourism development funds (such as the U.S. Agency for International Development and the Tourism Sustainability Council) that can all provide seed capital.

o Capacity-building and Education:

A destination seeking private-sector investment should ensure that critical information about the benefits and opportunities of green initiatives is widely available. In addition to targeting investors, educational and capacity-building campaigns can be used to train the local tourism community about best practices and encourage them to implement and promote green policy. For example, these programs can train local tour operators to choose environmentally friendly modes of transportation, limit tourists' contact with protected areas, and discourage littering.

o Marketing and Public Relations:

When embarking on a green initiative, a strong marketing and public relations campaign is essential. By raising awareness about upcoming changes, a campaign can attract ecologically oriented tourists. In addition, it encourages stakeholders to participate in the program and addresses potential investors.

However, destinations should be careful not to start a vigorous green campaign until they have made concrete progress and can demonstrate results. Otherwise, they risk losing credibility with tourists who are savvy enough to identify empty PR when they see it.

Each one of these components and enablers requires prioritization and commitment. What's more, they are all intertwined, making the creation of an environmentally sustainable tourism strategy a potentially daunting endeavor. How, then, should a destination begin to go about crafting such a strategy?

Green tourism and sustainable development

Environmental consequences of tourism

Ecosystems are the essential life-sustaining basis for the majority of the Earth's human population. Human intervention is destroying the environment and degrading natural resources at an alarming rate, increasingly jeopardizing efforts to attain sustainable development and effectively alleviate poverty. While an avalanche of tourists has a positive impact on the local economy, modern mass tourism also brings about negative externalities such as congestion, decline in quality of life, low access to socio-cultural amenities and loss of local identity, to the extent that the sustainability conditions of a locality might be endangered.

Tourist activities impact directly and indirectly on ecosystems. For instance, coral reefs can be damaged through trampling, buying, or collecting reefs species (a direct impact occurring locally), or through increased water temperatures as observed during El Nino Southern Oscillation (ENSO) phenomena. ENSO phenomena have increased in frequency and intensity in recent decades (International Panel on Climate Change 2001), which is likely to be a result of global climate change related to human activities including travel, an indirect impact occurring on large regional scales. Discussed how present tourism activities occur locally or individually initiated changes in the global perspectives, such as changes in land cover and land use, energy use, biotic exchange and extinction of wild species, exchange and dispersion of diseases, and changes in the perception and understanding of the environment. Infrastructure (accommodation, traffic structures etc.) for tourist destination significantly change land cover especially in coastal zones. Land alteration is an important cause for release of greenhouse gases like CO2, CH4, and NOx (International Panel on Climate Change 2001), thus interacting with other aspects of global environmental change. Those impacts are not limited to the built area only, but the residual impact often goes outside the boundary. Such impacts are quite extensive in developing countries because of their cheap land prices. For example, erosion rates in Bali, Indonesia is 2-7.5 m/year on the beaches. In the British Virgin Islands, the building of roads led to severe erosion and sedimentation problems. Energy consumption and emission of CO2 in transport and destination places activities are considered to be the long-term impacts of tourism on the local and global environment. About 40% of the distances covered in reforming countries are by car, 5% by aircraft, and 55% by other means of transport, while in developing countries, distances traveled by car are assumed to account for 20% and other means of transport are 80%.

Global tourism-related energy use and resulting CO2-e emissions in 2001

Category	Energy Use(PJ)	CO2-e emissions(Mt)
Transport	13,223	1263
Accommodation	508	81
Activities	350	55
Total	14,081	1399

Tourism activities are influencing export and import of species through international trade, as well as movements of species by tourists or tourist enterprise. This contributes to the extinction of species through disturbance, collection, alteration of habitat, and trading of animal and plant species especially coral reefs as souvenirs. It was estimated that about 12,000 flowering plants have been imported into Europe, out of which 687 have become naturalized. Locally, new species may contribute to an increase in species numbers, but from a global perspective transfer leads to the homogenization of the plant kingdom. Leisure-related transport of alien species can also significantly change the host species location and cause the destruction of native species. In the same way, tourism can contribute in different ways to the exchange and dispersion of pathogens and diseases from tropics to temperate and vice versa. In addition to these above impacts, local culture, tradition and ethnicity is significantly influenced by the incoming of outsiders and also creates local unemployment problem through bringing skilled stuffs from outsides to run tourism activities.

Tourism, particularly nature tourism, is believed to foster environmental consciousness and to result in an increased knowledge about the environment. However, while such changes of the perception and understanding of the environment have generally been understood as supportive of sustainable development, it is argued here that they may not necessarily lead to changes in attitudes and more environmentally friendly behavior. In fact, there is some evidence that a paradoxical situation occurs: even though the knowledge about the environment may increase among travelers, personal behavior may be characterized by increased resource consumption.

Linking green tourism and sustainable development

Since the introduction of the concept of sustainable development, it has been analyzed and discussed in a range of activities related to economic development to support the survival of the earth in the coming future.

The tourism sector is increasing steadily, and will likely become one of the largest economic sectors in our modern open global economy. Its importance has increased over the past decades, as a consequence of the rise in spending power of increasingly mobile consumers and households, the increasing accessibility of tourist regions or cities all over the world, the emergence of relatively cheap transport modes, and the changes in our lifestyles and the trend towards internationalization in modern societies.

These impacts occur because tourism, both international and domestic, brings about an intermingling of people from diverse social and cultural backgrounds, and also a considerable spatial redistribution of spending power, which has a significant impact on the economy of the destination.

It is evident that tourism creates a range of impacts and consequences, which we cannot prevent altogether because of its contribution to economic development. However, the importance of tourism does not mean that we cannot plan and manage this activity in order to minimize the negative impacts and accentuate the positive impacts of tourism. The importance of sustainability can be addressed as an integrated paradigm when considering relationships between tourism and the natural environment and in this century tourism must be redesigned with reference to the changing global relationships and social structures, technological innovations, growing spatial awareness and environmental concerns.

Integration of environmental activities into the broader development framework is at the heart of MDG Seven on achieving environmental sustainability. In fact, although the issue of tourism was not included in Our Common Future (World Commission on Environment and Development 1987), but since the Earth Summit in 1992, pressure has grown for the tourism industry to lift its environmental performance in common with other economic sectors, mobility towards green tourism development in every corner of the world. In addition to the three principles of sustainability viz., environment, economic and social, cultural sustainability is an important issue, particularly when the tourism practices in a certain location are based on local or indigenous culture and tradition. Although sustainable tourism development on a global scale remains a telic concept, the journey toward the goal of sustainability is vital for current and future economic, ecological, and socio-cultural well being and should be integrated with community based economics, conservation with equity, and integration of the environment with the economy.

Conclusion

Sustainable tourism has become part of sustainable development in the sector of tourism. The term sustainable tourism has been widely used and has been "officially recognized or 'institutionalized' among organizations both internal and external, of the tourism sector." The UN World Tourism Organization (WTO) defines sustainable tourism as tourism that meets the needs of present tourists and host regions while protecting and enhancing the opportunity for the future. Sustainable tourism is often mixed with responsible tourism or alternative tourism. The alternative tourism is the new forms of activity emerging like rural tourism, green tourism, nature tourism, urban heritage tourism, cultural tourism, industrial tourism, health tourism, political tourism, volunteer tourism etc.

Under the present world trend of sustainable development, ecotourism is the most noticed sector in tourism. In ecotourism, three elements are well connected. These are the preservation of nature and culture, benefit to local people and the development opportunity by tourism. Within that framework, the neo populism approach is gradually emerging. Neo populism is characterized by "small-scale community-based development, environmental sustainability and empowerment of the community."

But the majority of actual foreign tourists are mass tourists. Given the present reality and possible future of tourism, where the mass tourism will consistently predominate in the world tourism, as well as the hope of government and local people do hope to pursue that direction due to economic benefit and employment opportunities, sustainable tourism should be defined as the new type of tourism having the direction to improving the present mass tourism within the framework of sustainable tourism. The essence of this definition is to change the characteristic of present main stream of tourism and not to take over it. In reality, ecotourism cannot be distinguished from nature tourism. The Laos government has pursued to include some elements of ecotourism in mass tourism. Some local governments in Japan pursue "one day ecotourism" in the massive mass tourism as well.

Mass tourism is believed to be detrimental to the environment and not suitable for sustainable tourism. But the author would like to cast doubt to such a simple understanding. For example, tens of millions of tourists visit Kyoto, Paris, and Utsukushigahara highland, a beautiful highland in Japan, every year for example. But how the environment in these places was deteriorated? The problem lies in the good maintenance system. It is true that when tourists increase rapidly, there is a probable increase of criminals, pollution, traffic congestion and environmental degradation. But at the same time, as Salah Wahab insists, the merits should be considered also like upgrading of roads, water, sanitation, airport, etc. From the economic viewpoint, mass tourism is the desire of local people and government. There is no other way than adding the elements of sustainable tourism or ecotourism to mass tourism.

The cases of Cambodian ecotourism managed by an NGO and Bhutan shows that ecotourism itself is difficult to connect with profitable local business. Developing countries would like to make tourism as an important business sector for profit and employment opportunities. However, this direction needs to be connected with mass tourism. Pursuing ecotourism itself and other alternative tourism programs are necessary in upgrading the variety of tourism sector and tapping its potentials. But the combination or ecotourism/ alternative tourism - mass tourism synergy will be the main direction.

References:

Alhilal Furqan, Ahmad Puad Mat Som, Rosazman Hussin. Promoting Green Tourism for Future Sustainability.

Kimura Hirotsune. Tourism, Sustainable Tourism and Eco Tourism in Developing Countries, Graduate School of International Development, Nagoya University, Paper for ANDA International Conference in Nagoya, March 5-7, 2011.

Barnaa maulick, "Enlarging the Potential of Rural Tourism in India"Kurukshetra may 2012. Pg no 13-16.

David Weaver, 2006, Sustainable Tourism: Theory and Practice, p.10.

Jim Butcher, 2007, Ecotourism, NGOs and Development, p.5.

Das, Sandeep(Sep,2011), "Indian Tourism Sector: A Growth Story", Yojana, pp-49-51.

Honey, Martha and Gilpin, Raymond, Special Report, 2009, "Tourism in the Developing World - Promoting Peace and Reducing Poverty"

Krishna, A.G., 1993 "Case study on the effects of tourism on culture and the environment:

Market Research Division, Ministry of tourism, GOI, 2009 "Tourism Statistics 2008"

Parmar, Jaisingh (May, 2012), "Tourism: An Engine to Economic Growth In The Rural Economy of Himachal Pradesh", Kurukshetra, Vol (60)(7), PP. 17-20.

Dr. Jürgen Ringbeck, Amira El-Adawi, Amit Gautam, " Green Tourism A Road Map for Transformation"

Tenth Five Year Plan 2002-2007

Journal of Environmental Management and Tourism, Volume II Issue 1(3) Summer 2011, ISSN 2068 - 7729

www.ibef.org

www.incredibleindia.org

http://www.slideshare.net/zoeviney/sustainable-savings-green-tourism-business-scheme.

WEB PAGE DESIGNING FOR TRAVEL AND TOURISM ENTREPRENEURS: AN ANALYSIS

S.Mehdi Hasan Rizvi

Computer Programmer, Institute of Tourism Studies, University of Lucknow

Anupama Srivastava

Lecturer, Institute of Tourism Studies, University of Lucknow

Syed Ahmad Rizwan

Asst. Professor, Punjab University, Chandigarh

Abstract: The era of globalization has opened up several new vistas of reaching to people across the globe. Internet presence for any small or big business is one of them. A web page is the first step for any organization to mark its presence in a world where frontier exists only in the minds. Travel and tourism being one of the commodities that tops the preference of customers and consumers when it comes to online business. In such a scenario web page, its format, layout, designing, features, and add-ons attached to it become all the more important and requires a meticulous approach. This research note has been conducted to highlight the intricacies involved in designing a web page, its purpose and its effect on travel and tourism trade. This note will serve as basic guidelines for small and big organizations that are intending to make their appearance on the Net and help them by assessing the web pages of organization who already have made their presence felt.

Keywords: Web designing, Globalization, Travel and Tourism Business.

Tourism is increasingly expanding under the impact of 'Global Cosmopolitanism'. Cosmopolitanism here, referred to 'a capacity in people to open out to others who are often geographically distant' (Lash and Urry 1994:225), or an 'orientation, a willingness to engage with the other' (Hannerz 1990). It can also be taken up as an ability to reflect upon and judge aesthetically between different nature, places and societies (Lash and Urry 1994). With the concept of global cosmopolitanism, a totally new space is being created for tourism. In this space, tourist travels in a 'space less world where the only frontiers are in his/her mind'. Web page, of any organization is one such world.

The present paper discusses the impact, role and designing of web page for travel and related services. Definitely web pages have played a crucial role in bringing openness about people and objects, people travel for.

Advantage of web page publishing

With the advent of internet came an opportunity to heap shape the future of newly emerging communication medium. Never before an organization have been able to reach to literally millions of people without having to go to the expense of inventing in a press and paper hiring a staff, advertising and distributing, nor would have to apply for a license, purchase a tower, transmitter and staff, a radio or television station.

With the advancement in technology and introduction Property Management Systems, Computerized Reservation Systems, improving efficiency, facilitating control, reduction of personnel, channel enabled personalized services and relationship marketing (CHERVENAKL 1993:113-120) it is no longer a question 'whether to become technological savvy or not'but which technological advantage to select so as to provide the most competitive advantage and should be incorporated first.

The advantages of web pages are numerous, and extend beyond the peripheries of the present paper yet just to applaud some can be:

- o Distribution of electronic brochures.
- o Distribution of booking forms to both travel trade partners and direct consumers.
- o No concept of an advertising agency or a Public Relation Agency in between, which act as a barrier to the direct contact between the producers and consumers.
- o Cost cutting in terms of brochure printing and its distribution through traditional methods, e.g.: Snail Mail.
- o Direct contact between the suppliers and the customers or consumers resulting in lesser number of intermediaries indirectly saving financially and faster communications.
- o Facilities of electronic-booking resulting again in commission cost cutting (SAS and Lufthansa airlines have reduced commission to 5% on electronic tickets).
- o Tapping customers and potential customers at their leisure time rather at organizations' own fixed time.
- o Even the cost per individual can be reduced from US$ 10-US$ 15 up to US$ 0.25 shifting from voice based reservation to World Wide Web (BEAVERA 1995).

Creating a web page for travel

The presentations of Forrester research that web generated global sales have risen from US$ 2 billion in 1996 to US$ 61 billion in the millennium year. The best that it came out was the top three sectors for on-line shopping is computer products, travel and entertainment respectively. (Forrester research and consultancy organizations, that has carried out extensive internet analysis).

The first and the most basic commitment that a company can make to the internet is the establishment of its own website, which starts with a web page. A telephonic survey was conducted to add primary research data to the note, of major travel agencies and travel service providers. Study area taken was Lucknow, a city of India forming a part of South Asian market.

Illustration 1

Your Organisation Would Like To Get Its Web Page Designed 'In House' Or Would 'Outsource' To Any Bureau? Give Reasons?

INHOUSE: 20%

OUTSOURCE: 80%

Source: Primary Survey

Survey was necessary to adjudge the most fundamental issue that should the site be created and maintained in house using the organizations own system labor or should be outsourced to some core Information Technology organization? The survey brought a very clear picture.

Majority, who went for the 'In House' option the reason favor their choice was existence of a cost effective in-house IT department. These were top shots and big organizations. Smaller organizations favoring this option were doing so they couldn't support outsourcing. As labor in developing countries is cheap, so these organizations were ready to engage an employee for week.

Preparing an ordinary web page is becoming a common place (Michael C.; Rivard J; and Branscomb E. 1997). New software is a blessing; especially for financially weaker organization as they allow writing ones own web page without botheration of a separate browser and editor. With Netscape Testing Navigator Gold it is no longer necessary to be well versed with H.T.M.L but yes for perfection and complexity it is essential.

The concept of Macintosh and Window's "drag and drop" technology by which web page and its designing attained a new definition through this by click and drag, the objects that one wants to place on the page and the program inserts the codes behind for the designer which in computer slang is known as WYSIWYG (what-you-see-is-what-you-get).

Naming a web page

A major step and an important decision to be made are to name a site. It should be such so that it can be held into memory and should be a part of lingua franca. They are important as they provide an identity and should be kept as close to the organization's identity.

For this aspect also a survey was done through personal interview method at various cyber cafes and Internet shops of travel site visitor and random sampling method was adopted. Study area here was again Lucknow.

Illustration 2

What Kind Of Names Appeals Most And Is Easy To Memorise?

O	Frequently Used Names	30.7%
O	Unique Name	10.3%
O	Product Related Names	20.0%
O	Supplier Related Names	20.7%
O	Others	18.3%

Source: Primary Survey

The maximum support in remembering names of web pages went to the frequently used names. The option 'others' was supported by mostly younger generations who suggested web pages should have 'funky names' or names based on 'famous personalities'. (Bizarre)

Designing a web page

Designing a web page is not a simple task. The intangible aspect of tourism and travel products makes the task arduous.

Illustration 3

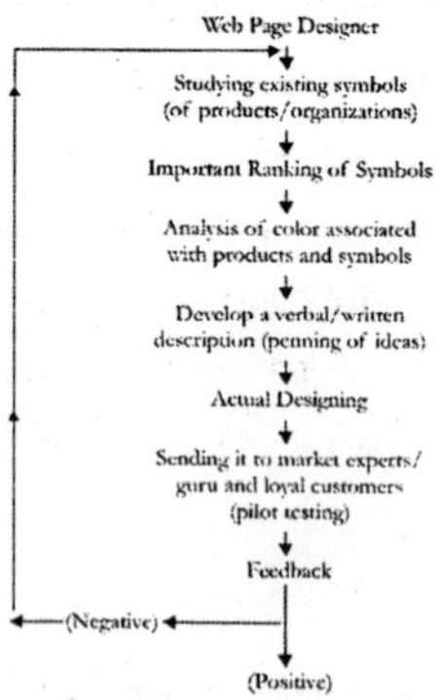

Implemenation

Source: Modified From Iso Sub Committee 'Development Of Public Symbols', Tourism Recreational Research Vol Xi No (1), 1986: 7

The existing symbol of the product has to be studied e.g. Beach Tourism, its sun, sand and sea, Dubai its shopping and modernity, Sydney its harbors, Kerala its Ayurveda, greenery etc. top all other symbolizations. If there are multiple symbols then the symbols placed higher up in hierarchy list has to be given prominence.

The color combination is also of utmost importance. Especially the contrast has to be taken care of the background. After all this, a verbal or written description, 'draft' is conceptualized. Once the actual designing takes place market gurus/experts and loyal customers are asked to judge the alotness of web page and are suit ability to the product. When this final feedback is collected, analyzed required modifications are done.

Designing : a mixture of creativity

Design does not stand-alone and extends beyond layout and information content.

Illustration 4

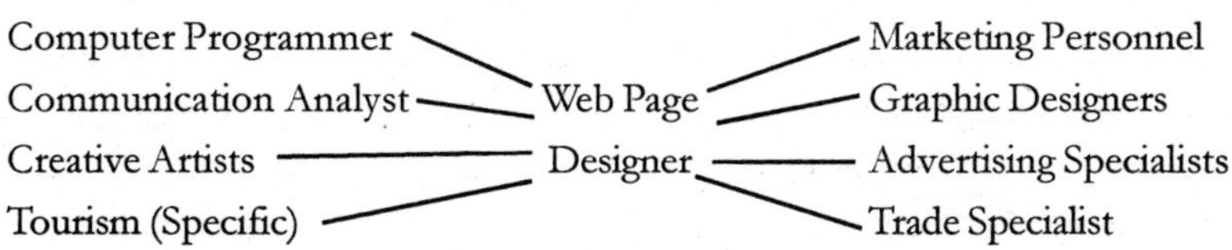

People involved in design of a web page

Source: Primary Research

The overall research appearance on the screen speaks a lot. As the illustration illustrates it is not confined to the domain cumulative supported by graphic designers, creative artists, people from the field of advertising, publishing, marketing and corporate communications. This is essential as web page holds a large responsibility to replace and support the impact to be produced by brochures, magazines, logos, hoardings, advertisement etc.

Things that can go wrong

Despite a mad rush yet it is one of the many which form a rapport between producers and consumers of travel related market,

It is appropriate, at this juncture to consider why do web pages do not have marked effect. The reason between hit and miss is:

- o The target market should be computer literate.
- o Easy accessible reliable and economical Internet services.
- o There can be folly in web page layout and symbols used (Modley 1976)
- o The web page does not express the object or the idea.
- o Page may be poorly designed e.g.in terms of aesthetic appeal.
- o May give out conflicting messages.
- o Colors may not be used as per tier conventional meanings i.e. Yellow for friendship, Pink for care, White for purity.
- o Background shapes are not fully exploited.
- o Symbols used on the page which are unable to explain intended meaning.

Additional features of a web page

The home page is the site owner's e-mail. It is an interaction tool with target market. E-mail feature provides an attraction to web page and enhances its value in terms of interaction and information, simultaneously adds to organizations' existing responsibility. It must answer its duty of answering of mail queries. A demarcation in the eye of the organization is essential (see illustration 5).

The organizations to turn lookers into bookers have to target seriously, serious browsers. With a bit of coaxing they can convert curious browsers into the category of bookers but a good rapport is essential even with casual browsers.

Illustration-5

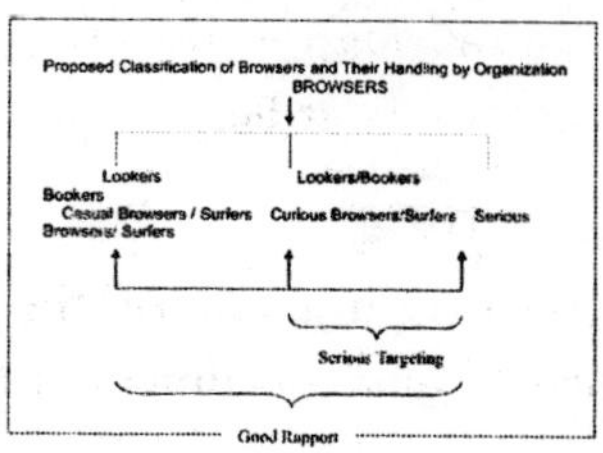

Suggestions

Compartmentalize the web pages under different services eg. Car Hire,. Ticket Reservations etc. So as to make it easy for the virtual visitors, to find what they want. Use of head lists and other design features also assist in the task of highlighting ideas and organizing the material into related groups. For very large graphic display be it of conference hall, banquet, beaches, themes parks there should always be a thumb-nail version display available as to give choice between the two. As often 'visitors' or 'cyber visitors' hate 'graphic interference'. Each page should have a direct connection to go back to the main page. To provide attractiveness to the web page it is mandatory to provide links to other parts of the sites and the related sites. This not only adds to the attractiveness but can help to generate advertisement fee (Inkpen, g. 1998). Each travel service provider can connect its website with other service provider. A heading of FAQ's Frequently Asked Questions can kept under separate head to instant response to commonly asked questions.

Conclusion

With the advent of web pages a new market has ushered where frontiers exist psychologically. Tourism market has become "an oyster for the small, innovative, flexible and networked enterprises" (Poon 1998).

Even in web page publishing and designing in the environment of ever-changing taste of customer, opportunities and challenges lie for those who understand that only 'change is constant', in this highly susceptible industry. This era is opening up new vistas for professionals who not only have command over web designing but are 'jack of all trades', efficient in advertising, business communication, customer relationship marketing, creative aspects and graphics.

Therefore, all small and big organizations of travel trade should consider innovativeness and mark their presence in the unlimited world of World Wide Web through web pages, where only frontiers existing, exist in the minds.

References

Beaver, A. (1995). Lack of CRS Accessibility May be Strangling Small Hoteliers. The Life Blood of European Tourism. Tourism Economies 1(4):341-355.

Buhalis, D. (2000). Tourism and Information Technology. Tourism Recreation Research 25(1): 41-58.

Chrvenak, L. (1993). Hotel Technology at the Start of Millennium. Hospitality Research Journa1 17(1). 113-120.

Hanner,Z. (1990). Cosmopolitans and Locals in the World of Culture. In Featherstone. (ed.) Global Culture. London. Sage: p. 239

Inkpen, G. (1998). Information Technology for Travel and Tourism. England. Pearson Education Limited.

Lash and Urry. (1994). Economies of Science and Space. London. Sage: 255-256.

Michael, C., Rivard, j., Branscomb, E. (1997). Quick Guide to the Internet and Mass Communication. Massachusetts. Allyn and Bacon: 35-38.

Modley, R. (1976). Speaking of Sign Language. Industrial Designs July-August: p. 62.

Poon, A. (1998). Flexible Specialisation and Small Size- The Case of Caribbean Tourism. SPRU. DRC Discussion on Paper No. 57

Tourism Recreation Research. (1986). Vol. 11(1): p.7

PERCEPTION OF COMMUNITY TOWARDS COMMUNITY BASED TOURISM: A STUDY OF NAGGAR, KULLU VALLEY

Sandeep Walia

Assistant Professor, Maharaja Agrasen University, Baddi, Himachal Pradesh. Sndp.walia551@gmail.com

Prashant K Gautam

Assistant Professor, University Institute of Hotel Management and Tourism, Panjab University, Chandigarh. Prashant.k.gautam@gmail.com

Abstract: Community Based Tourism is gaining popularity all over the world as a major form of Tourism. This new type of Tourism shows a contact with the local community and the experimentation of different new sensations. This paper discuss about a study carried out about the opinion of residents in order to develop a tourist destination based on the remarkable ecological resources of the area and the role of the residents and their importance for the development of touristic activities in the particular area.

The Study is an empirical study, guided by a theoretical approach of Murphy's book, tourism: A Community Approach (1985) and was conducted in Naggar village of Kullu Valley of Himachal Pradesh.

The Study concluded the perception of local community that the development of touristic activities can create jobs and generate wealth to their area as well as to the community concerned with that respective area.

Keywords: Community Based Tourism, Local Development, perception, touristic activities, Naggar, Kullu Valley.

Introduction

It is observed a change in tastes of tourists in 21st century. Despite from the traditional forms of tourism the tourists have moved towards the other forms of tourism (Guzman et.al 2011). Studies explored that this could be a result of discovery of new places or destinations or may be due to the knowledge of new destinations, may be of that point unexplored by tourists and may be because of a search for new destinations with greater emphasis on Local Customs, Traditions, History and the particular Culture of that destination.

Thousands of grass root, low impact, high sustainable initiatives all over the world struggle to tell tourists that they exist. Very few of these inspirational initiatives have the resources and skills to market themselves in an industry dominated by existing traditional forms of tourism. So in this way cultural diversity can be looked upon as a means of enriching the experience of active tourists who are looking for new experiences and new Horizons in tourism.

On the one hand at the local level opportunities can be observed to develop plans for the participation of new plans and strategies and also for the involvement of civil operations in the development. On the other hand tourism can be linked to a community's hidden culture and natural resources which are on the recurrent factors in fostering the development of the associated/ concerned communities.

The World Tourism Organization (2002) points out that sustainable development in certain geographical areas may become a fundamental tool for the economic development of the particular area and the reduction of poverty in certain areas. It is possible to create tourism products and services by means of areas own cultural and environmental resources, offering job opportunities for job creation especially for young people and women of the respective areas.

Thus, tourism is also considered as a tool in fighting poverty with the initiatives such as the World Tourism Organizations

Sustainable Tourism Eliminating Poverty (ST-EP) Program. This would always be a complementary activity and is never a substitution for primary touristic activities. In this respect that the promoting tourist exploitation of undeveloped rural areas of the developing countries is not good or bad but it depends on different Political, Social Economic, Environmental and Cultural factors.

Thus several tourist destinations can be established through the structuring of tourism supply and demand. The new need to break in Traditional tourism is observed and the change in monotony has fostered the local initiatives which incorporate the natural attractions and the leisure activities at the local level. The effect of all these activities is that the rural undeveloped areas are undergoing through a phase of transformation and this transformation is changing both the local economic structure on the first hand and their traditional production on the second hand.

And these kind of new initiatives in the field of Tourism, travel and trade have caused a natural repositioning of market destinations in accordance with the fluctuating demands that have led to make a route/way to certain emerging destinations which are becoming more attractive for increasingly specialized markets.

Community based tourism initiatives in the region can reap the benefits of the partnership with tourism for sustainable future alternatives and transforming the lives of people in the host communities. Thus it is more evident that there are opportunities for new projects, such as tourist exploitation of natural, local and cultural resources are to be coordinated at local level and it will help to boost local economic structure that is primarily based on agriculture and live stock farming. So this shows that in order to implement a certain tourist product there is a need to establish a suitable regional tourism policy which is based on the three activities (Bringas & Israel, 2004) first- training of local people and raising awareness. Second- infrastructure and Equipment. Third- Promotion.

There should be two essential components which should be taken into consideration firstly the level of involvement of local community and secondly the Number and type of the tourists.

This paper presents a study in which the extent of this new form of tourism could generate vast incoming economic resources and create employment. Similarly a revision of the existing literature in this field related to relationship between tourists and local community which is more interesting than it was in case of the traditional tourism (Zorn and Farthing, 2007) mainly because of the involvement of host and contact with other cultures for its own development..

The concept of Community Based Tourism (CBT) can be found in the work of Murphy in his book A Community Approach (1985) where aspects concerning tourism and developing communities are analyzed and was a catalyst for the discussion in this area. It provides an important platform for debate and change at a key stage in the development of the tourism industry and the further study by the same author in 2004(Murphy and Murphy).

At that time when leisure travel was expanding in terms of both visitors numbers and the amount of more easily accessible destinations, the emphasis on considerations such as local initiative, a tourism product being in accord with the community and local benefits being integrated into the principles of tourism planning and management was refreshing and stimulating (Blank,1989: haywood,1988). Studies like Guzman, Canizares and Pavon (2001) has also noted that Community Based Tourism is gaining Prestige all over the world as a major form of Tourism.

The concept paves the way for new lines of investigation and for the possibility of tourism development together with other alternatives such as community benefit tourist initiatives (CBTI's) (Simpsons,2008) or community based Enterprises (CBE's) (Manyara and Jones,2007). All these agree that the local community should be a part of the planning and decision making process so that they can easily adapt to the changes and also open their horizons. The most important feature of this type of tourism is to make a healthy relationship between the visitors and the local people, this is why creation of community events favors this type of tourism, because community based tourism is actually based on the active participation of the local community. The community also perceive this form of tourism beneficial for job creation (Guzman et. al,2011)

The study will take example from Indian perspective. The main aim of study will be to identify some applications of theoretical model of Community Based Tourism and to give appropriate suggestions for the development of Tourism In Harmony with local community, since Batta and Pathak(2009) through their case study; have advocated the models of community based tourism in compare to other small and medium scale enterprises in tourism especially in Himalayan region.

There is a close link between community and tourism. Tourism helps a community become more attractive and prosperous. It is more attractive because a community must be appealing to draw and satisfy visitors and it is more prosperous because these visitors spend money. With this money spent in community, the community gets development. The main benefits of community based tourism are that they provide direct economic benefits to the families, socioeconomic developments to the communities and to the respective areas. It also shows sustainable diversification and improvement in the life styles of the communities concerned and the concerned area (Manyara and Jones; 2010 Rastegar,2010)

Community based tourism is also an effective way of exchanging knowledge, analyzing and implementing policies, establishing coordination and avoiding conflicts among visitors and the local people (Kibicho,2008). The study tells about that how a community as a whole can plays a decisive role in the development of the area as a tourist destination. The attitude of local community can make a base for the perception and evaluation of tourism including the factors involving infrastructure, environment and events.

The involving and participating nature of local communities in community based tourism exerts a strong impression on visitors experience and thus the tourism planning benefits the whole community which is involved. However some negative results of community based tourism can be seen as it may affects the lifestyle of the concerned community or tourism can result or even can destroy the local culture of the community. There can be a loss of Cultural identity of the concerned area. The large number of tourist volumes can affect the development of tourism product and the destruction of natural resources as well (Teye et al., 2002). In this case the local populations of the area have five ways to cope up with the problem and minimize its effect on the community- resistance, retreat, boundary maintenance, revitalization and adoption (Dogan, 1989).

Community Based Tourism is based on the introduction of new tourist products with the help of community involvement and participation. Community participation (which can mean a level of control, ownership or influence) in a tourism appears to be closely linked to the derivation of livelihood and other benefits from the tourism to that same community (Murphy, 1985; Scheyvens, 2002: world Wide fund (WWF).2001).

The issue relating to the strengthening of communities and their livelihoods through tourism are important and require further analysis; for example, how essential is community participation, ownership or control to the delivery of benefits to the community from the tourism and what role the visitors play in enhancing and conveying benefits to the community? Community Based tourism can also be a best solution to minimize the negative impacts of mass tourism in the developing nations and can also help to attain better standards of living as the visitor tourist also plays the equal role for the exchange of ideas and knowledge sharing with the host community visited. Community based Tourism is projected and promoted by several International Organizations, such as WTO (2002) keeping the view in mind of so many objectives like ownership and empowerment of the concerned community. It also focuses on protection of cultural and natural resources, high quality visitors experience and social and economic development of the community and the area.

Geographical Description of the Area

Naggar is a very large village located at the height of 1000ft above the sea level in Kullu Valley of Kullu district of Himachal

Pradesh. The village is on a hill surrounded by apple orchids and pine forests. Most of the houses are traditional madc up wooden and stone roofs. The village has a quite peaceful environment. Naggar remained the capital of the kullu valley for more than 1500 years. It has many old temples and a castle, which was Raja's headquarter 500 year ago.

Tourism is growing rapidly in Naggar. There are about six hotels and many smaller guest-house. The main tourist attraction, other than the castle, is the Roerich Art Gallery, which was previously the home of Nicolas Roerich, the Russian artist, explorer, botanist and mystic. In terms of facilities, Naggar has everything one needs for day to day living. There are several grocery shops that sell fruit and vegetables, there's a bakery, a tailor, an internet point and telephone booths. Manali is an hour's bus journey from Naggar if you need to change money, buy books, clothes etc.

Scattered throughout the hills of the Kullu Valley are beautiful villages, made up of ancient wooden houses where people still live a more or less traditional way of life. Often inaccessible by road, villages remain as self-reliant as they can, meeting their basic needs from the surrounding land. Naggar is still not so much known as a tourist destination at international level till now may be because of Kullu and Manali have a larger impact on the global map as being the famous tourist destinations in the state. But some NGO's like 'Ananda' are continuously working for the betterment and upliftment of the local people.

In table -1, we can see the number of foreign tourists visiting Kullu Valley of Kullu district in Himachal Pradesh.

Table 1 Foreign Tourists visiting Kullu Valley during 2009-2012

Year	2009	2010	2011	2012
Tourists	119514	133707	138488	143900

Source: Department of Tourism and Civil Aviation Government of Himachal Pradesh.

According to data provided by the Department of Civil Aviation Government of Himachal Pradesh, There has been observed a gradual increase in the number of foreign tourists visiting Kullu Valley every year. The main reasons for visiting the valley for a holiday and enjoy scenic beauty of the valley. The gradual increase year after year shows that the valley is loved and admired by the foreign tourists. This means that tourism produces more foreign currency income than traditional exports such as apple, which is the major source of income of people of the valley.

The research carried out to determine the perception of local community towards itself and its assessment about the tourism initiatives in the concerned area based upon the natural and ecological resources of the area. The subject of study were the local residents of the area and a sample designed was carried out by means of randomized sampling. The distribution of population was also taken into account. The survey statistics are listed below in the Table 2.

Table 2 Survey Statistics.

Area	Naggar Kullu Valley
Population	5800 people
Sampling	100 interviews
Procedure	Simple randomized sampling
Time Period	May-July 2013

The Instrument of research was a pre structured Questionnaire as was used by Bansal,S.P. & Gautam,P in their study in 2007. The questionnaire is divided into three sections:

Section A: Socio -demographic profile or the surveyed group

Section B: Analysis of the community's perception regarding the present situation of tourism and its potential development in the valley.

Section C: Evaluation of tourist resources and infrastructure in the area.

Data processing was carried out with the help of bivariant analysis of association or independence between variables by means of contingency tables (chi-square/X2 statistics).The aim is to evaluate gender as differentiating factor with the help of these tables, due to the importance of young people and women in the development of community based tourism.

The relevant socio-demographic variables of the sample are given in the table3.

Table 3 Socio-demographic profile

Variable	**%**	**Variable**	**%**
Gender		Place of Residence	
Men	50.9%	Rural areas	100%
Women	49.1%		
Age		Academic Level	
15-30	22.7%		
30-40	23.2%	Primary Education	60.9%
40-50	26.3%		
50-50	18.4%	Secondary Education	22.1%
60 and above	9.4%	Higher Secondary Education	17.0%

After identifying the tourist resources of the area the first step of the research was to ask the local community about the economic development of the area through tourism, which activities were increased or are considered to be increasing as a result of tourism development in the area. The responses found are given in the Table 4.

Table 4 Potential Development of Tourist activities

Activities	Men	Women
Accommodation	25.1%	27.6%
Food	13.6%	15.6%
Craftwork	33.3%	37.0%
Sports activities	20.2%	14.6 %
Other activities	7.8%	5.2%

As seen in table 4, the activities which are expected to grow the most are craftwork sales and creation of a network of accommodation for the visitors. It should be noted that the research carried out during the field survey of the concerned area it was found that the accommodation is normally provided by the local people of the area as the six hotels and a guest house is run by the people themselves. This means that the community based tourism could provide local people ample opportunities to start their own new hotels, with the aim of providing better accommodation facilities to the tourists visiting that area. Similarly, additional activities can also be offered, generally the development of sports activities like trekking, mountaineering and rock climbing was also observed.

The people belonging to the local community also believe that there is a strong need of improvement in the aspects of cleanliness and public safety. The third characteristic which was analyzed and put forward to residents in the area during this study was who would be benefited more if tourism was developed in the area in their opinion. Precisely four possibilities were offered: the local community, the national government, Ngo's, or private companies. A fifth option which comprises all four as a whole was also offered.

Table 5 Beneficiaries of Wealth generation

	Men	Women
Local Community	13%	16%
National Government	10.8%	8.3%
NGO's	15.6%	11.2%
Private Companies	22.9%	22.5%
All of The above	37.7%	41.9%

According to the data collected and displayed in table 5, people in the Naggar area believe that tourism implementation in the area would mainly benefit private companies, although they also have a small opinion that this could have a very good impact on the local community. It is very important that the local community can see that the economic development of community based tourism generates benefit especially for the local community. It was also a result of former studies conducted by Briedenhann and Wickens,2004 ; Christou and Saveriades, 2010.

The fourth aspect studied and analyzed in this investigation was the opinion of residents on the thought that whether the creation of a tour route would generate wealth and create employment. Therefore, only the percentage of positive evaluations highlighted by the residents in the local community with respect to these two economic aspects is presented, since more than 90% believes that it would generate and 87.4% are of the opinion that it would create employment. It is interesting to discover that majority of the people have a opinion that the establishment of tour routes are beneficial for the area.

The fifth aspect under analysis is the knowledge of residents in the area with respect to the level of training and ability in matters directly related to touristic activities. The results are displayed in the table 6.

Table 6 Perceptions of Knowledge of tourist matters

	Men	Women
Non Existent	6.3%	5.9%
Poor	50.9%	52.4%
Adequate	42.8%	41.7%

The result of the table 6 shows that the community does not perceive its training and adequate knowledge is sufficient for the development of tourist activities in the area managed by its own residents. Therefore this kind of response highlights a link between the community- based tourism activities and improvement in quality of life through education. It is better noting that the important role is to be played by NGO's and Local Governments in the improvement of the educational levels of the local people to make them more skillful and technologically sound.

Conclusion

Community based tourism is now present in different geographical areas of the world and it is very particular in developing countries. It is also an alternative way to traditional mass tourism. It is giving rise to specific new tourist destinations which permits the job opportunities and generation of wealth to the local communities. This study was aimed at to find out the opinion of community regarding the impact of Community Based Tourism on the development of the local community of Naggar Village of Kullu Valley. It can be concluded out of the study that tourism has served as a means of cultural revitalization as dying customs were rejuvenated for tourists, leading to increased cultural pride. Socially and culturally, it has been reported that, rather than acting as a "vital force for peace" tourism has often been the source of economic benefits to the community. The significance of tourism can be studied in relation to its contribution to increased foreign exchange earnings, conservation of resources, utilization of wastelands, and increase in employment opportunities and income of local people. Tourism provides the major source of earning opportunities to the people in the region. A number of authors (Ashley & Roe, 2002; Ashley & Goodwin, 2001; Mahony & van Zyl, 2002; Scheyvens, 2002) have also alluded to the importance of community-based tourism in improving the poor's access to assets which improve their livelihoods and develop their communities.

It is evident from the above study that tourism is supposed to be an economic indicator and it is responsible for growth in the employment and other regional development in the region. But as tourism grows at the large scale it can lead towards some negative impacts. Primary study shows that local people in urban areas are aware of negative impacts of tourism, while people in rural area are quite optimistic about the positive impacts of Community Based Tourism. One of reason may be that there are lesser occupational opportunities in these areas.

The people who are having link with the tourism industry are also having positive attitude about tourism impact on the local community. Tourism is also credited by the local community for generating new employment opportunities for the host population. However, some people think that uncontrolled tourism development on a massive scale generates employment for migrants/immigrants and expatriate labor, rather than the local population.

Finally it can be said that Community Based Tourism provide a concept by which the private sector, governments and NGOs (Non Governmental Organizations) can deliver a range of livelihood and other benefits to communities without, necessarily, carrying the potential baggage of significant community ownership or involvement. Another important area of Community Based Tourism development therefore, is the introduction of the concepts and practicalities of Community Based Tourism to private investors, existing tourism operators, NGOs and government bodies; an education and awareness raising process should be undertaken to present the concepts and management implications to these stakeholders.

The Community Based Tourism in Himachal Pradesh are enjoying a very good image regarding bringing the good effects of tourism to the local community. Need is to maintain this situation and thus making tourism - an industry for all.

References:

Bringas, N. & Israel, J.I. (2004). El turismo alternative: una opcion para el desarrollo local en dos comunidades indigenas de Baja California. Economia Sociedad y Territorio, Vol. 4, No.15,pp.551-588.

Dogan,H.Z. (1989). Forms of adjustment: Socio- cultural impacts of tourism. Annals of Tourism research, Vol.16, No.2,pp.216-236

Kibicho, W. (2008). Community-based tourism: a factor- cluster segmentation approach. Journal of Sustainable tourism, Vol. 16,No.2,pp.211-231

Manyara, G. & Jones, E. (2007). Community-based tourism enterprises development in Kenya: An exploration of their potential as avenues of poverty reduction. Journal of Sustainable Tourism. Vol. 15, No.6,pp.628-644

Murphy,P.E.(1985). Tourism: A Community Approach. London, Methuen.

Murphy,P.E. & Murphy, A.E. (2004). Strategic management for tourism communities: Bridging the gaps. Clevedon, Aspects of Tourism series Channel view Publications.

Simpson, M.C. (2008). Community benefit tourism initiatives- A conceptual oxymoron? Tourism management, Vol.29,No.1.pp.1-18

World Tourism Organization. (2002). Tourism and poverty alleviation. Madrid, World Tourism Organization.

Rastegar,H.(2010). Tourism development and residents' attitude: a case study of Yazd, Iran. Tourismos, Vol.5, No.2, pp.203-211.

Zorn, E. & Farthing, L.E. (2007). Communitarian tourism. Hosts and mediators in Peru. Annals of Tourism Research, Vol. 34, No.3, pp. 673-689

World Wildlife Fund (WWF). (2001). Guidelines for community-based ecotourism development. WWF International

Scheyvens, R. (2002). Tourism for development: Empowering communities. Harlow, England: Perason Education Limited.

Bansal, S.P. & Gautam, P. (2007). Sustainable Tourism Development-Himalayan Experience, Indus Publication: New Delhi.

Batta, R.N. & Pathak, R.D. (2009). Community Benefit Tourism Initiative (CBTI) Model for Sustainable Tourism development: A case study of Major Tourist destinations in Northern Indian state of Himachal Pradesh, Case study presented at conference, Finding solutions to Global problems through Stakeholders Engagement, New Social Partnerships and Strategic Alliances for a Sustainable Enterprise, Griffith business School,226 Grey street, Southbank, Brisbane, Australia, available at http:/www.apabis.org/asset/media/rbatta.pdf accessed on dated 30/12/2012.

Tourism Policy, (2005). Department of Tourism and Civil Aviation, Government of Himachal Pradesh.

Suansri, P. (2003). Community based tourism handbook. Responsible Ecological Social Tours (REST) Project, Thailand. Tourism Series Channel View Publications.

Boyd, S. W. & Singh, S. (2003). Destination communities: Structures, resources and types. In S.Singh, D.J. Timothy, & R.K. Dowling (Eds.), Tourism in destination communities. pp.19-33. Oxford, England:CAB International.

GOING GREEN IN THE HOSPITALITY INDUSTRY

Saurabh Rawat

Research Scholar Institute of Tourism Studies University of Lucknow. vicious_saurabh@yahoo.com

Anushree Banerjee

Research Scholar Institute of Tourism Studies University of Lucknow. 08anushree@gmail.com

Abstract: Tourism & Hospitality is one of the leading growth sectors of the global economy, bringing in billions of dollars annually and its growth through the years has created an increasing amount of stress on the environment. According to Wikipedia, "Environmentalism is a broad philosophy and social movement centered on a concern for the conservation and improvement of the environment. Environmentalism is associated with the color green."

These days "Going Green" has not only become a social responsibility but is also important for social acceptability, hence Hospitality Industry is actively contributing towards such activities. Focus of the study is on the initiatives taken by the Hospitality Industry towards being green.

Green hotels conserve and preserve by saving water, reducing energy use, and reducing solid waste. They have seen benefits such as reduced costs and liabilities, high return and low-risk investments, increased profits, and positive cash flows. Identifying these benefits and incentives has allowed the popularity of green hotels to grow. This research is based on meeting people from the hospitality Industry asking them about the various ways that they are using to be more environmentally friendly also going through various articles and case studies on the Internet.

Keywords: Green hotel, Green hotel knowledge, Tourism & Hospitality.

Introduction

There are many definitions of sustainability in use today. One such definition is from the United Nations' World Commission on Environment in 1987. The U.N. states sustainability is "meeting the needs of the present generation without compromising the ability of the future generations to meet their needs" (Morris, 2004).

Another definition from the Forum of the Future in 2008 is "sustainable development is a dynamic process which enables all people to realize their potential and to improve their quality of life in ways which simultaneously protect the Earth's life support systems" (Ricord & Smith, 2009).

'Both of these definitions explain the basic thought: to sustain all generations to come. These definitions explain why it is necessary for both businesses and individuals to make changes within their lives and environment. Each group or individual is responsible for taking action to help our environment as a whole and to allow each generation to live with the required amount of food and energy to advance the next generation.

The hospitality industry has started doing its part in recent years to sustain the environment while maintaining the integrity of the industry. However, many more steps need to be taken by hotels, meeting planners, associations, attendees, etc. Hotels need to become green buildings and make their locations energy efficient, which permits planners to run more sustainable conferences at the hotels. This allows for the companies and associations contracting these meetings to take the initiative in booking these hotels for their meetings so they can say to the shareholders that sustainability is a top priority. The responsibility for making changes lies with every shareholder.

History of Sustainability in Hospitality

In the past, going green was seen as a fad within all industries, especially the hospitality industry. However, some of these "fads" have proven the critics wrong through the years. There are some green hotels that have been in existence for more than three decades (Pizam, 2008). Choosing to be a green hotel is a very significant decision.

According to the Alliance to Save Energy, the lodging industry was the fourth largest user of energy among businesses in the United States (Fedrizzi and Rogers, 2002). Fortunately, the lodging industry is making changes to facilitate environmental upgrades.

One such change, which began in 1996, is a program to allow for certification in the travel and tourism industry. The organizations involved created a program called "Agenda 21 for the Travel & Tourism Industry: Towards Environmentally Sustainable Development" (Hospitality Going Green, 2008). This title pays homage to the Agenda 21 created at the Earth Summit in 1992. The program created a "Green Globe" certificate for hotels that address the issues of greenhouse emissions, energy efficiency and water management. This is just one of the many types of certification processes that are available in the United States. Another is to be LEED certified. For a building or hotel to be considered green, it needs to be recognized by the U.S. Green Building Council, or USGBC, and certified for Leadership in Energy and Environmental Design, or LEED. The USGBC was formed in 1993 to define what eco-friendly within the building development community is and what needs to be done to help the initiative (Holtmann, 2008). LEED is the rules that builders follow to have a certified green building. There are five areas that LEED certification uses as criteria to judge hotels sustainability: sustainable site development, water savings, energy efficiency, materials selection and indoor environmental quality (Katz, 2008). The LEED standards were first used in 2000 and now there are at least 60 hotels that are applying to be LEED certified (Butler, 2008).

The federal government and 23 states in the U.S. have put their weight behind LEED buildings by giving tax credits and incentives to those that build according to the standards (Butler, 2008). California leads other states by passing AB 32, which will require the state to reduce greenhouse gases by 80 percent below the levels in 1990 by the year 2050 (Butler, 2008). This will affect all industries within the state and change the way companies do business. Without conforming to the changes, hotels and other businesses will not be able to meet these standards and will have to face the consequences.

These are a few examples of how the hospitality industry has changed over the years. The world is starting to make bigger leaps into a more environmentally friendly existence. These processes will obviously help the environment, but may also help the businesses with their energy costs, and as a side effect, the public appeal of hospitality companies.

Responsibility of Environmental Sustainability in the Hospitality Industry

The environmental debate has many leaders explaining what needs to be done and how it should be completed, but there are very few individuals actually taking charge of the situation. The responsibility is passed from the individual to the businesses and back to the individual. This is where corporate social responsibility, or CSR, comes into play. CSR is the idea that companies should exist for more than just making a profit (Bohdanowicz and Zientara, 2008). While for the most part, CSR concerns community service and volunteerism, the phrase can also be used to describe environmentalism. This can be seen within the hospitality industry.

In the 1990s, the hospitality industry started being concerned about their CSR and focused it on environmental concerns, technology usage and the use of energy (Holcomb, Upchurch and Okumus, 2007). These are positive ways to focus the responsibility, but according to Paulina Bohdanowicz and Piotr Zientara, CSR has everything to do with brand management and nothing to do with caring about an actual cause (2008). And this is the main concern with CSR. If a company is only doing a good thing because it makes them look responsible, then is it really a good thing? Should it be the responsibility of the individual? In the hotel business, if the cost of the hotel is noticeably higher because of an environmental initiative, then the guest does not have a positive attitude toward the environment (Verbeek and Mommaas, 2008). Jim Butler says the hospitality industry has been somewhat slow in responding to the global warming warnings as the guests do not seem to care about anything more than recycling, so the hotel does not see the need to invest in the future (Butler, 2008). Basically, these data are saying that while the responsibility should be on the guest as well as the hotels, the guest would like the hotel to take charge without being involved in the change.

Implementing Green Initiatives

While many companies and individuals talk about ways they can help the environment, it is still only a few that are actually creating a plan of action. Meeting Professionals International, or MPI, took its first step in 2006 at the Professional Education Conference, a convention of meeting planners from around the world. MPI worked with the convention center to recycle products from the meeting by donating leftover food to a food bank, donating signs to local schools for art projects and using green catering for conference events (Gardner, 2006). These are simple ways to add a green initiative to your meeting and incorporate a no-waste practice at little cost.

One way meeting planners can learn what a hotel provides in terms of green practices is by placing green requests into the RFP, or request for proposal. Some planners are asking for recycling programs to be in place. Planners are also requesting that hotels have complete green programs in place or their hotel will not be chosen for an event (Gardner, 2006).

Banquet Department, Staff Areas and Meeting Space

According to Nancy Wilson of Meeting Strategies Worldwide, these are some steps that can be taken to green your company and your company's meetings: Use e-mail instead of paper mail, use an online registration system and forgo handing out conference bags unless they are made of recycled materials. Another major paper saver is to limit the amount of paper handed out at the conference.

This can be done by using flash drives or posting presentations to a Web site prior to the conference. A really interesting thought is to choose hotels either near the airport or close to all activities relating to the meeting (Gardner, 2006). This will limit carbon dioxide emissions by limiting the need for vehicular transportation from one location to the next.

As for food service, the banquet department should update how food and coffee breaks are presented to the attendee. Instead of individually wrapped sweets, honey, jams and cream, the hotel needs to switch to bulk containers that can be reused many times, creating less trash (McPhee, 2006). In addition, instead of throwaway utensils, silverware should be supplied to stir coffee and tea. Refillable water jugs that can be set up sporadically throughout the meeting space with real glasses available should be used in place of bottled water.

Changing the lighting to energy-efficient bulbs in the meeting space, fitness center and employee-only areas of the hotel will be a high priority. Groups have specific lighting needs for the meeting space, but the fitness center and back of house do not need to have many different types of lighting. Fortunately, there are many new efficient bulbs that can now be dimmed and adjusted to the groups' needs in the event space (Fedrizzi and Rogers, 2002).

The more intense project will be installing motion sensors throughout the meeting space and back-of-house. These areas are used for a large amount of time each day, but there are times when no one would be in the areas at all. If the sensors could turn the lights on and off when someone walks in or out of a room by detecting body heat, then the energy would be reduced in comparison to when the lights are left on continuously (Serlen, 2008).

Guest Rooms

The guest room is a difficult location to implement changes, as it requires the guest to believe in what the hotel would like to change. If the guest wants new sheets each day, then the hotel most likely will oblige the guest to make them happy. That being said, many initiatives can be taken to make it easy for the guest to participate in the new policies.

The Talbott Hotel in Chicago has incorporated going green into its guest rooms by installing INNCOM International's e4 Smart Digital Thermostat with the ecoMode add-on. This allows for smart technology to control your temperature in the guestroom, but with the add-on, the guest can decide if they want to participate in their hotel's energy program by using a touch screen in the room. The guest can choose to not have housekeeping each day, when they want the lights to go on and off by setting a timer, and more control over the temperature at anytime throughout the day (Kirby, 2008).

Along with controlling housekeeping needs, the hotel can place recycling containers in the guest rooms labeling and explaining the recycling program. A program instituted by the Muse Hotel in New York City has installed designer recycling bins for guest rooms so they can be functional as well as fashionable (Kasavana, 2008). Guests can recycle glass, plastic and paper, and this will allow the bins to blend into the decorations in the guest rooms.

Another aspect is how to save energy in empty guest rooms. According to Jeff Sobieski, hotel guestrooms are unoccupied approximately 60 percent of the time (2008). This means that for 60 percent of the time, the hotel can be in control of the temperature and lighting of a guestroom and manage how much energy is being used during that time without interfering with the guest's comfort.

The following are two examples of energy saving scenarios that can take place in guest rooms. The first is to change light bulbs to energy-efficient light bulbs that will last longer and use less power. The other change is the "turn off" program. This program will have the Thermostat linked to the hotel database so the temperature can change when the guest checks in and out. This system can also reset itself anytime the guest leaves the room (Freed, 2008). Also, if the room has a balcony, anytime the balcony door opens, the temperature will reset itself.

Housekeeping/laundry

The energy saving in the laundry area will require some installing of new appliances and systems. While there will be an initial cost associated with the new appliances, it will save money and energy in the long run. The first change will be to install new gas dryers that can dry fabric more quickly and use less energy. The other new system is a heat recovery unit that can save the heat from the old water cycle in the laundry and transfer the heat to the clean water being used in the next cycle (Fedrizzi and Rogers, 2002). Both of these options are creating new ways to conserve energy, but not changing the actual process of doing laundry.

The initial charges would be from installing Energy Star washers and dryers that will reduce wastewater that is created by the dirty laundry, detergent and water. If the appliances use less water, money will be saved from smaller consumption in the beginning. Also, less wastewater would be released into the environment (Riggs, 2007).

This can be used in conjunction with a linen reuse program. While many hotels have instituted a towel reuse program for years, the new addition is to not change sheets every day unless it is requested. The easiest fix for water conservation in the hotel is to fix leaks. The hotel's housekeeping staff would be responsible for watching for leaks throughout all guest rooms and hotel space. According to Ashwin Patel, a single leak can waste 10,000 liters annually; all sinks, showers and toilets need to be checked for leaks (2008). These are initial steps and easy fixes that can be taken while waiting for larger initiatives to take place.

Restaurants

The areas of restaurants and kitchens that are not seen by guests can save energy through a study of how the appliances are used and comparing that to how they are supposed to be used. The main way to save energy in the kitchens is to teach the staff the proper way to use the equipment (Jones, 2002). One example of this is to teach the staff to close the refrigerator door when not in use. In addition, keeping the equipment cleaned and maintained will make sure that the equipment is running at its best level; this will help ensure the lowest amount of energy would be used (Lawn, 2008).

The idea of replacing the appliances in the laundry area also can be applied to hotel kitchens. For example, a new Energy Star steam cooker can be 60 percent more efficient than the regular models available (Brodsky, 2005). This type of savings can be applied to all the appliances in the kitchen. Energy Star products really can make a difference throughout each division of the hotel.

Positive Aspects of Going Green

The most important side effect of going green is to create a more sustainable environment. This is the main goal of all the aforementioned initiatives. Also, the previous examples of changes have shown the savings that can be achieved for the hotel.

However, one main positive aspect may seem a little selfish. There are many reasons why a company chooses to do the projects they do, and for the most part, it is because the company wants to be viewed positively by clients. With positive marketing, the shareholders in the company will see greening as a way the company is doing well by their customers. This has an interesting effect. According to Patrick Hartmann and Vanessa Ibáñez, if the brand is considered green, then consumers are willing to pay more for that product (2006). This allows the individual to feel as if they are doing something good for the environment while attending the conference they planned on attending. However, there is contradictory information on this.

Negative Aspects of Going Green

One of the shareholders in any hotel is the consumer who is choosing this hotel as their destination for work or play. Unfortunately, those staying in the hotels may have unrealistic expectations of what the hotel can do according to the going-green principles. Many guests want their luxury services while helping the environment and some of these services will have to be changed to accommodate the environment. Will the guests accept the changes or will they want the luxury and forget about environmental needs (Butler, 2008)? While the guest can prove to be selfish in their wants while staying at a hotel, the hotelier must also be responsible in the changes they make. The hotel can not negatively impact the guest when it comes to saving money (Olesen, Seppanen, Boerstra, 2006). This contradicts the previous statement of individuals paying more if something is green.

A major barrier to becoming an environmentally friendly hotel is not seeing the urgency to go green from the guests. The consumers, for the most part, do not want to be involved in the changes, but just know they are occurring (Butler, 2008). According to the article, "Becoming an Ecologically Sustainable Organization," one of the top five reasons sustainability fails is the lack of buy-in from shareholders (2008). Without the support of the shareholders, whether they are the owners, managers or customers, no project will succeed.

While there are industry standard certificates available, unfortunately, there are many hotels that are just calling themselves green to appear more environmentally friendly and to sway the consumer (Pizam, 2008). This is a problem similar to the organic food market as there is not a standard set of rules and regulations. Along with this problem, hotel industry personnel know about the different certificates available for their buildings; however, the general public is not aware of the certificates and are not as educated in what makes a hotel green. And with the growing amount of certificates available, the credibility of these certificates has been reduced (Ricord and Smith, 2009).

Financial Aspects

The biggest financial problem to date is the economy. With no way of knowing when the economy will rebound, the industry does not know when and where to spend its money. With the rate of meetings and conferences decreasing every day, the hotels have seen a major decrease in sales. However, now is the time to make a change to get noticed?

One of the largest concerns for the companies is the financial savings that can be seen from going green. For example, in the restaurant industry, energy-saving equipment may cost more to begin with, but the savings will appear within eight to 10 years (Bentley, 2007). This is the challenge with all the new energy-efficient materials. They will save money later, but it is hard to create a business model to spend the money now. Unfortunately, while you may save energy from the products, if you choose to participate in a renewable energy program from the electric company, this may cost upwards of 20 percent more than regular energy (Elan, 2009). However, a renewable energy program is a much more forward-thinking approach. This illustrates that the most negative aspect for a business in creating an environmentally friendly program is the upfront costs. Many in the hospitality industry are wary of spending the money needed to implement the plan now even if it saves them money in the end (Paton, 2007). In the recession the world is experiencing today, it is hard for a company to spend money that may take years to recoup.

Conclusion

This paper has shown that there are many ideas that will not be as much of a financial burden as some may believe. The changes can be subtle and will still make a massive difference in the hotel. These ideas will affect many areas of a hotel and will make the hotel a more responsible business in the community.

References

Morris, N. (2004). Sustainability: What is it? Power Engineer, 18(5), 11-11. Retrieved December 1, 2008, from Academic Search Premier Database

Ricord, P. & Smith, T. (2009). Pulling together or pulling apart? The sustainable debate. Cavendish Square, London: HVS.

Pizam, A. (2008). Green hotels: A fad, ploy or fact of life? International Journal of Hospitality Management, 28.

Fedrizzin, R. & Rogers, J. (2002). Energy efficiency opportunities: The lodging industry. The Center for Energy and Climate Solutions

Holcomb, J., Upchurch, R. & Okumus, F. (2007). Corporate social responsibility: What are top hotel companies reporting? International Journal of Contemporary Hospitality Management, 19(6), 461-475.

Holtmann, A. (2008, February). Going Green. Casino Journal, 22-30.

Hospitality going green (2008). Global Hospitality Insights, 1-13.

Olesen, B., Seppanen, O., & Boerstra, A. (2006). Criteria for the indoor environment for energy performance of buildings. Facilities, 24(11/12), 445-457.

Patel, A. (2008). Green practices benefit world, bottom line. Hotel & Motel Management, 223(18), 10.

Elan E. (2009). Adverse economy has restaurateurs re-evaluating green-focused initiatives. Nations Restaurant News, 43(5), 4-12.

Serlen, B. 2008). Consumer appeal of green means more of it soon. Hotel Business, 17, 18.

GUEST ATTITUDE AND BEHAVIOUR TOWARDS GREEN HOTEL PRACTICES: AN OVERVIEW OF HOSPITALITY INDUSTRY.

Shefali Saini

Assistant Professor, Department of Tourism, Hospitality and Hotel management {THHM}, Punjabi University, Patiala, shefalisaini1988@gmail.com

Abstract: The available literature suggests that there is lot of increase in the interest of guest towards green hotel practices. Green awareness is becoming more and more mainstream and hoteliers must consider guest demand in relation to this increase of public awareness of environmental concerns. Hotel guests have indicated their preference for hotels that 'take care of the environment'. For hospitality in particular, an industry that is often characterized by indulgence and luxury, customer surveys reveal an expectation that hotels will implement behind the scenes conservation initiatives that will reduce a guest's environmental impact, without having any affect on their personal guest experience.

In spite of this, most studies on green practices in hotels have centred on programmes and initiatives undertaken by management with little focus on the attitudes and behaviour of guests. Guest awareness towards green practices has popularise the movement of going green and are starting to alter their purchasing behaviour to a more environmentally friendly way. This has provided the impetus for the 'greening' of hotels Thus, the objective of this study is to investigate guest attitude and behaviour towards the green hotel practices.

Keywords: Guest perception; Going green; Environment; Behaviour; Attitude; Hotel.

Introduction

"Green" Hotels are environmentally friendly properties whose managers are egger to institute programs that save water, save energy and reduce solid waste-while saving money-to help protect our one and only earth!

The term "green hotels" describes hotels that strive to be more environmentally friendly through the efficient use of energy, water, and materials while providing quality services. Green hotels conserve and preserve by saving water, reducing energy use, and reducing solid waste. They have seen benefits such as reduced costs and liabilities, high return and low-risk investments, increased profits, and positive cash flows. Identifying these benefits and incentives has allowed the popularity of green hotels to grow.

A green hotel is one that is environmentally friendly. It does not harm local, regional, or global ecosystems. Instead, it works continuously to improve its environmental relations, reducing its "ecological footprint" and giving back to the environment in beneficial ways. When located in degraded areas, the green hotel often seeks to improve the health and vitality of those areas upon which the health of both economy and environment depend.

Hotels are consistently becoming greener. The most costly and wasteful use of resources in hotels are usually in the consumption of non-renewable energy, excessive water use, and the generation of waste.

The Green Hotel is a new notion, which requires hotels to include environmental management as part of hotel management in general. Taking environmental protection as the starting point, it is necessary to adjust hotels' mindsets, development strategies, management modes and service, to implement pure production, to supply products that are healthy and safe for human beings, to build up public consciousness of environmental protection, to change traditional notions of consumption and to encourage "green" consumption. The idea of the Green Hotel is to provide guests with high-quality products that satisfy requirements for environmental protection and to also conserve energy sources and resources, reduce letting, prevent environmental pollution and improve product quality. The Green Hotel is a kind of direction and goal.

The buzz words have been around for years - green, environmentally friendly, eco-friendly - all used to describe companies that are doing their best to save resources in a world of limited natural ones. The hospitality industry was relatively quick to jump on the environmentally-friendly bandwagon. Today it is almost unheard of for any property to fail to offer the basic initiatives such as towel and bed linen re-use programs, recycling programs, or low-flow shower heads and toilets.

The Seaport Hotel, Cochin opened in 1998, when sustainable design was not a significant consideration. The hotel was designed with Sarnafil Energy Smart Roofing system, which reduces atmospheric heat and conserves energy. Thermo-glass windows were installed in guest rooms and public spaces, further conserving energy by diffusing upwards of 70% of the sun's radiant energy. It was one of the first hotels in the country to offer an entirely smoke-free environment.

At the time, the green movement had not caught the attention of the industry, and properties were not being planned and constructed with LEED certifications in mind. Guests were interested in a hotel only if it met their needs: Does the hotel have the amenities and services needed? Is the price right? Is it conveniently located? Guests were not overly interested in whether the hotel had a recycling program.

Fast forward to today, and whether guests are with you for an overnight, with a large group for a major business function or family event, or are in town for an extended stay for business, there has been a noticeable shift in the mindset about visiting a hotel that is environmentally friendly. Oftentimes, guests want to replicate their lifestyle at home when they travel. This includes having access to all the 'bells and whistles' of their home high tech equipment while also looking for the capacity to practice the same environmentally friendly initiatives while travelling.

As part of their decision making, guests, meeting planners and travel agents now inquire about a property's green efforts. They ask upfront about recycling programs and energy saving initiatives, how hotel work with clients to reduce food & beverage excess and waste, and how hotel reduce the amount of paper that is often heavily used during meetings. A hotel also receives feedback from guests, almost on a daily basis, regarding the property's environmentally friendly initiatives. Comments range from compliments about the in-room recycling program to encouraging remarks about the liquid soap containers and wall dispensers in the bathroom. Guests appreciate the conservation and savings that these dispensers provide in comparison to individual travel size containers. When considering new initiatives, it is important to review guest feedback. Talk with your frequent customers and find out what is important to them. What do they want to see? Armed with that information, you are able to research options and implement initiatives that make sense for both the property and guests. Doing so will encourage future business that likely would have been lost if the concerns gleaned from this dialogue were not addressed.

The importance of green hotels

Though few hotels can claim to be truly green, many of the world's hotels are making efforts to become greener, or more environmentally friendly. Although hotels can take advantage of greening the most when designing a new facility, there are many actions they can undertake to green existing facilities. Creating greener hotels is important for several reasons. First, it demonstrates the hotel's commitment to environmental responsibility. This helps to establish trust as guests recognize that the hotel is concerned with more than merely making profits. Second, it helps to protect or enhance the natural beauty that draws guests to many hotels. Third, certain greening activities, such as reducing energy and water waste, can reduce the hotel's expenses. Fourth, greening hotels is important for environmental health. Particularly on Malta, where large numbers of tourists tax a small nation's resources, any greening activities can have a positive impact.

Review of literature

- Kamal Manaktola, Vinnie Jauhari, (2007) stated in their study that guests which are using hotel services are conscious about environmentally friendly practices in India. They would prefer to use those hotels that follow green practises and are willing to pay extra for these services. The hotels would have to invest in environmentally friendly practices and look at long-term gains. The government needs to acknowledge and institutionalise the practice by instituting rewards and offering benefits in taxes.
- Md. Humayun Kabir (2011) focused on the corporate social responsibility (CSR) practices by the hotel industry in Swaziland. In his study the results pointed towards the involvement of the community is higher than other categories. There are no mandatory regulations in Swaziland requiring companies to practice social responsibility. However, while there is no specific legislation to enforce companies to practice social responsibility, the Swaziland Environmental Authority is trying to encourage hotels to show social concern.
- Shruti Gupta, Denise T. Ogden (2006) framework contributes to the environmental consumerism literature by proposing the moderating influence of level of involvement and perceived consumer effectiveness on the attitude behaviour link. In their review of the literature the understanding of notable research in this area can be seen. For managers, this framework provides additional information to help segment the green consumer market. With increasing environmental consciousness, hotels need to understand green consumers' behaviour by examining factors that influence 'green' purchases. This helps managers of green products understand the green consumer by identifying factors that elaborate on the process of environmental consumerism.
- Golnaz Rezai, Phuah Kit Teng, Zainalabidin Mohamed, Mad Nasir Shamsudin (2013) study's revealed that socio-demographic variables such as education levels and age have a significant effect

on consumers' perceptions as well as their attitude towards going green and becoming environmentally friendly. The results also show that subjective norms (environmentalists and the green society) are important determinants of consumers' intention to go green. Their study indicated that the majority of the guests are aware of the green concept but only a minority of them has availed green hotels in the past. Consumers believe that going green is costly but they also understand the green process can save the planet. The educational level of the respondents was an important determinate for the consumers' level of environmental concern as well as their perception and intention to go green.

- Jacob Cherian, Jolly Jacob (2012) Hotels are looking towards gaining an edge in the green market industry by trying to provide environmental friendly services. They are cutting down on extras and wasted materials and turning their operations into more efficient and green operation. Hotels are also starting to educate the masses with an increase in advertising that puts emphasis on green hotels and how they are more beneficial for the consumers. This kind of advertising goes a long way in educating the masses and promoting the concept of green hotels among the people. With more and more consumers willing to pay a little extra towards green services, organizations are taking notice of the demands and behaviour and attitude of the consumers.
- Stuart E. Levy and Philippe Duverger (2010), Findings reveal that while hotel green efforts impact key marketing outcomes such as satisfaction, retention, positive word of mouth, and price premiums, higher level constructs including respect for heritage and community are suggested to mediate the relationship between these green efforts and the marketing outcomes, implying a hierarchy of effects.
- Nicolai V. Kuminoff, Congwen Zhang, and Jeta Rudi (2010) they stated that twelve states have developed certification programs. After describing the new market for green hotel, data on prices and amenities of "green" and "brown" hotels in Virginia to estimate a hedonic model of hotel room pricing. They found that travelers

can expect to pay a significant premium for a standard room in a green hotel. An internal meta-analysis is used to evaluate the robustness of this result to subjective econometric modelling decisions.

- Orie Berezan, Michelle Millar, and Carola Raab (2010) in their study they revealed what motivates guests to participate in environmental programs and whether they will pay a premium for an environmentally friendly room. Furthermore, the measured impact of environmental hotel practices on guest satisfaction will reveal the items that are significant to customers.

Limitations and future research

- Hotels should balance being 'green' with their own brand experience. Not all environmentally friendly practices are right for every brand.
- This study is examined of customers' eco-friendly experience and its effect on purchase intention future research should examine the relationships among study constructs in other products/ services context to validate the current model.
- There may be more existing variables that are important in explaining relationship between green experience and green consumption not considered in the present study (e.g. personal characteristics, environmental consciousness and values etc.).
- Lastly, for future research, cross-cultural studies using the proposed model are recommended to validate this study across nations and cultures.

Conclusion

Perhaps most importantly, a new initiative should always be tested on a small scale first before launching it throughout the hotel. Implementing cutting edge technology is exciting but it is important to perform the appropriate due diligence upfront to ensure that your latest initiative will succeed on a larger scale. Talking to guests and customers may tell you what outcome they are looking for, but we must figure out the best way to achieve it ourselves. The results of this study will help hoteliers and hotel developers that are unsure about what environmentally friendly attributes guests would like to have in their hotel room. By providing them with such a list, hoteliers can begin to understand that such attributes are important to their clients and that they can be incorporated into the guest room.

In addition to understanding environmental attributes, hoteliers have a new description of what a green hotel may encompass. It is a definition that they can incorporate into their own business practices. It also provides potential hotel guests with a clear picture of what a green hotel is. Hoteliers again can use this to their advantage by tapping into that market, i.e. the younger travelers. Finally, the results of this study give a clear picture of the concerns, in particular environmental concerns that future hotel managers will face. Agreement on the future concerns is a stepping-stone to discussions and forums that hotel managers can utilize to better understand how to cope with those concerns. Because the research about environmentally friendly hotel attributes, or green hotels in general, is limited, the results of this study enable researchers to develop future research projects relating to environmental hotel attributes. For example, a future study could assess either environmental attitudes or personal values of travelers in order to obtain both a better understanding of the characteristics of travelers that care about the environment, and how values or attitudes influence choice of green hotels. Also, participants in the study were not very open to refillable dispensers or low flow showerheads. Further qualitative research that delves into why this is so may help hoteliers come up with alternatives for both items that are both environmentally friendly and acceptable to guests. Finally, in order to validate the list developed in this study, it can be incorporated into other studies assessing different populations of travelers, such as leisure travelers, business travelers, or international travelers. Also, as the green hotel movement continues to grow, the list of environmentally friendly attributes will continuously evolve and need to be updated. This study, very exploratory in nature, was conducted at a conference that focused on green development in the hospitality industry. As a result, the sample may be biased towards environmentally friendly activities. Many of the respondents were architects and developers currently working in the hospitality industry.

They may therefore already have knowledge about environmentally practices in the industry and welcome them in a hotel room. This in turn may influence their level of agreement with having such attributes in a hotel room. In addition, the results are not generalizable to the entire population. The sample in the present study is small and rather homogeneous. The results, therefore, cannot be applied to the general travelling population. They can however, provide stepping stones for future research.

References

Golnaz Rezai; Phuah Kit Teng; Zainalabidin Mohamed; Mad Nasir Shamsudin (2013)"Going Green: Survey of Perceptions and Intentions among Malaysian Consumers" International Business and Management Vol. 6, No. 1, 2013, pp. 104-112 DOI:10.3968/j.ibm.1923842820130601.1125.

Green Hotel Association Retrieved October 30, 2007 from http://www.greenhotels.com/whatare.htm

Gustin, M. & Weaver, P. (1996). Are hotels prepared for the environmental consumer? The Cornell Hotel and Restaurant Administration Quarterly, 20(2), 1-14.

International Tourism Partnership "Going Green: Minimum standards towards a sustainable hotel". Retrieved October 30, 2007 from http://tourismpartnership.org/downloads/Going%20Green.pdf

Jacob Cherian, Jolly Jacob (2012) "Green Marketing: A Study of Consumers' Attitude towards Environment Friendly Products" Asian Social Science; Vol. 8, No. 12; 2012.

Kamal Manaktola, Vinnie Jauhari, (2007) "Exploring consumer attitude and behaviour towards green practices in the lodging industry in India", International Journal of Contemporary Hospitality Management, Vol. 19 Issue: 5, pp.364 - 377.

Md. Humayun Kabir (2011) "Corporate social responsibility by Swaziland hotel Industry" International Conference on Asia Pacific Business Innovation & Technology Management Procedia - Social and Behavioral Sciences 25 (2011) 73 - 79.

Michelle Millar and Seyhmus Baloglu "Hotel Guests' Preferences for Green Hotel Attributes"

Nicolai V. Kuminoff, Congwen Zhang, and Jeta Rudi (2010) "Are Travellers Willing to Pay a Premium to Stay at a "Green" Hotel? Evidence from an Internal Meta-Analysis of Hedonic Price Premia" Agricultural and Resource Economics Review 39/3 (October 2010) 468-484.

Orie Berezan, Michelle Millar, and Carola Raab (2010), "Hotel guests' perceptions of sustainable hotel practices in a Mexican destination" (June 8, 2010). Caesars Hospitality Research Summit. Paper 9. http://digitalscholarship.unlv.edu/hhrc/2010/june2010/9.

Shruti Gupta, Denise T. Ogden (2006) "The attitude-behaviour gap in environmental consumerism" APUBEF Proceedings - fall 2006, pg 199-206.

Stuart E. Levy and Philippe Duverger (2010), "Consumer Perceptions of Sustainability in the Lodging Industry: Examination of Sustainable Tourism Criteria" (July30, 2010). International CHRIE Conference-Refereed Track. Paper 31. http://scholarworks.umass.edu/refereed/CHRIE_2010/Friday/31.

Vora, S. (2007, June 25). Business travellers go green. Forbes. Retrieved October 30, 2007 from http://www.msnbc.msn.com/id/19417697.

Watkins, E. (1994). Do guests want green hotels? Lodging Hospitality, 70-72.

World Travel and Tourism Council (2007). United States: The 2007 travel & tourism economic research. Accessed November 11, 2007 from http://www.wttc.travel/bin/pdf/original_pdf_file/1unitedstates.pdf

FACTORS AFFECTING INBOUND TOURISTS: ASSESSMENT OF TOURISTS' ATTITUDES TOWARDS TOURISM IN INDIA

Shikha Misra

Research Scholar, Punjab Technical University, IITTM Centre, Gwalior.E-Mail: profshikha@gmail.com

Abstract: This paper aims at measuring satisfaction level of tourist coming to India. The measurement has empirically been done on the basis of 112 observations collected from Agra, India using onsite interview and mail back questionnaires. The study provides a theoretical frame work of the perspectives of the tourists on the destination attributes. The study ends with possible implications to avoid different fees for Indian and foreigners, better hygienic conditions of public places and transportation facilities. The study concludes to improve the quality of experience for the tourists visiting India.

Keywords: Tourist satisfaction, foreign tourist arrivals, word of mouth, moment of truth.

Tourist satisfaction

The concept of tourist satisfaction has been drawn from customer satisfaction. Customer satisfaction is conceptualized as been transaction -specific, meaning it is based on the customer's experience on a particular service encounter (Cronin & Taylor, 1992). Customer satisfaction is the foundation for customer loyalty and highly satisfied customers turns into "apostles". Joseph Benoy (1996) cites a study by American Society of Quality Control which found that when consumers were asked what quality in services meant, the largest group of responses cited employee contact skills such as courtesy, attitude and helpfulness. The research above clearly indicates the expectations of a customer from a service provider. Also some authors explain customer satisfaction as cumulative based on the overall evaluation of service experience (Jones & Suh, 2000).

Customer satisfaction related to any buying is always associated with customer's expectations. If the consumer's experiences do not meet with the expectation the customer will be dissatisfied, if those are met the customer will be satisfied, if those are met and the experience is beyond expectation then the customer will be delighted. The destinations must develop service culture because tourists make their buying decisions based on these judgments. If any country wants to know how satisfied are its tourist? This objective can be achieved by knowing how well it treated its tourists and whether it has improved the quality of a tourist experience with time.

International tourist arrival in India

The year 2012 has seen an annual growth rate of 4.3% with 6.58 million tourist arrivals in India while the foreign exchange earning has seen an annual growth rate of 7.1% with USD 17.74 billion. During the same period the world tourist arrivals have been 1035 million and international tourism receipt has been USD 1075 with annual growth rate of 3.2%.India's share in international tourist arrival is only 0.64% which is significantly low and it stands at a petty 41st position. But if we look at the share of India in international tourism receipts then it is 1.65% and it ranks at 16th position in the year 2012 (India Tourism Statistics at a Glance, 2012 Published by Ministry of Tourism, Government of India) (Government of India, 2012). The given data somewhere justifies that the average expenditure done by per tourist coming to India is higher with respect to the average worldwide.

Ministry of Tourism has predicted total 3.31 million @ 2.6% change over the previous year in foreign tourist arrivals by June, 2013 for the same time. Table 1 shows the foreign tourist arrivals in India from the year 1997 -2013 (till June):

Table 1

Foreign Tourist Arrivals and percentage of change over the previous year

Year	Foreign Tourist Arrivals (M)	%Age Change (Over The Previous Year)
1997	2.37	3.8
1998	2.36	-0.7
1999	2.48	5.2
2000	2.65	6.7
2001	2.54	-4.2
2002	2.38	-6.0
2003	2.73	14.3
2004	3.46	26.8
2005	3.92	13.3
2006	4.45	13.5
2007	5.08	14.3
2008	5.28	4.0
2009	5.17	-2.2
2010	5.78	11.8
2011	6.31	9.2
2012	6.58	4.3
2013 (Prediction Till June)	3.31	2.6

Sources:

(1) Bureau of Immigration, Government. of India, for 1997 -2012 (Government of India, 2011) (Government of India, 2012)

(2) Ministry of Tourism, Government. of India, for 2013 (Government of India, 2013)

The future

India has set a mission to attain 11.24 million Foreign Tourist Arrivals by 2016. It also plans to position and maintain tourist development as a national priority activity. Enhancing and maintaining the competitiveness of India's tourism industry requires developing not just infrastructure and superstructure but it also requires a well oriented society which welcomes a foreign tourist. This will be the result of an integrated development of major tourist destinations and circuits. With the launch of the campaign of "Atithi Devo Bhava" (Guest is God) in electronic media one can expect an improved participation from the host community side in conducting international tourism in India in terms of quality. Ministry of tourism has also been giving trainings to human resource employed in hospitality sector under "Huner Se Rozgar" scheme. As of now total 14962 candidates are trained and it plans to train further 11000 in financial years 2013-14 and 2014 -15. It also plans to train 180 tour guide per financial year from 2012-13 to 2014-15. During the same time frame 324 tourist facilitators will be trained every year.

As the level of knowledge of a tourist if he is visiting a destination for the first time is generally very limited and his decision is largely influenced by the image and attitude of the host community largely influence the destination choice of a tourist (Um & Crompton, 1990). Since last three financial years the top seven positions in terms of foreign tourist arrivals in India are fixed and are occupied by U.S.A., U.K., Bangladesh, Sri Lanka, Canada, Germany and France, which altogether constitute little more than half of the total tourist arrivals. Therefore, one can understand the importance of feedback and "word of mouth" given by tourists, as from the same origin places India is getting the maximum number of repeated tourists. Table 2 shows the position, owned by the country, arrivals in terms of numbers and share in percentage for the foreign tourist visited India in the year 2010, 2011 and 2012 respectively. The data clearly indicates the importance of word of mouth for the destination India as only top seven countries constitute more than half of the total tourist arrivals. A superior quality tourist experience helps in image building and influences the decision making of the tourists.

Table 2

Top seven tourist generating countries for India

Rank	2010			2011			2012		
	Country	FTAs	%share	Country	FTAs	%share	Country	FTAs	%share
1	USA	931292	16.12	USA	980688	15.54	USA	1039947	15.81
2	UK	759494	13.15	UK	798249	12.65	UK	788170	11.98
3	B'desh	431962	7.48	B'desh	463543	7.35	B'desh	487397	7.41
4	Sri Lanka	266515	4.61	Sri Lanka	305853	4.85	Sri Lanka	296983	4.51
5	Canada	242372	4.20	Canada	259017	4.11	Canada	256021	3.89
6	Germany	227720	3.94	Germany	240235	3.81	Germany	254783	3.87
7	France	225232	3.90	France	231423	3.67	France	240674	3.66
	Total	318361	53.4		3279008	51.98		3363975	51.13

Source: Bureau f Immigration, India (Government of India, 2010) (Government of India, 2011) (Government of India, 2012)

Literature review

Tourists' level of satisfaction is determined by their cumulative experiences at all the points of contact with the country they are visiting. People like to tell their friends and relatives about their experiences at the destination they visited and hence affecting their decision significantly. This is called "word of mouth" (Lewis, Chamber, & Chacko, 1995; Murphy, 2011;). Organizations (or destinations in case of this study) that consistently satisfy their customers enjoy higher retention levels and greater profitability due to increased customer loyalty, Wicks & Roethlein, (2009, p.83). Tourist creates an image in his mind with the help of what he has learnt from word of mouth and from his own experience. Tourist will directly correlate his quality of experience with this image and hence these images will directly affect the satisfaction level of the tourist are of crucial importance for marketers.

Carlzon (1987) describes moment of truth as every point of contact between the customer and the employee of a company which plays a role in defining the overall experience of a tourist. Applying this concept on tourism industry one can conclude that "Destinations which can create positive moments of truth for its tourists consistently can enjoy repeated tourist due to increased customer loyalty / satisfaction". Some researches reveal that tourist with the experience to the destination are more likely to visit it again with respect to the one with no experience (Milman and Pizam, 1999). One may argue here that once delighted by the tourism experience why the same tourist will come back to the same destination, the tourist may come back provided the destination offers variety in its offerings.

Some of the factors which affect the satisfaction level of a tourist, have been identified by Bailey et al., 1983 (p.532); Karen, 2001 (p.306); Shi et al., 2005 (p. 1440) are quality of services, the user friendly nature of goods and services and comfort assurance. Although, the factors are determined but the combination of these factors varies from customer to customer.

Williams (1988) argues that customer experience based on the perception created by others experience must at least match with the perception in order to get satisfaction. Else it will lead to dissatisfaction but if it exceeds it will delight the consumer, therefore, one may conclude that the level of satisfaction out of any purchase is highly dependent on the perception created from that particular purchase. In addition to this, we might further discern that whereas service quality is based on a perception, i.e. how a tourist rates excellence in service, satisfaction is a feeling, a frame of mind that arises when the service received meets or exceeds expectations. Berry et. al. (1989) defines service as, "service is what customer feels about it so customer assessment of the service quality is the only assessment of the quality of services". Rao and Das (2003) argues that in tourism being a service oriented industry, there are several moments of truth, so the satisfaction level of a customer is highly dependent on the employee relationships and responses towards the customer.

Lots of researchers have done studies on tourists' experiences at destinations, but most of them have followed case study method. This method although describes each situation well in depth but it fails to generalize and correlate the cases with each other (Yin, 1994 for a discussion of case study method in social science research). Graefe and Vaske (1987, cited by Page, p. 24) cited that a tourist's experience is important to identify a tourist's generalize experience which is the result of the tourist experiences on factors like "individual, environmental, situational and personality" as well as the extent and experiences of communication with host community and services suppliers. With a complex list of factors and multiple moments of truth a tourist satisfaction related research becomes difficult to implement.

Research objectives

1. To study the experience of foreign tourists visiting India on the quality of various services being offered to them.
2. To study the views of foreign tourists regarding the quality of services in India
3. To suggest some measures for improvement of tourist services in the country and to enhance the competitiveness of India as a destination.

Research methodology

This research is the result of data collection from tourist using non probability judgmental sampling method, with 112 valid responses, as well as compilation of secondary data from sources available like research journals, travel magazines, news papers and books on tourism, annual reports of Department of Tourism, Government of India, and web portals etc. Quantitative data is used for the analysis. The target population consists of tourists above the age of eighteen. The secondary data is also collected from the research papers and journals available on search engines like Google and Yahoo, etc. Study has used the primary data collected from the foreign tourists visited India. The sampling unit is Agra, India. The tool which has been used is structured questionnaire.

The data has been checked for reliability and the Cronbach's Alpha value has been found to be 0.755, which is higher than the recommended value. The questionnaire includes both open ended and closed ended questions. The responses are collected using modified Likert 5 point scale ranging from "much better than expected (5 points) to much worse than expected (1 point). The questionnaire is divided into seven sections. The first section requires the respondents to give details about their experiences on parameters like services of the travel facilitators, experiences while obtaining visa, communication skills and language of the hotel staff, behavior of local transport driver, local guides' availability, local guides' knowledge, local guides' language, safety against eve teasing, etc. From second section to the last two sections the questionnaire is open ended. Second section of the questionnaire needs the respondent to give detail about problem(s) faced by the respondent during their stay in India, third section about the suggestions on how the quality of the experience on the destination can be improved. Fourth and fifth sections require respondents to give response on the aspect which they give maximum emphasis while deciding a destination and the frequency of the visitations of the respondent. Last two sections epitomize the entire experience of the respondent by requesting them to respond on their intention to come back to India again and if they would recommend India as a tourist destination to others.

Scope of the study

Despite the growing literature in the field of Consumer Behavior, Customer Satisfaction and the field of tourism, there is currently a significant gap between theory and practical. All our understandings on tourism is growing there is a definite need for research on the consumer satisfaction of international tourists, to ensure that we have a tourist friendly environment, leading to increase in the number of tourists visiting India. The present research therefore, provides ways to not only evaluate the current satisfaction level but also give directions on the additional measure to be employed to increase tourist satisfaction.

While visiting a destination a tourist several times interacts with the local host community. Sometimes this interaction is for information collection (e.g. interaction between local guide / local transport driver or with a public helper) while sometimes the interaction is largely to know about the destination (interaction with the local community or with a shop keeper). The study attempts to summarize the entire experience of the respondent during his / her stay in India.

Analysis of Tourists' Demographic Profile

Age	**No. of respondents**	**Percentage**
15 -25 years	7	6.2
25 -35 years	56	50.0
35 -45 years	28	25.0
45 -55 years	8	7.1
55 -65 years	10	8.9
65 -75 years	3	2.7
Gender		
Male	80	71.4
Female	32	28.6
Marital Status		
Married	70	62.4

Unmarried	21	18.8
Single	21	18.8
Budget		
USD 1500 -2000	32	28.6
USD 2000 -2500	18	16.1
USD 2500 -3000	31	27.6
USD 3000 -3500	7	6.2
USD 3500 -4000	7	6.2
USD 4000 -4500	10	8.9
USD 5500 -6000	7	6.2
Duration of stay in India		
1 -8 days	10	8.9
8 -15 days	4	3.6
15 -22 days	24	21.4
22 -29 days	17	15.2
29 -36 days	32	28.6
36 -43 days	6	5.4
43 and above days	19	17.0
Type of Accommodation used		
Star property (1-5*)	89	79.5
Budget (Non -star)	13	11.6
Supplementary Accommodation	10	8.9
Total	112	100.0

Age and gender:

Almost three fourth of the tourist visiting India are from twenty five to forty four years while number of male respondents is more (71.4%).

Marital status:

There were more married tourists (62.4%) while unmarried and singles which were equal in composition.

Budget per person:

Almost one third of the tourist have budget USD 1500 -2000 and 2500 -3000 per person.

Duration of stay:

Maximum tourists (28.6%) stay in India for a time period of five weeks and the second highest duration preferred by tourist to India is three weeks by little more than one fifth tourists.

Type of accommodation used:

Four fifth of the tourist prefer staying in star properties while remaining tourist equally prefer non -star budget properties and supplementary accommodations.

Findings

For measuring the nature of data Standard Deviation, Skewness and Kurtosis are calculated. Data is found to be negatively skewed which generally a higher satisfaction level. Chi square value has been calculated and found significant.

Table 3

Tourists' Responses

	Mean	Std. Deviation	Skew ness	Kurtosis	Chi-Square
Information about the destination India	4.45	.745	-1.208	.836	84.64
Services of the travel facilitators	3.71	.788	-1.021	3.574	111.04
Experiences while obtaining VISA	3.56	1.097	-.141	-.811	39.70
Choices of the accommodation	3.53	1.154	-.317	-1.026	28.80
Quality of the accommodation	3.67	1.226	-.835	-.088	34.34
Hygienic conditions of the accommodation	3.73	.958	-.374	-.479	49.07
Cost of accommodation	3.62	1.141	-.607	-.120	57.82
Communication skills of hotel staff	3.75	1.000	-.358	-.678	42.02
Behavior of the hotel staff	3.83	1.003	-.577	-.228	46.84
Choices of inbound transportation	3.76	1.068	-.497	-.440	38.80
Quality of inbound transportation	3.69	1.074	-.633	-.054	39.34
Availability of seats	3.54	1.056	-.236	-.437	42.11
Interconnectivity between destinations	3.69	1.023	-.521	-.422	46.30
Choices available for local transport	3.67	1.126	-.664	.505	67.25
Reasonability of Cost of local transport	3.52	1.074	-.759	1.039	77.43
Safety in local transport	3.63	1.116	-.400	-.335	60.29
Behavior of the driver	3.73	1.022	-.521	-.395	43.45
Quality of public transport	3.42	1.190	-.573	.460	72.39
Variety of food	3.43	1.206	-.473	-.173	46.46
Hygienic conditions of food	3.55	1.199	-.639	.115	53.00
Cost of food	3.49	1.349	-.799	.025	41.96
Drinking water quality	3.37	1.238	-.732	.533	64.25
General hygienic condition of the eating joint	3.53	1.154	-.532	.151	57.18
Availability of medical facilities	3.21	1.383	-.689	.106	45.61
Local guides' availability	3.94	.883	-.596	.135	67.91

Source: Data collected through questionnaire

Information about the destination India:

As indicated by the table a very high mean value (4.45) and the least standard deviation, clearly indicate that the information about destination India is easily available on net, through travel retailers and through other tourist visited earlier.

Services of the travel facilitator:

The data indicates overall satisfaction level as better than the expectations of the respondents (3.71) meaning the companies selling India abroad are not able to delight their customers. Hence there still exists a scope for improvement on the quality of services provided by them.

Experiences while obtaining Visa:

It is observed that most of the tourists face some kind of difficulty while obtaining visa the overall experience is better than expected (3.56) but it is a clear indication to Indian embassies abroad to mend their ways and make their processes tourists' friendly.

Quality of Hotel accommodation:

The behavior (3.83) and communication skill of the hotel staff (3.75) are the attributes which have given the highest satisfaction to the tourists. Hygienic condition of the accommodation used is only satisfactory (3.73) while in quality (3.67), cost (3.62) and choices (3.53) of accommodation are those factors on which tourists are lesser satisfied.

Quality of experience on inbound transportation:

The choice of inbound transportation mode is rated the highest (3.76), while quality (3.69) and availability of seats (3.54) are the attributes which are rated comparatively lower.

Experiences on local transportation:

The respondents show a highest satisfaction level for the behavior of the driver (3.73) which was followed by Interconnectivity between destinations (3.69), Choices available for local transport (3.67), Safety in local transport (3.63), Reasonability of Cost of local transport (3.52) and Quality of public transport (3.42) were those attributes which have just been able to satisfy the inbound tourist.

Local cuisines and eating joints:

Although the tourists usually find the variety in the food (3.43), but at the same time they look for more variety of genuine Indian food. Cost (3.49) and hygienic condition of food (3.55) are satisfactory but they certainly look for better hygienic conditions at the eating joints (3.53).

Local Guide facilities:

The tourists find the availability (3.94) and languages (3.96) used by the local guides to be much better than their expectations although some respondents indicated that the supply is more than the demand. Local guide's behavior (3.81) and knowledge (3.74) are rated comparatively lower with respect to other attributes of the local guides.

Experience with local public:

It was observed that the general behavior of the local public has been found to be better than expected (3.57) but on the parameter of the languages spoken by the local public the satisfaction level was comparatively lower (3.46).

Shopping experiences and Currency conversion facility:

Shopping experience in India was one of those which had delighted foreign tourists (4.07). The data indicates that respondents find currency conversion facilities satisfactory (3.70) though most of the agreed have brought enough foreign exchange along with them.

Safety against eve teasing and safety against terrorism:

While observing the respondents towards the factor teasing or as popularly known as public sexual harassment the mean was found to be 3.33, which indicated better than the expected behavior of general public towards tourists. In spite of larger world issues like 09/11, and Indian issues like terrorism in Jammu and Kashmir and 26/11 the tourist in India found India a safe and free from terrorism destination which survey found to be 3.61.

Experience with public help facility:

It was observed that the respondents found to be equally satisfied with knowledge followed by control over bribery and they found them satisfactory with the mean score 3.49.

General ecological conditions:

It had been evolved that the respondents find to be more satisfied with the general ecological conditions which have been prevailing in India, with a mean value 3.53.

Conclusion and possible implications

On most of the attributes there is a lot of scope for India to improve on its services. Quality of public transport, variety of food, cost of food, drinking water quality, availability of medical facility, compatibility of languages spoken by general public and tourists, safety against eve teasing, control over bribery, knowledge of public helper are those where more quality improvement is required. On rest of the attributes (except shopping and bargain) there is a higher satisfaction level. Litter thrown by the passerby as plastic bags, used disposable glasses and bottles, spitting, etc create an unwelcoming surroundings near the sites and needs to be controlled by imbibing a sense of belongingness in the local public. This will also create a better civic sense in general public. Availability of good shopping options and bargains and information about India as a destination are the only two parameters which are able to delight the tourist.

Suggestions and recommendations

1. India has a dual fee structure at monuments and tourist sites where in different fees are charged from local public and foreign visitors. Foreign visitors find it unwelcoming, though they do not have any objection in India making more money from tourism. To avoid it India can impose tourism / travel tax on foreign visitors, hence still making money from tourism but invisibly.
2. The quality of public transportation needs to be improved and easily accessible to be able to serve its foreign tourists.
3. The quality of tap water to be unfit for drinking which needs an immediate attention of the authorities.
4. Some indication on the food items which will direct on the level of spices in the food. This will help the tourist in identifying the edible items as per their choice also genuine Indian taste is to be

served to a foreign tourist and not always plain, low on fat and boiled food, as is generally served to them.

5. The hygienic condition of public areas and eating joints needs to be improved.
6. To have better understanding of life and culture of India should offer more home stay with local families.
7. Tourist sites to be absolutely honk free areas.
8. Higher pollution level is another issue to be addressed.

Limitations of the study

This study is restricted to the samples collected from Agra. The paper does not show emphasis on the demographic details of the respondents. The study does not divide the total experience of the respondent on the basis of the cities visited by them. The data was collected during November and December months of 2013, therefore the views expressed by the respondents may be more pertaining to that time period.

Scope for further study

1. A further study can be conducted taking the similar attributes but larger sample size and sampling area in to consideration.
2. A further study can be conducted taking a larger population and more sample units where in more research tools can also be applied.
3. If the researcher takes the origin country of the respondents in to account and correlates them with the satisfaction level of the respondents of different parameters then the findings of this research will be very useful for the promotion of Indian tourism products.
4. If the data can be collected for a larger time span and repeatedly for the same time then the results may be more intense and useful. Further the researcher will also be able to throw light on the impact of the measures taken by Government for improvements.

References

Carlzon, J. (1987). Moment of Truth. MA: Ballinger.

Government of India. (2010). New Delhi: Ministry of Tourism.

Government of India. (2013). New Delhi: Ministry of Tourism.

Government of India. (2012). Domestic and Foreign Tourist Visits. New Delhi: Department of Tourism.

Government of India. (2011). FTA 2011. New Delhi, India.

Government of India. (2012). India Tourism Statistics at a Glance, 2012. New Delhi, India.

Government of India. (2011). Top 15 in 10-11. New Delhi: Ministry of Tourism.

Government of India. (2012). Top 15 in 11-12. New Delhi: Ministry of Tourism.

Graefe, A. R., & Vaske, J. J. (1987). A framework for managing quality in the tourist experience. Annals of Tourism, 14, 389 - 404.

Kincaid, J. W. (2006). Customer Relationship Management. New Delhi: Dorling Kindersley (I) Pvt. Ltd.

Lewis, R. C., Chamber, R. E., & Chacko, H. E. (1995). Marketing Leadership in Hospitality (Second ed.). New York: Van Nostrand Reinhold.

Ministry of Tourism. (2011). India Tourism Statistics at a Glance. New Delhi, India.

Murphy, L. (2011, January). Exploring social interactions of backpackers. Annals of Tourism Research, 50-67.

Um, s., & Crompton, J. L. (1990). Attitude determinants in tourism destination choice. Annals of Tourism Research, 17, 432-448.

Wiiliam, D. R. (1988). Great expectations and the limits to satisfaction: A review of recreation and consumer satisfaction research. Outdoor Recreation Benchmark: Proceedings of the National Recreation Forum (pp. 422-438). SE: US Forest sservice.

Yin, R. (1994). Case Study Research: Design and Methods (Second Edition ed.). London: Sage.

AN APPROACH FOR HERITAGE TOURISM DESTINATION DEVELOPMENT AT SHIMLA

Shikha Sharma

Research Scholar, Institute of Vocational Studies (MTA), Himachal Pradesh University, Summer Hill, Shimla, 171004. Himachal Pradesh

ssharma.shimla@gmail.com

Abstract: Shimla, the capital of Himachal Pradesh has the potential of heritage as it has all the aspects of heritage tourism destination. The main component required to be a heritage destination is its legacy of the past and its reflection as being enriched with tangible, intangible heritage forms. The purpose of this study is to analyse current situation of Shimla as a tourism destination and describe its potential areas of heritage tourism development to make the hill station an attractive international heritage tourism destination. The research is based on the literature review that includes the subtitles of tourism destination development, destination development on the basis of heritage, history, attractions and facilities at Shimla. The methodology of the research is a descriptive study. During the study some conclusions were reached. The different elements and variables were analysed which could help Shimla to grow more and more as heritage destination. The heritage tourism at the destination is described as the product, and the measures that should be taken to develop Shimla on some new lines have been suggested. The paper also tries to highlight a link between the tourist and the destination .The link can be studies by understanding the nature of heritage site and perception of the site .The rich cultural and heritage aspect has not been fully utilized along with the nature based tourism to enrich the experiences of the tourists. The paper tries to highlight the need of the importance of heritage tourism along with other forms of tourism to add to the tourism experience of the tourist. The colonial past is a rich source of generating more tourists to the place.

Keywords: Heritage tourism, potential, elements, variables, importance.

Introduction and Literature Review

A destination is known by the attributes and assets it possesses. The flow of the tourists is largely influenced by the promotion of the destination in the global market and the kind of tourists that the destination is targeting for. According to (WTO 2001) the most important niche market is the market of heritage tourism. There cannot be any rising of tourism without heritage and culture at its base. A destination is a sum total of the culture and traditions amalgamated with the essence of natural beauty. There has been a close relationship between heritage and tourism and heritage has always been a grand source of tourist inflow to most of the places in the world.

Shimla is also one of the destinations in the world which before its development as hill station was in the form of a small village. It was named after the Goddess Shyamala located in the village .In 1817; it emerged as a middling village. According to W. H. Carrey the village was situated towards east of present secretariat buildings .Shimla became the summer Capital of Britishers in 19th century. Shimla has always been known as the "Jewel of the Orient". It is a beautiful hill resort for the tourists around the globe. It is also called as the "Queen of Hill Stations". It has distinct British heritage.

(Ritchie and Goeldner, 1994, p. 72) has defined Tourism is considered as a phenomena that represent the sum of industrial and commercial activities which produce goods and services wholly or mainly consumed by foreign and domestic tourists'. Seaton and Bennett (1996.p.4) argued that tourism is not a homogeneous market rather a heterogeneous sector which consists of products having degree of linkage. Heritage is associated with inheritance which is transferred from one to another generation. Heritage is the carrier of historical value and part of cultural society. In the last three decades heritage and tourism have become inextricably linked with each other. Tourism is economic justification for heritage and it preserves artefacts (Timonthy, 1997). According to Balcar and Pearce (1996, p.203) heritage tourism is a range of concepts and definitions, involving case studies and discourses. According to (Stewart et al., 1998), heritage tourism refers to historic sites and buildings and the experiences which people seek to have in them.

Destinations have always been important for tourism researchers. According to Medlik(1993,p.148) Destination may be defined as countries, regions, towns, or other areas which are visited by tourists throughout the year, the facilities serve their residents and working population, but some time or other they are also used by the tourists.

According to Smith (1995, p.199) there are number of criteria that can be used to identify the destination zones:

1) The region should culturally, physically, socially able to create sense of regional identity.
2) There should be adequate tourism infrastructure like utilities, roads, business services, social services which should support tourism business and cater to tourists' needs. The region should
3) The region should be larger than just one community or one attraction.
4) The region should have attractions or potential to develop attractions to draw tourists.
5) The region should have tourism planning agency and marketing initiatives for further development.
6) The region should be accessible to a large population base. It should be accessible to all modes of transportation.

In Shimla Heritage Zone has been formed in order to ensure conservation of heritage along the Mall, i.e. the stretch from Chhota Shimla to Vice-Regal Lodge along with single building depth and up to 25 metres distance already been notified as Heritage Zone. In this

Heritage Zone only reconstructions on old lines are permitted under the Heritage Regulation. The wealth of Heritage that Shimla has inherited from the years needs to be protected over the years. Shimla has a name in the international market, due to its unique architecture and beautiful buildings that dot the cityscape.

Potential Areas in Shimla

There are two types of heritage in Shimla which serve as the main potential for destination' tourist inflow. These are natural and built heritages of Shimla. Amongst the natural heritage are the Acer ablongum Ushan, white oaks and rhododendron. Pinus Excelsa, St. Helena weeping willows, Himalayan Holly which are much commoner in Shimla. Deodars, large oaks, interspersed with hilly shrubs gives Shimla rich natural heritage. Amongst the built heritage of Shimla which can serve as major potential areas is the Mall which starts from Boileauganj covering many heritage monuments on the way joining Cart road at Chhota Shimla.

From Mall the entire view of snow clad Greater Himalayas and outer Himalayas are visible. The walk up to Mall is 6km long which can make tourist fully satisfied along with the lush green Deodars, parks, open spaces, heritage Buildings and shopping centres. The Ridge on the other hand is located in the centre of Lakkar Bazar, Library and Christ Church, Town hall and providing the view of Himalayas from here also. The Kalka Shimla Railway Line which is 96.5 km long and now a UNESCO world heritage site also serves as an important attraction for the tourists. It is an important part of northern Railways and world renowned for the toy train. It was constructed in 1903.The Railway station of summer hill is also an important heritage site as when the railway line between Kalka and Shimla was commissioned in 1903; it was the first station from the direction of Shimla. The town hall is the best example of the British Architecture and imperial planning of Central city.

Another important monument is the Railway Board Bhawan which is a unique colonial style cast iron and steel structure constructed in the year 1896-97 and The vice Regal Lodge which is built in Neo-gothic style of architecture. Elements of Scottish Baronial Architecture are also visible in the building .Another heritage monument is the Gorton Castle which was constructed in neo-Gothic style and the most oldest buildings of Shimla is the Telegraph Office Buildings near Scandal point. It is constructed in the Swiss Bhavarian style of architecture. The oldest post office of Northern India is also situated in Shimla. The building in which it was constructed was known as Conny.

Another heritage monument is the Ellerglie in which the present H.P.Sectariat is occupied. Barnes Court is another masterpiece of British in -Chief of colonial architecture. The Grindlay's Bank Building is another fine example of the Colonial Architecture. The post Office of Chaura Maidan is neo-Tudor in construction. It was constructed in 1910.The Carton House is now turned into the hospital in Shimla .The Clermont i.e. Labour Bureau Office at present still houses many offices in it. The race view building derived its name from its view of Annandale which was the place of gymkhanas', fancy dress parties, polo, cricket and football.

The other important monuments in Shimla are the Council Chamber i.e. also known as the Vidhan Sabha, the Dalziel House i.e. the state Bank of India at present, the Cedars, Crow Borough, Winter field, YMCA,YWCA,Walsingham which is now the D.C.Residence,Thistle Bank, Benmore, Jammu Castle, Torney house, Green Gate, Pari Mahal, Gaiety Theatre, U.S.Club,Muncipial Corporation Library ,at Ridge ,Band stand, Jesus and Marry School ,Chaps lee, The Chalet, Parkash Niwas, Dharbanga House,Torrentium and many more monuments are still prevalent to give the proof of extensive heritage at every nook and corner of the place. All these important and valuable monuments which give Shimla a look of the European city has great potential and can serve as major elements to attract tourists for reasons other than a hill station destination. Though that image of Shimla is an important one but the time now demands to understand the other areas, elements and variables on which Shimla can grow as a major heritage destinations of the world rather than just being a hill station fit for honeymooners and bunch of youngsters who come to Shimla for pleasure and enjoyment.

Variables and Elements of heritage tourism in Shimla

Shimla as a destination has variety of heritage and there has to be a link between the heritage and tourist at the destination so that more and more tourists could relate themselves with the destination. Heritage at a destination is not just the monument possessed by the destination but the religion, history, archaeological importance traditions, culture, language, folkdances and perceptions all come under the umbrella of heritage tourism. It is the treasure of the legacy passed from the previous generations to the future generations. The perceptions about the heritage site, the nature of the site, the age group of the tourists, purpose of the visit of the tourist, have to be understood .The perception plays an important role in forming a strong linkage between the heritage site and the tourism destination.

The tourist should be able to relate to the heritage site, gain knowledge some may be emotional visitors. The nature of the site is also very important to understand. Depending upon the type of heritage it possesses a site is always rated in the eyes of the tourists. For example, if it is a battlefield the emotions would be different and if it is a religious place the emotions vary. The age groups also play an important role like each age group perceives heritage in a different manner. The last important element for the linkage is the purpose for the visit to the destination. It is mainly the purpose which decides the type of growth of a particular kind of heritage in destination.

Heritage tourism and tourism as identity

Tourism has always been understood a setting, which provides the space to relate, become closer distinct, having inherent identity related dimension (Abram, Waldren, & Macleod, 1997; Urry, 1990, 1994). When tourism focuses on heritage and culture, a link between tourism and identity is established even further (Stebbins, 1997). In heritage tourism local heritage plays a very important role as it is the centre of focus of the various activities the link between heritage tourism and identity has been explored in diverse directions and in the most varied of contexts.

The way in which heritage tourism contributes to the formation of the tourists' and visitors' identities has been analysed by many researchers such as (Bessie` re, 1998; Chronis, 2005; Palmer, 1999, 2005; Pretes 2003; Stebbins, 1997), as has the transformation of the identities of the hosts (Boissevain 1996; Brown, 1999; Chambers, 1997; Howell, 1994; Prats 1997; Rogers, 2002; Smith, 1989; Valcuende del R?´o, 2003) and even as a way of generating and consolidating new identities and images (Ashworth & Larkham, 1994; Bessie` re, 1998; Doorne, Ateljevic, & Bai, 2003; Kroshus, 2003; Le Che^ne & Monjaret, 1992; Light, 2001; Pritchard& Morgan, 2001; Thierry, 2003).

Heritage tourism favours identity polyphony (Bajtin, 1982): the same heritage stimulates different identities both for its depositaries and for tourists. However, all these approaches consider almost exclusively the influence of tourism on identities, but not that of identities on tourism. An open and procession view of notions relating to identity and community, together with a more recursive consideration of cause/effect relationships (Morin, 1990), invite a different analytical approach. According to (Palmer, 1999:315, Alzua, O'Leary and Morrison 1998; Herbert 1995) heritage, which was a buzz word in 1990s is regarded as one of the fastest and significant components of tourism .Heritage has been referred by Cheung 1999 as something which needs to be managed, and marketed according to (Bennett 1995).According to Hewison 1987 ,Nuryanti 1996 Heritage is a subject which ranges from a social behaviour of individuals and society as a whole. According to Colin 20001; Hewison many researchers have focused on the growing heritage industry where differentiation has been made between culture (Richards 1996), natural (Hall 2000) ,and built (Laws 1998)elements.

Research methodology

The purpose of the study is to analyze the current situation of Shimla as a tourism destination and describe the potential areas of heritage tourism development, to make the city an attractive international tourism destination based on heritage. In order to examine this analysis literature about the destination development based on heritage was reviewed. The goal is to explore the potential of Shimla as tourist destinations.

Strengths

- Shimla has rich colonial heritage tourism product.
- It has wide variety of natural resources
- It has favourable climatic conditions throughout the year
- It has rich diversity of green vegetation especially oak and deodars which keeps the city evergreen.
- It has rich variety of flora and fauna.
- It has unique colonial past and history of association with the Britishers.
- It has rich cultural and tradition values.
- The INTACH has identified 329 Heritage buildings in Shimla alone.
- It has state level museums in the town.
- The community of Shimla is quiet hospitable and peace loving.
- Easily approachable hill station from Punjab, Chandigarh and for entire north region.
- It has got the benefit of Kashmir terrorist attacks.
- It has unique handicrafts like Woollen Shawls, Pattu, Patti, Caps, Mufflers and wooden items.
- Infrastructure to support current flow of tourists.

Weakness

- Insufficient high-quality accommodation facilities.
- It is perceived as a short trip destination.
- Non availability of trained guides.
- It has become overcrowded.

Opportunities

- It can serve as a centre of cultural exchange as it has rich cultural diversity.
- Involving locals in the phenomena called tourism

- o It can focus on other forms of tourism such as adventure, ecotourism, sustainable tourism.
- o Organising heritage walks on regular basis.
- o Organising exhibitions, festivals and entertainment driven events from time to time.
- o Building a museum that can demonstrate the live history and heritage of the place.
- o Improves marketing and promotion of the destination.
- o Potential for rich shopping and cultural hub.

Threat

- o Competition from other destinations like Kashmir, Uttrakhand.
- o Overcrowding
- o Pollution
- o Shortage of water
- o Littering
- o Congestion and traffic

Conclusion and recommendation

According to the SWOT analysis and historical past available in Shimla it has an important potential to be developed as a heritage tourism destination. Sustainable tourism can be reached in the site but there is a need to improve the infrastructure. The main component that makes a destination as a heritage tourism destination is its reflection through heritage. Findings can be read, that the attitude of local people towards tourism and foreign tourists are very positive. Accessibility to Shimla is one of its greatest assets but efforts should be made to improve the air transport to Shimla. Local art, culture and handicrafts should be promoted to the international level so that authenticity and uniqueness of the culture should be maintained and heritage should be made more pronounced in the world.

The heritage aspect should be kept in the forefront for promotion, marketing and advertising of the place. The beauty of the old houses and architecture that reflect the glorious past should be protected by preparing some kind of guidelines. The unique and interesting history of the place due to the exchange of populations and positive effects of people exchange on tourism could be used as a tourism motive. A museum could be established and gift shops, cafes, and tea rooms should be installed in this museum. Shopping items and souvenirs should be made available to the tourists at reasonable rates rather than high pricing them in order to achieve target market, promotion and sales through tourists. Amenities are sufficient for current population but as population increases due to the tourism activities some problems like lack of water, pollution, littering, traffic, could emerge. Local should be involved in each and every policy of the government in order to provide them benefit at the root level. Heritage should become the prime focus element rather than just being an element of admiration. It should be the tourist attractor of the destination and tours to such sites which hold importance in the history of Shimla should be highlighted to the tourists in order to provide better image to the destination. Different incentive schemes should be started by the HPTDC for the promotion and upliftment of local heritage sites of the place. Awareness, heritage walks should be organised by the government organization from time to time. Shimla has the great potential to develop on historic city grounds but the need is to utilize the assets in a planned and systematic manner.

References

Abram, S., Waldren, J., & Macleod, D. (Eds.). (1997). Tourists and tourism. Identifying with people and places. Berg

Alzua, A., J. O'Leary, and A. Morrison 1998 Cultural and Heritage Tourism: Identifying Niches for International Travelers.The Journal of Travel and Tourism Studies 9(2):2-13.

Ashworth, G.J., (1997), Elements of Planning and Managing Heritage Sites. What? Where? How Much? Whose? For Whom? Two Different Paradigms; Two Different Answers. In: Nuryanti, W., (Ed.). Tourism and Heritage Management. Yogyakarta: Gadja Mada University Press. Development: 10th General Assembly, Bali, Indonesia. Madrid: WTO.

Audrerie, D., Vilar, L., (1999), Heritage Conservation: Examples of Practice and of Voluntary-Sector Initiative. Council of Europe.

Batra G S, Tourism in the Twenty First Century, Anmol Publications Private Limited, New Delhi, 1996. http://epubs.surrey.ac.uk/1103/1/fulltext. Pdf

Bayraktar, B. (2002), Osmanl?'dan Cumhuriyet'e Ayval?k Tarihi. Ataturk Arast?rma Merkezi. Ankara.

Bennett, M. 1995 Heritage Marketing: The Role of Information Technology. Journal Of Vacation Marketing 3:272-280.

Bessie` re, J. (1998). Local development and heritage: Traditional food and cuisine as Tourist attractions in rural areas. Sociological Ruralis, 38(1), 21-34

Bhatia A K, Tourism Development Principles and practices, Sterling Publishers Private Limited, New Delhi, 1997.

Boissevain, J. (Ed.). (1996). coping with tourists: European reactions to mass tourism. Providence, RI: Berghahn Books.

Brotherton, B., (Ed.) (1999), the Handbook of Contemporary Hospitality Management Research. Chichester: John Wiley and Sons Ltd.

Brown, D. (1999). Mayas and tourist in the Maya world. Human Organization, 58(3), 295-304. Chambers, E. (1997). Tourism and culture. An applied perspective. New York: State University of New York Press.

Chambers, E. (1997). Tourism and culture. An applied perspective. New York: State University of New York Press.

Cheung, S. 1999 The Meanings of a Heritage Trail in Hong Kong. Annals of Tourism Research 26:570-588.

Chronis, A. (2005). Coconsturcting heritage at the Gettysburg story cape. Annals of tourism research, 32, 386-40

Conlin, J.2001 the Art of Dining. The Times (August 13):52-53.

Davidson, R., Maitland, R., (1997), Tourism Destinations. Holder and Stoughton, London Du Cross, H., (2001), A New Model to Assist in Planning for Sustainable Cultural Heritage Tourism. International Journal of Tourism Research, 3(2) 165-170. Chichester: John Wiley & Sons.

Erim, H. (1948), Ayval?k Tarihi, Güney Matbaac?l?k ve Gazetecilik T.A.O. Ankara.

Gartner, W., C. (1996), Tourism Development: Principles, Processes, and Policies. Van Nostrand Reinhold, NY.

Gunn, C.A. (1994), Tourism Planning: Basics, Concepts and Cases. Washington: Francis and Taylor.

Hall, C.2000 Tourism and the Establishment of National Parks in Australia. In Tourism and National Parks, R. Butler and S. Boyd, eds., pp. 29-38.Chichester: Wiley.

Hall, C. M. (2000), Tourism Planning: Policies, Processes, and Relationships. Prentice Hall, Harlow.

Herbert, D., Prentice, R. C., Thomas, C.J. (Eds.), (1989), Heritage Sites: Strategies for Marketing and Development. Aldershot: Avebury

Hewison, R.1987 the Heritage Industry: Britain in a Climate of Decline. London: Methuen

Howell, B. (1994). Weighting the risk and rewards of involvement in cultural conservation and heritage tourism. Human Organization, 53(2), 150-159.

Inskeep, E., (1991), Tourism Planning: An Integrated and Sustainable Development Approach. Van Nostrand Reinhold, New York.

Laws, E., (2001), Management of Cultural and Heritage Destinations. In: Drummond, S. and Yeoman, I., (Eds.). Quality Issues in Heritage Visitor Attractions. Oxford: Butterworth-Heinemann.

Laws, E.(1998) Conceptualizing Visitor Satisfaction Management in Heritage Settings: An Exploratory Blueprinting Analysis of Leeds Castle, Kent. Tourism Management19:545-554.

Medlik, S. (1993), Dictionary of Travel, Tourism, and Hospitality, Butterworth Heinemann, Oxford.

Nuryanti, W. 1996 Heritage and Postmodern Tourism. Annals of Tourism Research 23: 249-260.

Ortega, M., L., G., (2001), Managing Heritage Tourism: Challenges For The Management of Urban Heritage Cities and Attractions (Case Study of Madrid).

Palmer,Contemporary Issues in Heritage and Environmental Interpretation. London: TheStationery Office.

C. (1999). Tourism and the symbols of identity. Tourism Management, 20, 313-321.

Palmer, C. (2001). Ethnography: A research method in practice. The International Journal of Tourism Research, 3, 301-312.

Palmer, C. (2005). Ethnography of Englishness. Experiencing identity through tourism. Annals of tourism research, 32(1), 7-27.

Pearce, D., (1997), the Roles of the Public Sector in Conservation and Tourism Poria,Planning. In: Nuryanti, W.,(Ed.). Tourism and Heritage Management. Yogyakarta:Gadja Mada University Press

Y., R. Butler, and D. Airey 2001a Clarifying Heritage Tourism: A Comment. Annals of Tourism Research 28:1047-1049.

Prats, Ll. (1997). Antropolog?´a y patrimonio. Barcelona: Ariel.

Prentice, R., (1989), "Sales Promotion in Tourism" in Stephen F.W., Moutinho, L., Tourism Marketing and Management Handbook, Hertfordshire, Prentice Hall.

Rogers, S. (2002). Which heritage? Nature, culture and identity in French rural tourism. French Historical Studies, 25(3), 475-503.

Smith, S. L. J., (1995), Tourism Analysis: A Handbook. Longman, Harlow.

Smith, V. (Ed.). (1989). Host and guests. The anthropology of tourism. Oxford: Blackwell

Stebbins, R. (1997). Identity and cultural tourism. Annals of tourism research, 24, 450-452.

Swarbrooke, J., (1999), Sustainable Tourism Management. Oxon: CABI Publishing.

Timothy, D. 1997 Tourism and the Personal Heritage Experience. Annals of Tourism Research 24:751-754.

Tinsley, Lynch, P., (2001), Small Business Networks and Destination Development. Hospitality Management, 20, 367-368.

Thornburg, A., (1986), Marketing Cultural Heritage: Does It Work Within Europe? Travel and Tourism Analyst, 39- 48.

World Tourism Organization (2001), A Report on Heritage Tourism, WTO, Canada. www.culturalheritagetourism.org/annualreport/ 07.01.2008

GREEN TOURISM - SUSTAINABILITY IN TOURISM

Sunil Upadhyaya

Assistant Professor, Manyawar Kanshiram Institute of Tourism Management (Uttar Pradesh Tourism), sunilupadhyaya@gmail.com

Abstract: A green economy can be thought of as one that is low carbon, resource efficient and socially inclusive. In a green economy, growth in income and employment should be driven by investments that reduce carbon emissions and pollution, enhance energy and resource efficiency, and prevent the loss of biodiversity and ecosystem services.

Green tourism is defined as environmentally friendly tourism activity. Green tourism is about being an environment friendly tourist or providing environment friendly tourist services. The green tourism concept would be highly appealing to tourism enterprises and operators owing to increasing governmental pressure to improve environmental performance by adopting effective and tangible environmental management techniques.

Furthermore, achievement and promotion of internationally recognized environmental awards would be instrumental to the tourism enterprises in marketing their services. As a result, many concerned and responsible parties put forward recommendations for green tourism products to regulate tourism's negative impacts. This conceptual paper attempts to discuss green tourism concept, green tourism certification and its processes as well explain the comparative approaches of green tourism. Towards the end, by this green labelling, the industry can legitimately open up new areas for the more discriminating and wider range of the market, and tourists or visitors can enjoy the holiday they want with a clear conscience.

Keywords: green, tourism, certification, sustainability

Introduction

There are a myriad of definitions for Sustainable Tourism, including eco-tourism, green travel, environmentally and culturally responsible tourism, fair trade and ethical travel. The most widely accepted definition is that of the World Tourism Organisation. They define sus- tainable tourism as "tourism which leads to management of all resources in such a way that economic, social and aesthetic needs can be fulfilled while maintaining cultural integrity, es- sential ecological processes, biological diversity and life support systems." In addition they describe the development of sustainable tourism as a process which meets the needs of present tourists and host communities whilst protecting and enhancing needs in the future (World Tourism Organisation 1996).

Tourism is one of the world's largest industries. For developing countries it is also one of the biggest income generators. But the huge infrastructural and resource demands of tourism (e.g. water consumption, waste generation and energy use) can have severe impacts upon local communities and the environment if it is not properly managed.

To reach this current state, we have witnessed an exponential growth in global tourism over the past half century. 25 million international visitors in 1950 grew to an estimated 650 mil- lion people by the year 2000 (Roe et al 1997). Several factors have contributed to this rise in consumer demand in recent decades. This includes an increase in the standard of living in the developed countries, greater allowances for holiday entitlements and declining costs of travel. Tourism is an important export for a large number of developing countries, and the principal export for about a third of these. Statistics for domestic tourism are not so easily available. However it is certain that domestic tourism is also growing rapidly in many Asian and Latin American countries (Goodwin 2000).

World Travel and Tourism Council (WTTC) estimates show that in 2002 travel, tourism and related activities will contribute 11% to the world's GDP, rising to 12% by 2010. The industry is currently estimated to generate 1 in every 12.8 jobs or 7.8% of the total workforce. This percentage is expected to rise to 8.6% by 2012. Tourism is also the world's largest employer, accounting for more than 255 million jobs, or 10.7% of the global labour forces (WTTC 2002).

It is clear that ecotourism, in the strictest sense of the word, still only accounts for a small proportion of the total tourism market. Current estimates are between 3-7% of the market (WTTC, WTO, Earth Council 1996). Taking the WTO's full definition of tourism, there's a risk that ecotourism alone will fail to fully realise the potential to support more sustainable development across the entire sector - suggesting that there may be real benefits trying to make all of the Travel and Tourism industry more sustainable.

Current Global and Regional Trends

The magnitude of the tourism industry can be clearly seen from the World Travel and Tour- ism Council (WTTC) statistics. The WTTC estimates that in the year 2002, travel, tourism and related activities will contribute to approximately 10% of the world's GDP, growing to 10.6% by 2012. The industry is currently estimated to help generate 1 in every 12.8 jobs, 7.8% of total employment. This will rise to 8.6% by 2012 (WTTC 2002).

Tourism has helped to create millions of jobs in developing countries. For example official estimates for 2002 suggest China has 51.1 million jobs associated to tourism and India 23.7 million jobs. In terms of the relative importance of different sectors for job creation, the larg- est contributors in travel and tourism employment are found in island states and destina- tions - ranging from 76.3% of the total number of people employed in Curacao, to 34.6% employment in Antigua and Barbuda. The top ten countries with greatest expected relative growth in employment over the next ten years are all developing countries. Vanuatu is pre- dicted an annual growth rate of 8.8% in employment and tops the list. The balance of benefits begins to tilt toward the developed countries in terms of visitor exports and capital investments, in absolute terms. The top ten list for visitor exports is led by the US. The rest are all European countries, except for China (at number 7). On capital investments, US receive an estimated investment of US$ 205.2 million - far ahead of all other countries. Japan with an investment of US$ 42.7 million and China with US$ 42.5 million follow. The expected growth rates for capital investments over the next ten years are significant for developing countries. Turkey has an annualised growth rate of 10.4% (WTTC 2002). Whilst it can be argued that tourism creates an incentive for environmental conservation, tourism is also responsible for damage to the environment. The phenomenal growth of the sector has been accompanied by se- vere environmental and cultural damage. The projected growth for the industry frequently occurs in destinations that are close to or have exceeded their natural carrying-capacity limits. The consequences are that short term economic gain clearly incurs long term environmental and social costs (European Parliament 2002). Beyond these environmental aspects, other issues of a more social, cultural and rights-based nature have gained increased attention since the mid- 1990's. These include financial leakages, disruptive impacts to local livelihoods and culture, gender bias, sexual exploitation, formal vs. informal sector, domestic vs. international tourism, the growth of "all-inclusive" package tours. Some of the key issues and challenges related to these problems are outlined in the sections below.

Issues: progress and challenges

Tourism and the Environment

The natural environment is an important resource for tourism. With increasing urbanisation, destinations in both industrialised and developing countries with significant natural features, scenery, cultural heritage or biodiversity are becoming increasingly popular sites for tourist destinations. Efforts to preserve and enhance the natural environment should there- fore be a high priority for the industry and for governments. But the reality is not quite as clear cut. Environments where past human interaction has been minimal are often fragile. Small islands, coastal areas, wetlands, mountains and deserts, all now popular as tourist destinations, are five of the six 'fragile ecosystems' as identified by Agenda 21 that re- quire specific action by governments and international donors. The biophysical characteristics of these habitats often render them particularly susceptible to damage from human activities. As the scale of tourism grows, the resource use threatens to become unsustainable. With a degraded physical environment, the destination is in danger of losing its original attraction, increasing the levels of cheaper mass tourism and forcing more "nature-based" tourism to move on to new destinations, which are likely to be even more inaccessible and fragile. Mainstream "ecotourism", as promoted after the Rio Earth Summit, hasn't always enjoyed a good reputation. Tour operators have used the concept merely as a "green wash" marketing tool. In reality it often meant introducing unsustainable levels of tourism into fragile areas, having scant regard for either the environment or for the residents of the destination areas. As the International Council for Local Environmental Initiatives (ICLEI) pointed out:

"Tourism in natural areas, euphemistically called "eco-tourism," can be a major source of degradation of local ecological, economic and social systems. The intrusion of large numbers of foreigners with high-consumption and high-waste habits into natural areas, or into towns with inadequate waste management infrastructure, can produce changes to those natural areas at a rate that is far greater than imposed by local residents. These tourism-related changes are particularly deleterious when local residents rely on those natural areas for their sustenance. Resulting economic losses can encourage socially deleterious economic activities such as prostitution, crime, and migrant and child labour" (ICLEI 1999).

Some of the different kinds of impacts that tourism development and operational activities can have include:

- Threats to ecosystems and biodiversity - e.g loss of wildlife and rare species, habitat loss and degradation,
- Disruption of coasts - e.g shoreline erosion and pollution, impact to coral reefs and fish spawning grounds,

- Deforestation - loss of forests for fuel wood and timber by the tourist industry also impact on soil and water quality, bio-diversity integrity, reducing the collection of forest products by local communities,
- Water overuse - as a result of tourism / recreational activities e.g. golf courses, swimming pools, and tourist consumption in hotels,
- Urban problems - Congestion and overcrowding, increased vehicle traffic and resultant environmental impacts, including air and noise pollution, and health impacts,
- Exacerbate climate change - from fossil fuel energy consumption for travel, hotel and recreational requirements,
- Unsustainable and inequitable resource use - Energy and water over consumption, excessive production of wastes, litter and garbage are all common impacts.

Further study could be carried out regarding the negative relationship between tourism and environment (Roe et al 1997), however the many examples across the globe indicate this scenario is quite typical and widely recognized, emphasizing the need to identify more mutually beneficial approaches in tourism development.

Tourism and Economics

Economic gains have been a major driving force for the growth of tourism in developing countries. The initial period of growth happened in the late 1960's and 1970's, when tourism was perceived as a key activity for generating foreign exchange and employment by both development institutions, such as the World Bank, as well as by governments (Goodwin 2000).

Despite the negative economic impacts of tourism (such as inflation; dominance by outsiders in land and property markets; inward-migration eroding economic opportunities for domestic industry including the poor) the demand for travel and tourism continues to grow. The WTTC has estimated there was an approximate 40% cumulative growth in tourism demand between 1990 and 2000. This demand was largely driven by economic gains at all levels, including in the communities in remote, and hitherto relatively isolated, destinations (Ashley, 2000). There is significant scope for enhancing the possible gains through addressing a number of issues that can help improve opportunities for entrepreneurs and the communities in the destinations, for the poorer sections within these communities, as well as at the macro leve l for the national economy. Some of these are options are discussed below.

Financial leakages

Powerful trans-national corporations (TNCs) continue to dominate the international tourism market. Estimates suggest that about 80% of international mass tourism is controlled by TNCs. These companies have an almost unhindered access to markets and use this to drive down the cost of supplies. The result is high levels of financial leakage, and limited levels of revenue retention in the destination or host countries. Financial leakages tend to occur due to various factors, including importation of foreign building material, skilled labour and luxury products, and packaged travel arranged with TNCs. This is as opposed to locally sourcing the necessary resources. It has been estimated that, on average, at least 55% of tourism expenditure flows back out of the destination country, rising to 75% in certain cases e.g. the Gambia and Commonwealth Caribbean (Ashley et al 2000).

During the seventh UN Commission on Sustainable Development (CSD) meeting (1999), financial leakages was identified as a key area for stakeholders to take action and work together in order to try and assess the situation, as well as seek solutions to better support local communities in host / developing countries. The CSD called upon the UN and the World Tourism Organization, in consultation with major groups, as well as other relevant international organizations, to jointly facilitate the establishment of an ad-hoc informal open-ended working group on tourism to:

- Assess financial leakages and determine how to maximize benefits for indigenous and local communities,
- Prepare a joint initiative to improve information availability and capacity-building for participation, and address other matters relevant to the implementation of the international work program on sustainable tourism development (UN CSD 1999).

Impacts on livelihoods in destination communities

In most tourist destinations of developing countries, the livelihood impacts of tourism, takes various forms. Jobs and wages are only a part of livelihood gains and often not the most significant ones. Tourism can generate four different types of local cash income, involving four distinct categories of people:

- Wages from formal employment.
  - o Earnings from selling goods, services, or casual labour (e.g. food, crafts, building materials, guide services).
- Dividends and profits arising from locally-owned enterprises.
- Collective income: this may include profits from a community-run enterprise, dividends from a private sector partnership and land rental paid by an investor.

Waged employment can be sufficient to lift a household from an insecure to a secure footing, but it may only be avail- able to a minority of people, and not the poor. Casual earnings may be very small, but more widely spread, and may be enough, for instance, to cover school fees for one or more children. Local participation in the industry can be categorized into three different categories; the formal sector (such as hotels), the informal sector (such as vending) and secondary enterprises that are linked to tourism (such as food retail and telecommunications). Experience from Asia suggests that:

- As a destination is developing, accommodation for tourists can be as simple as offering home stays at the early stage, with lodges, guest houses and hotels replacing more basic options as tourism grow, and some of these may include foreign companies. Once luxury resorts start to develop, the scenario becomes more complex with international investors beginning to play a much more dominant role.
- Transport tends to fall into a grey area between formal and informal sectors. Most destinations have taxis, jeeps or other motorized forms of transport, often driven by the owners. As things expand organized associations of owners, operating on a rotation system become more common.

- Data about employment in the formal sector is scattered and collection is often not very systematic. There are references of cases where high-status jobs in resorts typically go to non-locals, expatriate staff or foreign-trained nationals. However, there is almost no analysis of who is employed in middle and lower ranking jobs. The potential for employment of local staff seems to improve as one move away from the luxury resorts into less established areas.
- The informal sector includes activities such as vending, running stalls and collecting fuel wood for the tourist industry. The informal sector often provides an easy entry into the industry for the poor, especially for women. The incomes can be substantial but unreliable as it is often a seasonal activity. However it can still provide a substantial boost to the income of the poor.
- The informal sector tends to get the least attention when interventions are planned, and interventions such as planning permissions are frequently detrimental to this sector. However, there are cases where initiatives such as flexible licensing systems and cooperatives and associations have helped the sector.
- Causal labour and self-employment provide major opportunities for local communities to enhance their livelihood opportunities from tourism. Unlike formal employment, self-employment tends to highlight the entrepreneurial spirit of village communi- ties. Villagers are used to stringing together a livelihood from a diverse variety of sources, often giving them a knack for enterprise. Causal labour includes porters, cooks, guides, launderers, cleaners, caterer and entertainers. Nepal, for instance, has a well- organized labour market to employ porters, cooks and guides on a seasonal basis. An estimate made in 1989 showed that trekking alone generated 0.5 to 1 million person days of employment in a year in Nepal.
- Significant gains also accrue from economic linkages between tourism and other economic sectors such as agriculture, horticulture, animal husbandry and handicrafts. (Shah & Gupta 2000)

Tourism and Society/Culture

Tourism developments often stop people from having the right of access to land, water and natural resources. NGO's such as Tourism Concern and Rethinking Tourism have reported on examples worldwide where the articles in the UN Declaration of Human Rights are flouted, and where indigenous rights are lost or exploited. Adverse social impacts also include poor working conditions, low wages, child labour and sex tourism. The International Labour Organization and International Confederation Free Trade Unions (ICFTU) note that some parts of the tourist industry still degrades labour and drives workers to the lowest levels, exhibiting the worst side of unsustainable production.

Cultural transformation

Fears of tourism threatening local cultures can be misplaced and many cultures have proved resilient enough to be able to take rapid changes required by tourism in their stride. However it is true that popular destinations are typically transformed at a very rapid pace. Buzzing small towns can replace sleepy one lane bazaars. Areas where once only officials rode in motorised vehicles become a familiar site for traffic jams, and dealing with unknown faces can be- come a daily occurrence for people whose previous focus had been confined to a few score square kilometres to their home and work.

Communities visited by tourists can (or have to!) adapt surprisingly quickly. For example, they rapidly adopt business like attitudes to maximize profits. They are creative in inventing and staging events to entertain and provide in- formation on their culture. These attractions, while usually not explicitly developed to protect back regions (i.e. areas of a host society reserved only for local residents, where tourists are not welcome), can function to deflect the tourist gaze from private space and activities. Host communities take specific, active measures to protect their values and customs. This can either be covert action such as private communal functions, fencing off of domesticities but also overt ac- tion such as organized protests and even aggression to protect their interests (Harrison and Price 1996). Tourism development in remote areas can be positive however, bringing with it infrastructure, health services and education facilities. It could be a by-product, or a result of increased incomes, or as is happening increasingly, a result of corporate and customer social responsibility. Nevertheless, rapid tourism development can come at a price and often creates its own unique problems. Tourism activities can degrade the social and natural wealth of a community. The intrusion of large numbers of uninformed foreigners into local social systems can undermine pre-existing social relationships and values. This is particularly a problem where tourism business is centered in traditional social systems, such as isolated communities or indigenous peoples (ICLEI 1999). There are also examples in ecotourism segment, of communities becoming marginalized and forced out of traditional lands as protected areas and destinations become established. Involving host and particularly local communities in all stages of tourism development, from planning right through operations, will help to alleviate some of these issues - if their needs and perspectives are properly taken into account. There is growing amount of work in this area and an expanding body of good practice examples but such approaches needs to extend. In addition, programs which aim to train and assist communities adversely affected by tourism development i.e. pro- viding a social safety net need to be openly assessed for their suitability, and promoted where appropriate.

Solutions and partnerships-towards sustainable tourism

Tourism was only specifically mentioned in a few sections of 1992 Rio Agenda 21, despite its huge economic significance. Agenda 21 for the Travel and Tourism Industry was written in 1996 by the World Trade Organisation, the World Travel and Tourism Council and Earth Council to try and fill this gap. It noted that with a growing standing in the world economy the tourism industry has "a moral responsibility in making the transition to sustainable development. It also has a vested interest in doing so." The document highlights the vital importance of the environment as the main base upon which the market relies.

These and other activities have supported a growing awareness of the positive and negative impacts of tourism, including a growing realisation of the impact that a degrading environment has on the livelihoods of communities living in destination areas. This has contributed towards the initiation of positive actions for mitigating and minimising the more negative aspects. Various different approaches have been explored, especially in the last couple of decades. Emerging from these efforts is a better recognition of the importance of the role of local communities, their valuable knowledge base and understanding of local circumstances, as well as their strong vested interest in preserving a sustainable system. Establishing partnerships with local communities is being increasingly recognised as necessary for sustainable tourism. The trend now is moving towards more integrated approaches, which include communities working with governments. Some broad proposals and responses for moving towards more sustainable tourism, from various stakeholders, are out- lined below.

International institutions, agreements and action plans

International institutions such as UNEP are working in a number of ways (often in partnership) to promote sustainable tourism. This includes a proposal by UN Economic and Social Council to the UN General Assembly to designate 2002 the "UN International Year of Ecotourism". Though facing some controversy regarding the definition and breadth of the term "ecotourism", the idea was that the year would aim to recognise tourism's potential benefit as both a tool for environmental protection and development. For ecotourism, it is particularly seen as a means to advance three basic goals of the UN Convention on Biological Diversity: To conserve biological diversity; 2. To promote sustainable use of bio-diversity to generate income, jobs and business opportunities in ecotourism etc; 3. To share the benefits of ecotourism developments equitably with local communities & indigenous peoples). Other groups like the World Tourism Organization do work to try and encourage good practice in the sector. For example the World Tourism Organisation has produced a "Global Code of Ethics for Tourism in 1999 (an extension of the WTO "Manila Declaration on the Social Impacts of Tourism"

1997), as well as a "Compilation of good practices in sustainable tour- ism", and a practical guide for the development and application of indicators of sustainable tourism, "What Tourism Managers Need to Know".

Business activities and tourism

The Rio Earth Summit 1992 was a major turning point for the tourism industry. Environmental issues subsequently became an important part of the agenda for the industry. However, the approach has not yet generally been an integrating one. Instead the focus has been on minimising environmental impacts that the industry is directly responsible for. There is growing support by lead companies throughout the private sector to implement principles of Corporate Social Responsibility (CSR), Environ- mental Management and Auditing Systems (EMAS), "Triple Bottom Line" accounting procedures (Environment, Society and Economics) and Sustainability Reporting. Measures are predominately based on adopting a voluntary approach to tackling impacts rather than having regulations/legislation imposed on business by governments.

The action plan for the industry, "Agenda 21 for the Travel & Tourism Industry: Towards Environmentally Sustainable Development" contains a number of priority areas for action and suggested steps to achieve them. The importance of partnerships between government, industry and NGOs is stressed, along with the enormous benefits that will be obtained by making the tourism industry more sustainable. The document warns the industry not to under-estimate the challenge which requires "fundamental reorientation". However it also makes it clear that the long-term costs of inaction will far outweigh those for starting to act now. Companies are encouraged to set up systems and procedures to incorporate sustainable development issues into core management functions and to identify actions needed to bring sustain- able tourism into being. A long-term communications program was initiated after the document launch to increase awareness and promote regional implementation (WTTC). The 10 priority areas for action are:

- Waste minimization, re-use and recycling
- Energy efficiency, conservation and management

- Management of freshwater resources
- Waste water treatment
- Hazardous substances
- Transport
- Land-use planning and management
- Involving staff, customers and communities in environmental issues
- Design for sustainability
- Partnerships for sustainability

Another major voluntary activity highlighted by many companies is the use of codes of conduct and certification. However, even the voluntary codes lag far behind activities for environmental performance in the area of social responsibility (UNED 1999). The World Tourism Organization recently produced a study "Voluntary Initiatives for Sustainable Tourism" examining 104 schemes worldwide and gives recommendations to improve the conditions for voluntary initiatives and achieve better effectiveness in the operation and support of voluntary initiatives. In addition it gives a checklist for the planning and assessing of your own voluntary initiatives and makes recommendations for eco-labeling. The report states that voluntary practice has not yet had a significant impact on the mass market. The report recognizes that "their current impact has been minimal across the sector as a whole". It finds that 78% of tourism certificates focus on tourism within Europe and not further afield. However the report also says that "they are revealing tremendous potential to move the industry towards sustainability, but not without careful nurturing and support from key industry partners" (WTO 2000).

When it comes to building more mainstream corporate responsibility, the vast majority of tourist companies state that whilst they would like to do something they feel they are unable to do so because of being faced with 'cut throat' business competition. They argue that the costs involved in acting more responsibly would drive them out of the market, especially if they take unilateral action without wider industry support. Industry surveys have identified the need for establishing mandatory regulations, making it compulsory for everyone to meet the same standards and thereby incur similar costs. Legal and fiscal regulation of corporate sector includes market-based tools such as carbon trading, as supported through the Kyoto Protocol of the UN Framework Convention for Climate Change. Also environmental standards legislated by governments on water quality and waste management, labelling standards, are growing but need to be more widely implemented and effectively enforced.

NGOs are increasingly engaging with the travel sector. They have been playing an active role in addressing problems such as financial leakages and in trying to encourage greater corporate responsibility. Key activities involve consumer education about the potential impacts of tourism and about how local communities might benefit more from the industry. They actively lobby policy-makers on associated issues of trade liberalization, fair trade and globalization. There has also been a concerted effort to set up common certification standards, independent of the industry, along the lines of Fair Trade certification or eco-labeling. Initiatives include the International Fair Trade in Tourism Network, established by Tourism Concern (London-based) in 1999 and a feasibility study for setting up a Sustainable Tourism Stewardship Council being conducted by the Rainforest Alliance, New York.

Conclusion

As we've seen ecotourism is just one approach towards seeking sustainable tourism. Responsible and pro-poor tourism are emerging as new specialist approaches. And new initiatives which aim to push the mainstream tourism industry are building. One example is a new alliance between the World Tourism Organisation and UNCTAD aimed at "poverty alle- viation through tourism". The initiative was announced in July 2002 and it will be presented at the Johannesburg Summit in an attempt to gain wider support. Model projects and successful multi-stakeholder initiatives, albeit on a small-scale, are also beginning to grow. Even these few examples perhaps prove that tourism has the potential to meet many of the objectives of sustainable development - to revitalize economies, support local communities, protect the environment and even generate cost savings and efficiency gains for tourism companies.

Promotion of sustainable tourism, through the development of policy tools, capacity building and awareness-raising programmes, local involvement, guidelines for good practice and actual implementation remain essential goals. Sustainable tourism should aim to directly support poverty eradication and sustainable production and consumption - in line with the general aims of Agenda 21. Making progress on a larger scale will be a fine balancing act and will require a massive "sea-change" in approach from the entire Travel and Tourism industry but it is an approach that is clearly worthy of sup- port from all stakeholders interested and involved in the industry.

References

Ashley, C (1998) 'Tourism, Communities and National Policy' Development Policy Review, Vol. 16 (1998)

Ashley, C, Roe, D and Goodwin, H (2001) 'Pro-Poor Tourism Strategies: Making Tourism Work for the Poor, A review of experience' Overseas Development Institute, London, The International Institute for Environmental Development, London, and Centre for Responsible Tourism, London.

Baez, A (1996) 'Learning from Experience in the Monteverde Cloud Forest, Costa Rica' in Price, M (ed) 'People and Tourism in Fragile Environments' Chichester.

Boniface, P (2000) Information Technology, Tourism and Biodiversity: in Society, and in Relationship draft version. Global Information Society International Research Program.

ECPAT International (End Child Prostitution and Trafficking in Children for Sexual Purposes)

ECOSOC (1999) Chairman's summary of the dialogue segment on tourism and sustainable development at CSD7.

ECOSOC (1999) Multi-Stakeholder dialogue on tourism and sustainable development. Discussion paper contributed by the World Travel and Tourism Council and the International Hotel and Restaurant Association CSD 7 Background Paper no 1. The Global Importance of Tourism

ECOSOC (1999) Multi-Stakeholder dialogue on tourism and sustainable development. Discussion paper contributed by the ICFTU & TUAC. CSD 7 Background Paper no 2. Workers and Trade Unions in the Web of Tourism.

ECOSOC (1999) Multi-Stakeholder dialogue on tourism and sustainable development. Discussion paper contributed by the ICLEI CSD 7 Background Paper no 3.

ECOSOC (1999) Multi-Stakeholder dialogue on tourism and sustainable development. Discussion paper contributed by the UNCSD NGO Steering Committee. CSD 7 Background Paper no 4. Sustainable Tourism: A Non-Governmental Organization Perspective.

European Parliament (2002) European Union Action in the Tourism Sector Improving Support for Sustainable Tourism. Scientific and Technological Options Assessment Series. Working Paper. Directorate for Research.

Farsari, Y (2000) Sustainable Tourism Indicators for Meditarrean Established Destinations. Institute of Applied and Computational Mathematics. Foundation for the Research and the Technology Hellas

Hemmati, M, Shah K and Gupta G (1999) 'Summary, Conclusions and Recommendations' in: Gender & Tourism: Women's Employment and Participation in Tourism 186 - 205. London, UNED-UK

Hewett, C. 'Clear Trails?', Green Futures magazine, May/June 2001

ASSESSMENT OF GREEN PRACTICES IN EMERGING COSMOPOLITAN SHADE OF LUCKNOW'S TOURISM

Suyash Yadav

Research Scholar, Institute of Tourism Studies, University of Lucknow, India; yadav.suyash@gmail.com

Abstract: Natural resources are not infinite, secondly if resources are exhausted we have nowhere to go. The mother earth is in crisis due to environmental concerns. This gave rise to mother concept of Green Tourists Movement known as alternative tourism which later culminated into ecotourism. In 1950, international tourism was 25 million, and by 2010 it had grown to 940 million, generating over US$ 900 billion in export earnings. The WTTC ranked India as a tourism "hot-spot", with a very high growth possibility in the coming years. Lucknow was among world's 50 Greatest Cultural Destinations, according to a special supplement on Greatest Cultural Destinations brought out by The Sunday Telegraph, London and travel experts Page and Moy. The other two cities on the list are Agra and Jaipur. The modernization and population pressure, in the era of globalization, upon the cities are changing their façade, which, in, certain ways are better; but in other ways can be detrimental to the existence of the spirit of the city. Lucknow as a city has a personality of its own. No other city has experienced the Hindu rule, the Muslim rule, a passing Mughal touch, feudal lord's regime and colonial rule so closely. It is one of the fastest growing cities of the country in terms of population which is due to influx of people from the neighboring areas. The primary survey of the stakeholders' of hospitality sector in the city revealed that Lucknow is increasingly gaining MICE tourists apart from the existing tourist who visited the city primarily for its culture and historical relevance. Emerging Lucknow is characterized by construction of hotels primarily to serve Business clientale, therefore the researcher made an attempt to enquire into the aspects of Green Hospitality/practices in the city which has numerous benefits.

Keywords: Green Tourism, Alternative Tourism, Emerging Lucknow, Green Practices

Introduction

In terms of cultural heritage, India is a giant on the South Asian scene. Few countries, with the possible exception of China, in this entire region of South and Southeast Asia can match India's rich natural and cultural diversity, history, economy and heritage. Lucknow, the capital of Uttar Pradesh, was among world's 50 Greatest Cultural Destinations, according to a special supplement on Greatest Cultural Destinations brought out by The Sunday Telegraph, London and travel experts Page and Moy. The other two cities on the list are Agra and Jaipur.

Culture and tourism have a mutually beneficial relationship which can strengthen the attractiveness and competitiveness of destinations, regions and countries. Culture is increasingly an important element of the tourism product, which creates distinctiveness in a crowded global marketplace. At the same time, tourism provides an important means of enhancing culture and creating income which can support and strengthen cultural heritage, cultural production and creativity. Creating a strong relationship between tourism and culture can therefore help destinations to become more attractive as well as more competitive as locations to live, visit, work and invest in (OECD,2009).

The commonest sight anywhere you go in the city of Lucknow at any time is construction material and men at work. But the major chunk of all these activities is Shaheed Path. From housing projects to roads and from railway over bridges to IT parks, buildings are coming up around the 23 -km stretch from Faizabad Road to Kanpur

Road. Construction work continues at a hectic pace and every project is directed towards solving one urban problem or the other or creating one facility better than the previous. In times to come, Lucknow seems poised to be looked at as the hot new proposition for investors, the favourite destination of the immigrants and a provider of employment instead of the best of hands and brains. (Yadav ,2013)

The modernization and population pressure, in the era of globalization, upon the cities are changing their façade, which, in, certain ways are better; but in other ways can be detrimental to the existence of the spirit of the city. Lucknow is a unique city which portrays characteristics of 'traditionalism', roots of which can be traced in the life and times of people of old Lucknow (Luckhnawis) which was an affluent section of society in its search for knowledge, academic achievements and activities, hedonistic pastimes, social and religious ceremonies, and artistic pursuits. Largely free from struggles of existence the people of this class were able to engage themselves in the above mentioned activities (Sharar,1989). Lucknow as a city has a personality of its own. Rather than a monotonous history, passing through the alleys of Hindu princedom and Muslim rule; it encompasses much more. No other city has experienced the Hindu rule, the Muslim rule, a passing Mughal touch, feudal lord's regime and colonial rule so closely. The exception lies not only in the variety, but also in the manner, in which all the colours of these periods have been amalgamated, absorbed and exhibited, explicitly visible even in the present times (Rizwan,2006)

The turn of the century was a watershead year on Lucknow's development calendar .This was the time when the city's old master plan, drafted in 1992, was losing its relevance .The old city was bursting at the seams and even newer areas like Gomtinagar were fast approaching the saturation point. Lucknow was waiting for a new plan to tackle the population boom -triggered by steady influx of immigrants from eastern UP and Bihar-it was already witnessing .Then in 2001, a city road project-Shaheed Path -crossed the moorings of the conceptual stage. Nobody would then have imagined that it would become the new artery of the city of Nawabs in another 10 years around which all the major development would be positioned (Yadav ,2013). A smooth, planned and controlled pattern of development of a tourist destination along a predetermined and anticipated route is an exception rather than the rule (Butler,1980).

In the new master plan that came out in 2005, the area beyond Gomtinagar stretching between Faizabad Road and Kanpur Road was tuned in as new hub of development .The plan defined the way development had to be undertaken in the area. As on date a land bank of more than 12,000 acres has been created around Shaheed Path alone, with the help of private developers (Ansal API, Garv Buildtech) who are engaged in the development of hi-tech and integrated cities. The Sultanpur national highway would also witnesss a host of integrated townships. Some of the developers which are vying for the land includes ANS constructions, EMMAR-MGF, MTECH constructions and Rohtas. Integrated townships are also proposed on the Hardoi Road bypass and Faizabad Road(Yadav, 2013)

Tradition and modernity are viewed as a continuum (Shills, 2006) and the co-existence of two can be seen very uniquely in the city of Lucknow, which can be offered as a unique tourism product.The process of evolution has transformed the physical, social and cultural landscape of the people of Lucknow beyond recognition. The culture of Lucknow, therefore, like that of other countries at different times and places could not retain its status quo and 'modernity' seeped in ,more strongly with the advent of shopping malls, architectural structures erected by a democratically elected chief of the state with an objective to display power and position of a class which has been oppressed for years in the region, new colonies emerging in the periphery due to population explosion & the city being the capital was able to provide infrastructural base to prosper. Areas' exhibiting these features is popularly known as the 'New Lucknow', which has its own tourism edifices gaining popularity slowly and steadily (Yadav, 2013).WTO report says "There is no tourism without culture".

The management of cultural tourism is usually in the hands of many stakeholders, and the more intangible factors of the relationship between tourism and culture (quality of life issues, sustainability) are usually not taken into account in planning. Where countries used to concentrate on getting their national monuments on the UNESCO World Heritage List, they now seem to be jostling to have their intangible assets listed on the new UNESCO Intangible Heritage register. This is just one important sign that competition in the cultural arena is no longer just about culture, but also creativity (OCED ,2009). Despite all the efforts Lucknow still lacks a WHS (World Heritage Site) to its credit despite archaeological and cultural attributes.

Tourism is also a profitable economic endeavor, making it an economically enticing industry and a form of development for many countries around the world. However, the benefits of tourism are often accompanied by many negative environmental and social impacts. These include: revenue leakage from the community, air noise and water pollution, degradation and depletion of natural resources, biodiversity loss, labor issues, encroachment and overbuilding (Theobald ,1998; Bohdanowicz, 2005; Dodds ,2005; Graci ,2009).

Issues of Definition

Green Tourism is a form of alternative tourism; green tourism is generally related to rural tourism. It denotes a nature tourism seen to be environmentally compatible and with little or no ecological impact on the destination area. Like many other alternative tourism terms of the 80's it was merged with ecotourism (Oppermann ,2000). Green Tourism (used interchangeably here), has been identified as "tourism that consists of traveling to relatively undisturbed or uncontaminated natural areas with the specific objective of studying, admiring, and enjoying the scenery and its wild plants and animals, as well as any existing cultural manifestation found in these areas" (Boo, 1990).

Tourists practicing green tourism and green tourism ideology are known as 'Green Tourists'. It is not just a label, tag, fashion or fad rather a complete philosophy which encompass the traveler, host, society, organization, thought process and the suppliers and stakeholders.The growing economic importance of Green tourist cannot be ignored. For example, Green tourism generates billions of dollars globally and is reported to be growing at a rate of 10% to 15% annually, the fastest growth rate in the travel market. Much of this growth has been in travel to developing countries (20%) that offer ecotourists pristine environments often coupled with indigenous cultural experiences. Surveys of tour operators consistently suggest that green tourists are willing to pay for these experiences, with 7 million U.S. tourists willing to pay between $2,000 and $3,000 for a green tour (World Tourism Organization 1994).

In most cases, however, Green Tourists are: passive, non-consumptive observers rather than active resource users (Whelan ,1991; Kutay ,1989; Lindberg, 1991). In addition, tourists consistently report a willingness to contribute toward conservation in the area visited, thus financially strengthening conservation efforts. There are a number of additional large scale social trends that may have driven the development of Green Tourism. Environmental activism has grown significantly over recent decades (Weaver 2001, Fennell 2003), Green Tourism has been promoted as sustainable development opportunity in rural or remote areas sometimes as a substitute for declining agricultural and other rural activities (Rinnie and Saastamoinen ,2005) Tourism destinations that have suffered due to mass tourism may find refuge in Green Tourism (Fennell ,2003) At a broader societal level Saarinen (2005) suggests that interest in green tourism coincides with wider changes in consumption and economic production and with a move towards post-Fordism. This is represented by a trend away from packaged multiclient mass tourism, towards individual travelers and products that cater to highly segmented markets. The post-Fordist approach to tourism thus favours flexibility, individuality, hybridity and activity. Saarinen (2005) suggested that this is associated with the rise of discerning, educated and concerned travelers, who are more aware of their environmental and cultural impacts at tourism destinations. Post-Fordist patterns in product structures however are discernible irrespective of any possible change in traveller's attitudes.

Hospitality Perspective of Lucknow

The primary survey of the stakeholders' of hospitality sector in the city revealed that Lucknow is increasingly gaining MICE tourists apart from the existing tourist who visited the city primarily for its culture and historical relevance. Apart from the existing hotels in the city, Hilton group and Hyatt group are also coming up with their properties; both are in the construction stages. The hotel industry forms a large part of the tourism industry and if not managed properly, it has the potential to be detrimental to the social and natural environments within which it functions. Hotels are also resource intensive and in order to reduce their impact, it is imperative to go 'green'. Many greening initiatives are not expensive to implement and provide substantial benefits to the business. Emerging Lucknow is characterized by construction of hotels primarily to serve Business clientale.

Individually, hotels do not have a significant negative impact on the environment. Collectively however, they can be very wasteful and consume huge amount of resources. It has been estimated that seventy-five percent of hotels' environmental impacts can be directly related to excessive consumption (Bohdanowicz, 2006). This is wasteful in terms of resources and it creates unnecessary operational costs. The three key areas of environmental impact are energy, water, and waste.

Energy - Excessive energy use is extremely costly and with minor adjustments, it can lead to massive cost savings. According to (Gössling et. al. ,2005), "the average energy consumption per bed per night in hotels might be in the order of 130 Megajoules. Hotels generally use more energy per visitor than local residents, as they have energy intense facilities, such as bars, restaurants, and pools, and have more spacious rooms" (Gössling et. al., 2005). Studies have determined that a hotel emits an average 20.6 kg of carbon dioxide per night (Gössling et al., 2005).

Waste - A study conducted by (Bohdanowicz ,2005) also identified that hotels are not only resource intensive and that waste generation is one of the most visible effects on the environment. One estimate identified "that an average hotel produces in excess of one kilogram of waste per guest per day" (Bohdanowicz ,2005). Approximately 30 percent of waste in hotels can be diverted through reuse and recycling.

Water - Tourists and residents alike require a clean and dependable supply of water for survival including drinking, cooking and cleansing. However, water is integral to the amenities usually expected by tourists, such as swimming pools, landscaped gardens, and golf courses. Water also supports industries such as agriculture that support the tourism industry (Pigram, 1995). Thus, tourists demand more water than local residents on a per capita basis (Essex, Kent & Newnham, 2004). It has been estimated by (Salen ,1995) that 15,000 cubic meters of water would typically supply 100 rural farmers for three years and 100 urban families for two years, yet only supply 100 luxury hotel guests for less than two months (Holden, 2000). In dryer regions, tourists' water consumption can amount to 440 liters a day per tourist, which is almost double the average amount of water used by residents in Spain .

Facets of Change-Emerging Cosmopolitan Lucknow

Awadh had been a traditional stronghold of the Sufic doctrine of Wahdat-al-Wajid unity of being which made everyone believe in the essential unity of all phenomenon. Be it ethnic hindus, the minority Sunnis, the shiite rulers or the forced upon white races they all mixed up and amalgamated. There .were certain basic points around which culture nurtured and their relation with stae religion that helped this last composite city to develop (Rizwan,2006)

1. The Etiquettes were placed in the society. One had to wish salaam to everyone irrespective of gender, caste, social status etc.Islam says that a ruler should wish the passerby, the standing should wish the seated and even Sunnah practice emphasized that 'be first to say Salaam'.In a culture which was an amalgamation, Lucknow invented 'Aadab' keeping in the wish of Islam to Salaam.

2. The main lesson for a gathering for namaaz is that people can stand in straight queues despite their social standing. Even at Hajj, the pilgrimage people wear similar unseewn sheets of white. Lucknow provided a common costume Kurta, paijama, sherwani or Angarkha and a cap and was one which recognized Lucknowities.

3. It was the building that saw maximum impact. Be it Hammas, Mosques, Imambaras, Karbalas, Bazaars all were present and flourishing at Lucknow.Another aspect was intercommunity buildings like Pandaitain ki Masjid, Masjid Raja Tikait Rai, Hanuman Mandir of royal mother etc.Depsite Islamization of certain non-Islamic festivals and indianization of certain Islamic festivals the city provided a 'mourning festival', Moharrum as a common platform for all religion, sects and caste.
4. A new common language neither Sanskrit nor Persian but Urdu emerged. Today all the major theological books are in this language.
5. Quran says "What you consider good for thyself consider good for others"
6. Thus the 'Pehle Aap' was the proof not only of the commoners but of the Royalty also.

Lucknow is still a predominantly cultural tourism destination. Aspects of oriental era, which are potential tourism products, have been illustrated in the chapter. New forms of tourism, that are an offering of the modern times, especially Dalit Tourism and Ethnic Tourism/Indigenous Tourism (Kalagaon). Effort has been made to identify forms of tourism which can be developed in the city, for example-River Tourism (Gomti river), Fashion Tourism (Chikan works), Pro-Poor Tourism(SEWA), Wellness Tourism (Unani medicine), Educational Tourism ,Spiritual Tourism (dargahs) and Music Tourism, provided a holistic will from every stakeholder concerned is pooled in the right direction. The Heritage Walk of the UP Tourism Department along with the similar product offerings by private players like TORNOS are also given a space(Yadav ,2013)

City of Lucknow was initially conceptualized to be a tourist centre. It attracted, and attracts visitors both from domestic and foreign shores. In the fast pace of modernization, greater influx of population, it being the capital, the cultural landmark of the city had a tough time maintaining its identity .City developed across the other side of the river where every new ruler etched his/her mark by providing their own monumental edifice which can be embarked in the history. Initially it was of a conflict between the co-existence of two schools of culture developing side by side across a river. A transition has been the order across both the sides of the river, which with regards to tourism is healthy or unhealthy only time will be able to tell. The newer one trying to redefine the older one, or the older one providing a base to the newer one. With the passage of time somewhere the culture realized that they need to co-exist but with a demarcated boundary, and brought in a new challenge for the stakeholders.

It is important to accept the concept of city's transitory nature due to various factors and simultaneously conceptualize it as a product that is fit for tourist's consumption, and also it is in agreement with the stakeholders of the city. The study has delved deeper to suggest measures for promotion and development of tourism of the region which is complementary, research backed, sustainable, optimizes the resources of both forms of culture and can be replicated at destinations going through similar transition(Yadav,2013)More than a century back the definition of E. Tylor was formulated which is the first scientific definition of the culture. It states: (Tylor ,1871). 17 "Culture is that complex whole which includes knowledge, beliefs, arts, morals, law, custom and habits acquired by man as a member of society."

The researcher having spent his life in the city experienced and felt the mosaic of culture that exists in the city, which prompted the researcher to explore the transition and search for an opportunity in it for tourism purposes. Major potential tourism products of the transition are as follows (Yadav ,2013): Kalagaon- Presence of Ethnic tourism/ Indigenous tourism, SEWA (self-employed women's Association) - An Example of Pro-Poor Tourism, River Tourism-A potential game changer, Dalit Tourism.

Green Practices

Several studies have indicated that economic benefits can be gained in hotels through implementing environmental and social initiatives; many with little or no capital. In addition to cost benefits, there are also benefits to choosing an environmentally sustainable strategy. These include: Gaining competitive advantage by being a leader in the sector, Customer loyalty, Employee retention, Awards and recognition, Regulatory compliance, Risk management; Increased brand value. The hotel industry has been pursuing green practices since the 1990s due to fluctuating economic levels and a strong focus on customer service (Claver-Cortes et al., 2007).There are many green practices that hotels can implement as preventative measures to save unnecessary costs. Examples of these practices are: Pollution prevention such as waste discharge into waterways, Energy consumption, recycling. Other popular cost cutting measures for the short-, mid- and long-term include: Use of compact fluorescent lights - saves energy, Reuse of linens - saves water, detergent, energy and greenhouse gases, Low-flow shower systems - saves water and energy, Local products - save transportation costs, Installation of green roofs - saves energy, Installation of solar heaters or other renewable energy source - saves energy. The ultimate result of these actions is a win-win situation; to reduce hotel operational costs and harmful environmental impacts (Claver-Cortes et al., 2007).

Reports by hundreds of businesses around the world illustrate that by implementing appropriate management processes they have: Reduced energy and water consumption costs by more than 20 percent, Solid waste and waste water disposal costs by more than 15 percent, Improved the quality of the environment in which they operate, Improved staff motivation and community relations. A detailed description of the benefits is as under:

Cost Saving: (Brebbia and Pineda ,2004) claim that financial savings are one of the most significant factors that influence the implementation of environmental initiatives in a hotel. This is especially evident for hotel businesses that operate in a highly competitive market and where the cost of energy, water and waste disposal are high. Hotel operators that can maximize their efficiency and reduce waste will be more cost-effective than their competitors. For example, a hotel can reduce its energy consumption by 20-40% without adversely affecting performance. Some examples of environmental initiatives and cost savings include: Holiday Inn on King in Toronto reports saving Cdn $14,852 per year through the installation of low flow showerheads and faucet aerators (Graci ,2002).

Competitive advantage: Green programs can provide a competitive advantage to leaders as long as green activities continue to be voluntary. Over time, however, green practices in the hospitality industry will become a baseline requirement, particularly as the cost of non-renewable energy continues to rise, regulatory pressure increases, and consumers become more demanding. Therefore, hotels with business models that revolve around green practices will have the strongest opportunity to achieve a competitive advantage by being ahead of the emerging sustainability curve.

Customer loyalty: Over the past 25 years there has been a shift in the expectations and demands of consumers. The typical hotel guest of today is more sophisticated and to varying degrees is likely to be concerned about environmental issues such as recycling bottles, cans and paper at home as well as making greener lifestyle choices, such as organic food or fuel-efficient vehicles. Many guests however, make their decision to stay at a hotel facility based on location, amenities, and service. The implementation of environmental initiatives may play a smaller role in a guest's choice of a property. The influence from customers however occurs when their level of awareness increases and they come to expect environmental practices such as recycling. Despite first-time guests basing their decisions on location, amenities and service, customer loyalty may increase once they have experienced a hotel which has demonstrated a level of environmental commitment.

Regulatory compliance: Hotels must anticipate future regulatory changes and implement initiatives to mitigate the possible costly effects of emerging regulation. Savvy businesses are aware that regulations do not have to be a negative restraint on their daily operations - in fact; they can offer opportunities to gain an advantage over competitors. Some environmental regulations are good for economic competition as they stimulate innovation that can offset the cost of compliance. By implementing measures in the face of societal and regulatory pressures, unexpected, but substantial cost savings as well as potential new areas of profit may be found. The hotel industry worldwide is increasingly being regulated for Waste, Water,

Greenhouse gas emissions, Energy use. Being aware of pending rule changes will allow you to adopt measures in advance, and avoid potentially higher future costs which may be associated with compliance.

Risk management: Risk minimization is now viewed as increasingly intertwined with good corporate social responsibility and governance. Managing risk is as much about minimizing the potential damage from decisions and actions taken from within a company as it is about managing external exposure. Traditionally, a hotel's risk management strategy has been focused on health and safety concerns around food and water, pest infestation, fire or water damage, outbreaks of disease, and guest security and safety. In recent years however, environmental and social issues are emerging as a key risk issue for the lodging sector. Environmental risks include: Water and land contamination, Air and noise pollution, Supply chain environmental practices, Waste management. Environmental risks also have an impact on the cost of capital for businesses of various types and sizes, and may affect the value of a company over the long term. In addition, the investment community is increasingly regarding excellence in environmental management and performance as an indication of the quality and aptitude of management in general. Some insurance companies and lenders are beginning to selectively adjust their rates based on environmental criteria stipulated by ethical funds. Companies that integrate the environment into their business decisions and reduce their environmental risk and potential liabilities are in a better position to secure investment and reduce their financial and reputational market exposure (Graci and Dodds, 2009).

It would be nice and better perhaps if all tourism was "fair trade" tourism, if wage levels in the third world tourism operations were equal to those in developed countries if local communities had control over all operations and divided profits equally and fairly, but if we are honest, such a situation is highly unlikely to exist in any form of economic activity in many countries and the cost of such tourism would inevitably be beyond the means of most tourists, resulting in a reduction in numbers, in income and employment generation and financial viability. Fearing the above, the hospitality sector in the city agrees to the concept of green hospitality but seems unwilling to translate the same fully in day to day execution, as it will escalate cost and will make them uncompetitive.

It is the era of "adaptive management", "resilience" .It is hard to see sustainable development as anything other than conservation, "the wise use of resources", acknowledging that some of those resources will be exhausted over time, some should be protected and preserved and the rest used with a long term view for the greatest good for the longest time. If you think that is wishful thinking, it probably is, but sometimes dreams come true and survival has long been mankind's ultimate fantasy. To encourage the Stakeholders to promote and practice Green Tourism practices, the Ministry of Tourism, Government of India has included categories of awards " Best Eco friendly Hotel", 'Best Responsible Tourism Project", "Best Eco friendly Practices by Tour Operators" in the National Tourism Awards presented annually to various segments of travel, tourism and hospitality sector. But India needs a more market and political will on this. Green is not tourism or tourists only; it is a complete philosophy on which the existence of current residents of earth and the future of coming generations will depend upon. There are certain characteristics, demographics and profiles which make the Green Tourists distinct from others. Lifestyle changes have to be brought in so that global warming can be controlled. On one hand tourism is responsible for increasing global warming and pollution but on other hand there are examples of tourism acting as a savior. Government and market both are providing incentives to projects that are going green. Internet too is playing a major role in creation of awareness for green.

References

Boo, E. (1990). Ecotourism: The Potentials and Pitfalls Vol. 1. Washington,DC: World Wildlife Fund.

Bohdanowicz, P (2005), 'European Hoteliers' Environmental Attitudes: Greening the Business, Cornell Hotel and Restaurant Administration Quarterly, vol.46, no.2.

Bohdanowicz, P(2006), 'Environmental Awareness and Initiatives in the Swedish and Polish Hotel Industries - Survey Results' International Journal of Hospitality Management, vol. 25, no. 4.

Brebbia, C. A. and Pineda, F.D (2004), Sustainable Tourism. WIT Press, Boston

Butler, R.W. (1980). The Concept of a Tourist Area Cycle of Evolution: Implications for the Management of Resources. Sage Publications. London.

Claver- Cortes, E., Molina-Azorin, J.F. Pereira-Moliner, J., Lopez-Gamero, M.D(2007), 'Environmental Strategies and Their Impact on Hotel Performance' Journal of Sustainable Tourism., vol.15, no.6.

Dodds, R. (2005), Barriers to the Implementation of Sustainable Tourism Policy in Destinations. University of Surrey School of Management, Surrey.

Essex, S., Kent, M., & Newnham, R. (2004), 'Tourism development in Mallorca: Is water supply a constraint?' Journal of Sustainable Tourism, vol 12, no. 1.

Fennell, D. (2003). Ecotoursim (2nd Ed). London. Routeledge

Gossling, S, Paul Peeters, Jean-Paul Ceronc, Ghislain Duboisd, Trista Pattersone and Robert B. Richardson(2005), 'The Eco-Efficiency of Tourism.' Ecological Economics, vol. 54, no.15.

Graci, S. (2002), The Greening of Accommodation: A Study of Voluntary Environmental Initiatives in the Hotel Industry, University of Toronto, Toronto.

Graci, S. and Dodds, R. (2009), 'Why Go Green? The Business Case for Environmental Commitment in the Canadian Hotel Industry' Anatolia: An International Journal of Tourism and Hospitality Research, vol 19, no.2.

Holden, A. (2000), Environment and Tourism, Routledge, New York

Kutay, K. (1989). "The New Ethic in Adventure Travel." Ecotourism

Lindberg, K. (1991). Policies for Maximizing Nature Tourism's Ecological and Economic Benefits. Washington, DC: World Resources Institute WWF (2010). One Planet Living Campaign. Available at www.wwf.org.uk/oneplanet/ophome.asp. Accessed on November 2013

OECD (2009). Impact of Culture on Tourism. OCED Publications (2009)

Oppermann, M. (2000). In Jafar, J. (Ed.) Encyclopedia of Tourism. London. Routledge

Pigram, J (1995), 'Resource Constraints on Tourism: Water Resources and Sustainability' In R. Butler and D. G. Pearce (Eds), Changes in Tourism: People, Places, Processes, Routledge, New York.

Rinnie, P. and Saastamoinen, O. (2005). Local economic Role of Nature Based Tourism in Kuhmo Municipality Eastern Finland. Scandinavian Journal of Hospitality and tourism.

Salen, N (1995), 'Water Rights' Tourism in Focus, vol. 17.

Saarinen,J. (2005). Tourism and Touristic Representation of Nature. A Companion to Tourism. Oxford. Blackwell Publishing.

Sharar, A.H. (1989), Lucknow: The Last Phase of Oriental Culture.E.S Harcourt and F.Hussain (eds.) Oxford, Delhi.

Shills, E. (2006).Tradition.University of Chicago Press,Chicago

Theobald, W. F. (1998), 'Foreward' In W. F. Theobald (Eds.), Global Tourism, pp. ix, Butterworth-Heinemann, Oxford.

Tylor, E (1871). Primitive Culture. New York. Harper, Torch Books

Weaver, D. (2001). Ecotourism as a Mass Tourism: Contradictions or Reality. Cornell Hotel and Restaurant Administration Quarterly 42.

Whelan, T. (1991). Nature Tourism;Managing for the Environment NewYork: Island Press.

Witherspoon, S. (1994). The Greening of Britian: romance and Reality. Dartmouth. Aldershot

Yadav, S. (2013). Lucknow's Tourism in Transition: A Stakeholders' Perspective. Unpublished Thesis. University of Lucknow.

FOREIGN DIRECT INVESTMENT'S EFFECT ON HOSPITALITY AND TOURISM INDUSTRY: A REVIEW

Kalyani Singh

Faculty, Food Science and Nutrition, UIHMT, Panjab University, singh.kalyani26@yahoo.com

Tanvi Beniwal

Assistant Professor, UIHMT, Panjab University, tanubeniwal@yahoo.com

Abstract: Hospitality and retail sector holds immense potential for Indian economy. It can provide impetus to other industries through backward and forward linkages and can generate huge revenue earnings for the country. Tourism is one of the third largest net earners of foreign exchange for India and also one of the sectors, which employs the largest number of manpower. Liberalization policies have led to rapid growth in Foreign Direct Investment (FDI) flows in recent years. Basing on the benefits associated with FDI several developing, as well developed countries compete fiercely for FDI. They try to attract foreign investors by providing financial and fiscal incentives, undertaking corporate restructuring and economic reforms and inviting foreign investors in the privatization of hospitality units. The Indian hospitality industry experienced a growth of 24.6% during 2010-2011 timeframe. The industry is the third-largest foreign exchange earner; accounting for 6.2% of India's GDP and 8.8% of the total employment.100% FDI is permitted in the hospitality industry in India under various approvals. Restaurants, beach resorts and various retail outlets which facilitates accommodation, catering and buying various product to the tourist are the sectors which have been receiving the maximum amount of FDI inflows in past few years. According to Ministry of Tourism in India, in last four years (2008-2012), total 1901 Hotel and Tourism Projects have attracted a big amount of 11,110.98 crores under FDI.

Keywords: FDI, Hospitality and Tourism Industry, Medical Tourism, Developing Economy

Introduction

India is currently undergoing rapid economic and demographic transformation. Since 1980 average living standards have experienced a sustained and rapid rise. Real Gross Domestic Product per capita has risen at a trend rate of 4% annually and since 2001, this rate accelerated to more than 6%. Poverty declined at an annual rate of 0.88% during 1983-94 and at a slightly lower rate of 0.77% during 1993-2005. Rapid economic growth has been accompanied by rising urbanization. Between 1980 and 2000 the share of the urban population rose from 23% to 28%. By 2030, it is likely to be as high as 41%. As the global markets integrate and communication becomes better there is a move away from inferior to superior foods and a substitution of traditional staples by primary food products that are more prevalent in western diets.

One of the most notable features of economic globalization has been the increased importance of Foreign Direct Investment around the World. Some view it as an engine of economic growth and development while others look upon it as a panacea for all ills. It is, however, important to weigh the costs and the benefits of FDI to gauge whether FDI has positive impact on economic development. FDI has the potential to generate employment, raise productivity, enhancing competitiveness of the domestic economy through transfer skills and technology, strengthening infrastructure, enhance exports and contribute to the long-term economic development of the world's developing countries. India is seeing FDI as a developmental tool in whole hospitality and retail sector. The Indian hospitality and retail industry is interwoven with the country's monetary development. As GDP continues to mature, it increases deals in fundamental infrastructure like transportation systems, which is necessary to support more buying of food product and it will lead to increase the demand of the retail sector as well as hospitality industry. The hotel industry is directly connected to the tourism industry in India. Over the last decade, India has transformed into one of the most popular tourism destinations in the world, largely as a result of the government's ?Incredible India campaign which showed India in a new light to overseas tourists. Many worldwide hotel groups are setting up their businesses in India. India has also emerged as one of the world's most cost-efficient medical tourism destinations. Medical tourism in the country is a sunrise sector valued at more than US$ 310 million. Currently, India receives more than 100,000 foreign patients a year. It is expected that the Indian medical tourism market will register a compound annual growth rate (CAGR) of 27 per cent during 2011-15, according to a RNCOS report titled 'Booming Medical Tourism in India'.

Hotel(retail) and Tourism sector is declared as high priority sector and Foreign Direct Investment (FDI) up to 100%, under the automatic route is permitted in Hotels & Tourism Sector', subject to applicable laws/regulations, security and other conditional ties.

The hotel and tourism industries have been growing rapidly in recent years, bringing in huge revenues through overseas as well as domestic tourists in many parts of India. There was a key rush to inbound tourism in India in 2006 and a double-digit increase in the coming of overseas tourists to India in the same year. Tourism is one of the third largest revenue generators of foreign exchange for India and also employs one of the highest numbers of manpower.

The size of the Indian hospitality industry is estimated as a sum of revenues of two segments -

revenues generated from travel (business, leisure, visiting friends and relatives, religious, meetings and conferences) and revenue generated by consumers eating out at any form of outlet (restaurants, fine dining, quick service restaurants (QSRs), takeaways, or any other form of unorganized eateries).

Research Methodology

This paper is conceptual paper sole based on the secondary data and literature. Much of the paper has been derived from personal observation and discussion with expert in the field. This is a pilot study and will be taking up further at later stage.

Review of Literature

The Indian Retail Industry is the 5th largest retail destination and the second most attractive market for investment in the globe after Vietnam as reported by AT Kearney's seventh annual Globe Retail Development Index (GRDI), in 2008.The growing popularity of Indian Retail sector has resulted in growing awareness of quality products and brands. Indian retail sector specially organized retail is growing rapidly, with customer spending growing in unprecedented manner. It is undergoing metamorphosis. Till 1980 retail continued in the form of kiranas that is unorganized retailing. Later in 1990s branded retail outlet like Food World, Nilgiris and local retail outlets like Apna Bazaar came into existence. Now big players like Reliance, Tata's, Bharti, ITC and other reputed companies have entered into organized retail business.

Retailing is one of the pillars of the economy in India and accounts for 10% of Gross Domestic Product (GDP). The retail industry is divided into organized and unorganized sectors. Over 12 million outlets operate in the country and only 4% of them being larger than 500 sq ft (46 m2) in size. Organized retailing refers to trading activities undertaken by licensed retailers, that is, those who are registered for sales tax, income tax, etc. These include the corporate-backed hypermarkets and retail chains, and also the privately owned large retail businesses. Unorganized retailing, on the other hand, refers to the traditional formats of low-cost retailing, for example, the local kirana shops, owner manned general stores, convenience stores, hand cart and pavement vendors, etc. Most Indian shopping takes place in open markets and millions of independent grocery shops called kirana.

The multinationals with 51% opening of Foreign Direct Investment in single brand retail has led to direct entrance of companies like Nike, Reebok, Metro, McDonald's etc. or through joint ventures like Wal-mart with Bharti, Tata with Tesco etc.

FDI (Foreign Direct Investment) as defined in Dictionary of Economics is investment in a foreign country through the acquisition of a local company or the establishment there of an operation on a new (Greenfield) site. To put in simple words, Foreign Direct Investment refers to capital inflows from abroad that is invested in or to enhance the production capacity of the economy.

The foreign investors are free to invest in India, except few sectors/activities, where prior approval from the RBI or Foreign Investment Promotion Board (FIPB) would be required.

India is fast emerging as a key destination for Foreign Direct Investment. According to the FDI Confidence Index prepared by A T Kearney, India ranks third in Foreign Direct Investment attractiveness ranking, the first being China. Developing countries, emerging economies and countries in transition increasingly see Foreign Direct Investment as a source of economic development, modernization and employment generation, and have liberalized their Foreign Direct Investment regimes to attract investment.

High income and growing urbanization have also contributed to a shift in the traditional Indian food habits. High-income urban dwellers are seeking variety in their choice of foods and are willing to spend more in the international cuisine, including fast foods.

MNC's and Dietary Effect

Consequently, a growing number of domestic fast food outlets, home delivery, take-away restaurants, and American restaurant chains, such as Kentucky Fried Chicken (KFC), TGI Friday's, Domino's Pizza, Pizza Hut, McDonald's and Baskin Robbins, have opened in the last few years.

India has come a long way from opposing the entry of Multi National Companies to encouraging them to expand their business operations in India. An important reason for this shift in attitude is the ability if these companies to generate quality and long term employment opportunities for Indians. For e.g. McDonalds typically employs local people and the average. McDonald's restaurant in India employs more than 100 people in all kinds of positions-cashiers, cooks, managers, etc. besides, every expansion also brings additional income and employment opportunities to India's agricultural work force, which is very pleasing to government officials.

Rising disposable incomes in middle class and lower middle class with increase in employment opportunities for young adults in Indian Trade and Indian Trade enabled sectors are the major cause of retail growth in India.

Rapid economic growth, urbanization and globalization have resulted in dietary shifts in Asia, away from staples and increasingly towards livestock and dairy products, fruits and vegetables, and fats and oils. Besides, current consumption patterns seem to be converging towards a western diet. These dietary changes reflect interaction of demand and supply factors.

As incomes rise, exposure to the global 'urban' eating patterns increases. Recent evidence has pointed out to greater reliance of smaller and poorer households on street foods. Urban slums often mimic the branded products of fast food outlets. On the supply side, the main factors associated with the availability of food; liberalization of Foreign Direct Investment, with a new role of multinational corporations - especially supermarkets and fast food outlets, a sharp reduction in transportation costs.

Investment in Indian Hospitality and Tourism Industry: A Boon

The Hospitality and Tourism Industry is growing at a very fast pace in India, causing and showing large investments. Following are a few reasons for such boon:

- Economic liberalization has been a new force to the hospitality and tourism industry
- The Indian hospitality and tourism industry is increasing at a rate of 15 percent yearly depicting the manifold growth in the industry.
- India is ranked fourth among the world's must see countries
- The present government in its process has taken a few projects like opening of the partial sky

- policy as a result of which the private airlines are able to fly on skies of India increasing the tourism avenues.
- An increasingly growing middle class group, the arrival of corporate incentive travel, travel concessions and the multinational companies into India has opened up bright prospects for tourism.
- In the last few years India has seen a large inflow of business travellers in the country courtesy to relaxation of the government's stand on FDI for most of the sectors in the country

Conclusion

Hospitality and retail sector holds immense potential for Indian economy as it can generate huge revenue for India. Foreign Direct Investment aims to enhance the production capacity of the economy. The foreign investors are attracted by providing them with financial and fiscal benefits so that freely invest in India, except under few sectors/activities, where prior approval from the RBI or Foreign Investment Promotion Board (FIPB) is required. A large number of hotels and tourism projects have brought in a lot of investors under FDI. Hotel and Tourism sector is declared as high priority sector but however Foreign Direct Investment (FDI) up to 100% is permitted under the automatic route in Hotels & Tourism Sector' and subjected to laws/regulations, security and other conditions applicable in India.

With the step in of FDI and thus opening of food joints like Kentucky Fried Chicken (KFC), TGI Friday's, Domino's Pizza, Pizza Hut, McDonald's and Baskin Robbins, a shift in dietary habits has been seen from traditional foods habits among high income urban dwellers from staples to dairy products, livestock, fats and oils. The current consumption patterns seem to be converging towards a western diet. With increasing living standards, rise in GDP and rapid economic growth, and coming up of Foreign Direct Investment in India, a shift in consumption of traditional foods has been seen towards more food products of western diets.

References

1. Dash, K., (2005) McDONALD'S IN INDIA; Thunderbird, The Garvin School of International Management, 1-25, A-07-05-2015.

2. Purushothaman, R., (2007) Does Urban Development Drive Rural Growth in India?; IndiaKnowledge@Wharton, 212; 221-9595?407. Retrieved from, http://knowledge.wharton.upenn.edu/india/article.cfm?articleid=4224
3. Gupta. R., (2012) FDI IN INDIAN RETAIL SECTOR: ANALYSIS OF COMPETITION IN AGRI-FOOD SECTOR. Competition Commission of India, 1-57.
4. Kesari, R., Srivastava, AK., (2012) RETAILING IN RURAL INDIA:AN OVERVIEW OF MARKETS & OPPORTUNITIES. South Asian Journal of Marketing & Management Research, vol 12, issue 4 ; ISSN 2249-877X
5. Foresight Project on Global Food and Farming Futures. January 2011. The Government Office for Science. URN: 11/593. Retrieved from, http://www.bis.gov.uk/Foresight.
6. Labour_in_India.htm. Wikipedia.
7. RETAILING IN INDIA: A REVIEW OF PRESENT SCENARIO. (2012). Retrieved from, http://shodhganga.inflibnet.ac.in/bitstream/10603/3794/12/12_chapter%204.pdf.
8. Govt. to review FDI in Tourism Sector, News and Features, New Delhi, February 13, (2007), www.sarkaritel.com
9. Investment opportunities in Tourism Sector, Government of India portal Investment Commission http://www.investmentcommission.in/tourism.htm#v
10. Manpower recruitment in Hotel industry, A market plus report of Ministry of tourism, Government of India. http://tourismindia.com

BEST ENVIRONMENTAL PRACTICES: A REVIEW OF INDIAN SCENARIO

Tanvi

Assistant Professor University Institute of Hotel Management & Tourism Panjab University, Chandigarh tanubeniwal@yahoo.com

Gaurav Kashyap

Assistant Professor University Institute of Hotel Management & Tourism Panjab University, Chandigarh gauravkashyap@gmail.com

Abstract: This study examined best environmental practices adopted by hotel. It has been realized that objective of sustainable environment is turning out to be most important for the lodging sector for their growth and development. As the need of adopting the good environmental practices are considered important by government of India and then are followed simultaneously by hotels as well. This research paper is showing the various green practices adopted by hotels like waste reduction, water and energy conservation.

Keywords: Environmental Practices, Economic Scenario, Hotel

Introduction

Indian Economic Scenario and Hotel Industry

The hotel industry in India is among the fastest growing in the world. Nearly 60 per cent of the hotels in the country are less than five years old. Hotel industry in India is in a phase where national and international hotel companies are building hotels quickly in numbers, contemplating that the demand will rise in next 12 to 18 months time. However according to Krishna Kant, 2013 the hotel industry has been the biggest under-performer on the stock market in the last five years. The combined market capitalisation of the top seven listed companies, including Indian Hotels Company, East India Hotels, Hotel Leela venture and Taj GVK, a joint venture between Indian Hotels and Hyderabad-based GVK group, is a third of its peak of December 2007. "The Indian economy recorded its lowest GDP growth rate in a decade at 5.0% in 2012/13; a stark departure from the 9.3% growth rate achieved a couple of years ago, the country's current account deficit stood at 4.8% of the GDP in 2012/13 as against 4.2% in the previous year, the rupee has been volatile, depicted in the exchange rate to the US dollar fluctuating significantly in 2012/13. Domestic factors such as high inflation and an increasing current account deficit have caused the rupee to plummet.", yet the weighted room count for 2012/13 is 82,512, up from 72,267 for 2011/12. Also, the nationwide RevPAR recorded a 5.2% drop in 2012/13 over the previous year with the five-star segment registering the maximum decline (8.7%), followed by the three-star segment (4.0%). This downswing could be attributed to these two categories witnessing close to 60% of the new supply in 2012/13 as said by Kaushik Vardharajan, Juie S. Mobar in 2013 in annual report of HVS Hospitality Services of year 2012/13. So, it is not wrong to say that Indian Hotel Industry even though looking sluggish but indeed is evolving in spite of all odds and for that, development of hospitality products like rooms, restaurants, banquet halls, spa, etc is getting done at a fast rate.

The other positive news for Indian Tourism Industry has come on December 4th 2012 from Home Ministry of India who has lifted the restriction of the two-month gap on re-entry of foreign nationals coming to India on a tourist visa. The tourism ministry has a target of increasing India's share of global tourism arrivals from 0.64 percent to 1 percent. The visa relaxation would help contribute to a large extent in achieving this target. According to the ministry's latest figures, India received 3.24 million foreign tourists in the first half of 2012, earning the country $7.9 billion. Some 6.29 million foreign tourists arrived last year, bringing in some $16.5 billion. Now that tourists can use India as a hub while visiting other South Asian countries, officials are optimistic that numbers will be much higher in 2013 as by Mark Johanson, 2012.

India since Copenhagen Climate Change Summit & the Kyoto Protocol

Things have changed manifolds since the Kyoto Protocol globally not only in India, as decisions have been taken to protect the planet earth from the after-effects of industrialization, which are negatively impacting the atmosphere at pace and that there's a need to do the work collectively on the global level and for that United nation has taken an initiative. As of June 2013, there are 192 parties to the Kyoto Protocol to the United Nations Framework Convention on Climate Change. The Kyoto Protocol is an international agreement created by the United Nations for the United Nations Framework Convention on Climate Change, which asks its parties/countries to work towards reducing the emissions of Green House Gases they release into the atmosphere which eventually have disastrous effects on climate and are resulting in global warming. The Protocol was adopted at the third session of the Conference of the Parties to the 1992 United Nations Framework Convention on Climate Change Summit, held at Kyoto (Japan) from 1 to 11 December 1997. This led to Copenhagen Climate Change Summit in 2009. After this unique happening in the history, the economic growth of not only developed but developing nations has steered into a new direction. According to Tom Brookes and Tim Nuthall, 2009, "a very important change after the Copenhagen climate change summit is that green growth is now the prevailing economic model of our time. MICHAEL R. GORDON & JOHN M. BRODER, 2013 say that India is one of the fastest-growing sources of greenhouse gases in the world, and it has consistently rejected efforts by developed countries to slow down its energy consumption, fearing that it would retard its economic growth and hamper its drive to reduce poverty. India now ranks third in the world in production of carbon dioxide, the most prevalent heat-trapping gas, behind China and the United States.

The Prime minister's Council on Climate Change, in its first meeting on 13th July 2007, had decided that "A National document compiling action taken by India for addressing the challenge of climate change, and the action it proposes to take" be prepared (GOI, MOEF in NAPCC, 2008). In order to achieve sustainable development path that simultaneously advances economic and environmental objectives National Action Plan for Climate Change (NAPCC) is announced by Government of India in June 2008. There are eight National Missions which form the core of the National Action Plan. Those are National Solar Mission, National Mission for Enhanced Energy Efficiency, National Mission on Sustainable Habitat, National Water Mission, and National Mission for Sustaining the Himalayan Ecosystem, National Mission for Green India, National Mission for Sustainable Agriculture and National Mission for Strategic Knowledge for Climate change (GOI, MOEF in NAPCC, 2008). One of the components of National Mission for Sustainable Habitat is promoting the energy efficiency in residential and commercial sectors. Commercial sector comprises various institutional establishments such as banks, offices, restaurants and hotels etc.

Sustainable Development by Hotels in India - A changing trend

In light of the growing environmental degradation, society is becoming increasingly aware of the need of adopting and enforcing more effective measures of environmental protection. Sustainable development, including the development of a more sustainable built environment, has thus become a vital priority and a veritable challenge of our time. Hoteliers are increasingly aware that the environment and its protection are crucial to hotel industry development and performance. In the recent past, environmental responsibility has been receiving more attention in the hotel industry and is now increasingly becoming a corporate issue. However, in order to achieve greater environmental responsibility, proper implementation tools and strategies are necessary. The primary instruments of action include the enforcement of relevant laws and regulations (health and safety requirements, planning and building regulations, laws relevant to water utilization, waste generation and the release of emissions), the levying of environmental taxes (e.g. based on the amount of water and energy used), as well as voluntary standards (Paulina BOHDANOWICZ, Branko SIMANIC, Ivo MARTINAC, 2005). "Individually, hotels do not have a significant negative impact on the environment. Collectively however, they can be very wasteful and consume huge amount of resources. It has been estimated that seventy-five percent of hotels' environmental impacts can be directly related to excessive consumption (Bohdanowicz, 2006). As the concept of green hotels and Ecotels is gaining popularity globally, leading hoteliers in India are coming up with their very own environmental friendly hotels and adopting green practices (Sana Mirza, 2012). Hotels in India have long initiated the Best Environmental Practices with domains like water management and rationalization, energy efficiency and economy, wastes valorisation and recycling, purchasing policy and its ecological aspects, logistics and noise, air quality and land integration etc.

Review of Literature

For the last few decades, concerns about environmental degradation have been increasing (Chan and Lam, 2002: Laroche et al., 2001). As consumers have been recognizing the importance of protecting our environment, environmentalism has become a major issue in the marketplace (Brown, 1996: Kalafatis et al., 1999). An environment contributes to a healthy society by supplying its physiological needs in terms of water, food and even other aspects such as plants for the production of oxygen. The long term success of a healthy society, in turn, depends on economic development to avoid poverty and contribute to social welfare (Strange and Bayley, 2008). The Hospitality industry has not been immune from environmental scrutiny. For example, hotels consume substantial quantities of energy, water, and non-durable products that produce a negative environmental impact greater than other types of facilities of similar size (Robinot and Giannelloni, 2010). According to Hamele and Eckardt (2006) & Alexander (2002) "hotels are dependent upon environment as a result of the nature of service they provide. As an organization that provides high standard of accommodation to guests who, in turn, have high expectations of the service they receive, the use of water and production of waste is higher than what is usually produced domestically". Green hotels devote themselves to save energy and water and decrease solid waste, in order to minimize the impact on environment (Ayala, 1995; Ecomall, 2000; Green Hotels Association, 2002).

A green hotel is an environmentally friendly hotel establishment that practices green principles and programs (e.g., water and energy savings or the reduction of solid waste and emissions) to help save the environment as well as to improve the hotel's effectiveness (GHA, 2008). The term, "green" is alternatively called "eco-friendly", "environmentally responsible", or "environmentally friendly" (Kalafatis et al., 1999; Laroche et al., 2001; Manaktola and Jauhari, 2007; Pizam, 2009; Roberts, 1996). With the green concept, green hotels provide consumers green production and service by using eco-friendly facilities (Tourism Council Australia Jointly with Commonwealth of Australia, 1998). In addition, green hotels based on safety and health actively advocate green management and consumption, ecology protection, and resource conservation (The State Economic and Trade Commission, 2003). Green hotels, therefore, emphasize energy conservation, environmental protection and sustainable management by practicing recycling, reusing and resource saving. This study defines a green hotel as one that is successfully, "providing tourists with a comfortable, natural, healthy and safe lodging service infra-structure on the basis of environmental protection, focusing on sustainable development and minimizing the negative impact on the environment (T.Y.Hsiao et al., 2013). According to Delhi Pollution Control Committee (2010) guidelines, the five star hotels are advised to take appropriate Environment Friendly Measures, Waste Reduction Measures, Water Conservation Measures, Energy Conservation Measures and follow Environmentally responsible purchasing practices.

Environment Friendly Measures

These include Water treatment plant, Sewage treatment, Rain Water Harvesting, Alternative energy sources like solar energy, Waste management and alternative fuel source. Jiminez and Asano (2008) explain that water which is reused directly cannot serve a potable use but may be used for irrigation or other non-potable purposes. Rainwater harvesting provides a suitable substitute to surface water supplies as it may be used for non-potable purposes without treatment (Maunsel, 2004 & Sivanappam, 2006). Hotel managers, therefore need to make water conservation measures integral to their plans. Electric consumption is also very significant; particularly in tourist hotels that account for 70.8% of all energy usage in the hotel sector (Hsiao et al., 2002). Lighting consumes 33% of electricity used in commercial buildings. (Brian Liebel, P.E., and James Brodrick, 2005). Environmental man-agement systems (EMS) are important to evaluate hotels' practices regarding environmental protection. The idea of an evaluation sys-tem for assessing green hotels is to protect the environment by minimizing the negative impact of resource consumption (Chanand Lam, 2001; Chan, 2011; Dief and Font, 2012). Hotel managers would like to target their plans and activities by implementing an EMS that meets the Government's green hotel regulatory standards (Butler, 2008)

Waste Reduction Measures

Reducing and Reusing are the first two steps to decreasing a hotel's overall waste. Material reduction and reuse efforts focus on actions that staff can take to reduce their department or individual waste generation while at work. Recycling is the next step to take in reducing a hotel's trash. When developing a new, or improving an existing, recycling program it is important to know how much of the trash is recyclable (Mary Ann Remolador, 2011). Common recyclables found in Hotel trash are Paper Products, Food Waste and Bottle Cans. To reduce the negative impact of the trash on the environment hotels may compost food, paper, and landscape trimmings on site and use the resulting nutrient-rich humus as a soil amendment or mulch. According to (Mary Ann Remolador, 2011) green purchasing is defined as the purchase of products and services that have a lesser or reduced effect on human health and the environment when compared with competing products and services that serve the same purpose. The list of available green products is quite long. A short list of commonly used products in hotels which green versions are widely available include: Printing and Writing Paper; Envelopes; Toilet paper, Tissues, and Paper Towels; Office Supplies;

Office Electronics (computers, printers, copiers); Remanufactured Toner Cartridges; Cleaning Products; Janitorial Supplies; Lamps; and Appliances.

Water Conservation Measures

Water is an essential factor of production for the hotel industry (including hotels, boarding houses and campsites). Water consumption per person staying at these establishments tends to be high, and can be as much as three times the average consumption of people living at home (Ministerio de Medio Ambiente, 2007). According to (Meade and González-Morel 1999), introducing water conservation measures in rooms, such as low flow showers and aerators in taps, and projects to encourage the reuse of bed linen and towels when the same person spends more than one night in the same room; estimating consumption before and after these measures seems to indicate a 30% reduction. For the case of Spain, (Hamele and Eckardt, 2006) reveal that installing water saving devices in taps and dual flush toilets in a hotel on the island of La Gomera (Spain) produced a reduction of 33% in the first year. (Sarah Alexander, 2002) says in many water assessments, urinals and automatic flushing toilets are found to consume a great deal of water. The THC Rotorua Hotel in New Zealand had urinals that flushed automatically every nine minutes. Each flush used 10 litres of water. This added up to 66 litres per hour or 1,580 litres per day, regardless of whether the urinals had been used or not. The total consumption for three urinals was 4,740 daily. The hotel then installed detectors that sense when the urinals are being used and allow flushing to occur at a specified time after use. This program reduced water consumption in the three urinals from 66 litres per hour to 40 litres during the day and 20 litres in the evening. In addition to installing the urinal sensors the hotel installed low-flow shower heads at a cost of $3,060. The annual cost savings for the water conservation came to $5,244, with a payback of only seven months. As toilets and urinals are being recognized as high consumers of water, options are becoming available that have lower flush volumes, and systems are being introduced that separate solids from the fluids.

Energy Conservation Measures

Electricity is the primary form of energy used in hotels mainly for air-conditioning, space and water heating, lighting, lifts, kitchen equipment (Karagiorgas M et al, 2007). While natural gas, diesel and coal, only play a minor role (Onut S, 2006). Ali et al(2008) report that electricity used for running air conditioning systems corresponds approximately to 30% or more of total expenditures of energy consumption. According, however, to (Santamouris et al, 1996) air-conditioning systems increase the annual energy consumption by 29.77%, depending on the type of system. (Daskalaki and Balaras, 2004) report that in European hotels, 61% of the energy is consumed by space heating, cooling and ventilation, 25% by services and 15% by hot water production. Priority should be given to control energy use in guestrooms using popular room key-cards to ensure that practically all electrical appliances are turned off when guestrooms are unoccupied (Nikolaos Zografakis et al, 2010). Thermal insulation can reduce annual thermal energy consumption by reducing heat losses during winter and cooling load during summer. For insulated buildings, thermal energy consumption can be up to 20% less than the energy consumption in non-insulated buildings (Santamouris et al, 1996). Energy co-generation of heat and power (CHP) in combination with absorption chillers, compared to renewable energy technologies and demand side measures (DSM) is a solution examined in practice for a "green" large hotel (Mavrotas G et al 2004). Energy-saving related measures studied by specific software for energy management in hotels (XENIOS) for medium size Mediterranean hotels were (Daskalaki and Balaras, 2004):

1. Installation of solar collectors for sanitary hot water production
2. Installation of solar collectors for swimming pools
3. Hot water production
4. Solar cooling
5. Chillers with seawater
6. Installation of zoning and controls in the elevator system
7. Use of energy efficient equipment in the administration offices

8. Reduction of the energy consumption for lighting in specific areas
9. Daylight control in specific areas
10. Room key-card control.

Discussion & Conclusion

India being a growing economy and majority of hospitality unit beings very young has much to contribute to green practices and philosophy. Being young can be taken as a blessing as these hospitality units are in their development phases hence they can in their tactical and long term plans include steps to energy reduction, energy utilisation and overall environmental protection. As India has verbally agreed to cut down the green house gases emission to 25 % on the level of 2005 by 2020 and Prime minister's council on climate change has drafted a plan NAPCC in order to achieve sustainable development path including eight National Missions in this plan namely National Solar Mission, National Mission for Enhanced Energy Efficiency, National Mission on Sustainable Habitat, National Water Mission, and National Mission for Sustaining the Himalayan Ecosystem, National Mission for Green India, National Mission for Sustainable Agriculture and National Mission for Strategic Knowledge for Climate change. So, in order to achieve all the above mention mission the hotel also have started contributing by adopting green practices like Environment Friendly Measures, Waste Reduction Measure, Water Conservation Measure and Energy Conservation Measures etc. Hotels are playing their part well by coming up with different green programmes in association with various NGOs involving and motivating consumers to contribute in greener economy by becoming member of their respective programmes. So, all together a lot of effort is been put by hotel in adopting different practices and increase the interest of their guests as well. Hotels in order to spread more awareness amongst the customers must educate their employees and raise awareness through them so as to popularize the importance of green practices in public.

References

Alexander, S., 2002. Green hotels: opportunities and resources for success. Zero Waste Alliance, 5-7 September.

Ayala, H., 1995. Ecoresort: a 'green' master plan for the international resort industry. International Journal of Hospitality Management 14 (3/4), 351-374.

Bohdanowicz, P 2006, 'Environmental Awareness and Initiatives in the Swedish and Polish Hotel Industries - Survey Results' International Journal of Hospitality Management, vol. 25, no. 4, pp. 662-668.

Brown, M., 1996. Environmental policy in the hotel sector: "green" strategy or stratagem. International Journal of Contemporary Hospitality Management 8 3), 18-23.

Butler, J., 2008. The compelling hard case for green hotel development. Cornell Hospitality Quarterly 49 (3), 234-244.

By Tom Brookes and Tim Nuthall, 2009 The European Climate Foundation, What did the Copenhagen climate summit achieve? By BBC News, http://news.bbc.co.uk/2/hi/uk_news/8424522.stm, as on 12/12/2013, 16:05 PM

Chan, W.W., Lam, J., 2001. Environmental accounting of municipal solid waste orig-inating from rooms and restaurants in the Hong Kong hotel industry. Journal of Hospitality and Tourism Research 25 (4), 371-385.

Chan, W.W., Lam, J.C., 2002. Prediction of pollutant emission through electricity consumption by the hotel industry in Hong Kong. International Journal of Hospitality Management 21, 381-391.

Daskalaki E, Balaras CA. XENIOSda methodology for assessing refurbishment scenarios and the potential of application of RES and RUE in hotels. Energy and Buildings 2004;36(11):1091e105.

Dief, E.I., Font, M.X., 2012. Determinants of environmental management in the Red Sea Hotels: personal and organizational values and contextual variables. Journal of Hospitality and Tourism Research 36 (1), 115-137.

DPCC as on 8. 11. 2013 http://www.dpcc.delhigovt.nic.in/dpcc-categrstn_edit.htm

Standards for Hotels, Restaurants, etc. (DPCC board meeting dt. 06.10.2012).

GOI, MOEF, Ministry of Environment and Forests, Government

of India, Divisions/ Climate Change/ National Action Plan on Climate Change (NAPCC), 2008 http://envfor.nic.in/ccd-napcc as on 18.12.2013

Hamele, H., Eckardt, S., 2006. Environmental initiatives by European tourism businesses. Instruments, indicators and practical examples. A contribution to the development of sustainable tourism in Europe. ECOTRANS, IER., Saarbrücken.

Hamele, H., Eckardt, S., 2006. Environmental Initiatives by European Tourism Businesses: Instruments, Indicators and Practical Examples. University of Stuttgart, Stuttgart.

Hsiao, T.Y., Kuo, N.W., Chang, C.H., 2002. Analysis of feasibility of using solar and wind power electricity generation to improve total power consumption - using hotel construction as example. In: 15th Environmental Engineering Conference, Taipei.

Jimenez, B., Asano, T., 2008. Water Reuse. An International Survey of Current Practice,Issues and Needs, 20, pp. 166-176.

Karagiorgas M, Tsoutsos T, Moia-Pol A. A simulation of the energy consumption monitoring in Mediterranean hotels application in Greece. Energy and Buildings 2007;39:416e26.

Kaushik Vardharajan, Juie S. Mobar, 2013, HVS - Hotels in India Trends and Opportunities, www. hvs.com.

Krishna Kant | Mumbai May 13, 2013, Hotels pay a price for rapid growth published in in Business Standard as seen on 17.12.2013, http://www.business-standard.com/article/companies/hotels-pay-a-price-for-rapid-growth-113051301026_1.html

Laroche, M., Bergeron, J., Barbaro-Forleo, G., 2001. Targeting consumers who are willing to pay more for environmentally friendly products. Journal of Consumer Marketing 18 (6), 503-520.

Manaktola, K., Jauhari, V., 2007. Exploring consumer attitude and behavior towards green practices in the lodging industry in India. International Journal of Contemporary Hospitality Management 19 (5), 364-377.

Mark Johanson on December 04 2012 2:02 PM, India Relaxes Tourist Visa Rules to Boost Arrivals, International Business Times as on

12/12 2013 15:35 pm, http://www.ibtimes.com/india-relaxes-tourist-visa-rules-boost-arrivals-918653.

Mary Ann Remolador of the Northeast Recycling Council, Inc. (NERC) With Funding from EPA New England. Northeast Recycling Council, Inc. October 2011 GUIDE TO GREENING HOTELS THROUGH WASTE MANAGEMENT & GREEN PURCHASING http://www.nerc.org/documents/green_hotels_guide.pdf

Maunsell, F., 2004. Grey water recycling and rainwater harvesting at Birmingham Eastside. In: Feasibility Study Presented at Groundwork Birmingham, Birmingham, February 26, 2004.

Mavrotas G, Demertzis H, Meintani A, Diakoulaki D. Energy planning in buildings under uncertainty in fuel costs: the case of a hotel unit in Greece.Energy Conversion and Management 2003;44:1303e21.

Meade, B., González-Morel, P., 1999. Improving water use efficiency in Jamaican hotels and resorts through the implementation of environmental management systems. http://www.linkbc.ca/torc/downs1/jaimaca%20water.pdf. Lastaccessed June 2011.

MICHAEL R. GORDON and JOHN M. BRODER, Published: June 23, 2013 in The New York Times under the title: Kerry Prods India to Cut Greenhouse Gas Emissions. As on date :13.12.2013 time : 14.37 pm, http://www.nytimes.com/2013/06/24/world/asia/kerry-prods-india-to-cut-greenhouse-gas-emissions.html

Ministerio de Medio Ambiente, 2007. El agua en la economía espa˜nola: Situación y perspectivas. Ministerio de Medio Ambiente, Madrid.

Onut S, Soner S. Energy efficiency assessment for the Antalya region hotels in Turkey. Energy and Buildings 2006;38:964e71.

Paulina Bohdanowicz, Branko Simanic, Ivo Martinac, 2005, Sustainable Hotels - Environmental Reporting According To Green Globe 21, Green Globes Canada / Gem Uk, Ihei Benchmarkhotel And Hilton Environmental Reporting The 2005 World Sustainable Building Conference,Tokyo, 27-29 September 2005 (Sb05tokyo)

Pizam, A., 2009. Green hotels: a fad, ploy or fact of life? International Journal of Hospitality Management 28 (1) (editorial).

Roberts, J.A., 1996. Green consumers in the 1990s: profile and implications for advertising. Journal of Business Research 36, 217-231.

Robinot, E., Ginnelloni, J.L., 2009. Attitude toward environmentally friendly hospitality management: a measurement scale. Research in Applications and Marketing 24 (2), 29-50.

Sana Mirza, 2012, Indian hospitality going the green way, in features in India Hospitality Review.com as on 11/12/2013, http://www.indiahospitalityreview.com/features/indian-hospitality-going-green-way.

Santamouris M, Balaras CA, Dascalaki E, Argiriou A, Gaglia A. Energy conservation and retrofitting potential in Hellenic hotels. Energy and Buildings 1996;24:65e75.

Sarah Alexander GREEN HOTELS: Opportunities and Resources for Success and Edited by Carter Kennedy Zero Waste Alliance September 2002 http://www.zerowaste.org/

Sivanappan, R.K., 2006. Rain water harvesting, conservation and management strategies for urban and rural sectors. In: Paper Presented at the National Seminar on Rain Water Harvesting and Water Management, Nagpur, November11-12, 2006.

Source: LEED - India, Green Building Rating System - Abridged reference guide for new construction and major renovations (LEED-India NC) Version -1.0, January 2007).

Strange, T., Bayley, A., 2008. Sustainable Development: Linking Economy, Society, Environment. OECD Publications, France.

T.-Y. Hsiao et al. 2013 International Journal of Hospitality Management 36 (2014) 197-208 Establishing attributes of an environmental management system for green hotel evaluation

The State Economic and Trade Commission, 2003. Standards for Green Hotels Promulgated, Retrieved February 18, 2013 from http://www.cenews.com.cn

TOURISM SCENARIO IN HIMACHAL PRADESH WITH SPECIAL REFERENCE TO HIDDEN AND NEGLECTED TOURISM POTENTIAL

Tek Chand

Ph. D Scholar, Faculty of Commerce and Management Studies, H. P University, Shimla-5

Kulwant Singh Pathania

Professor, Faculty of Commerce and Management Studies, H. P University, Shimla-5

Abstract: Tourism is now well recognized as an engine of growth in the various economies in the world. Several countries have transformed their economies by developing their tourism potential. Tourism has great capacity to generate large-scale employment and additional income sources. Today the concept of traditional tourism has been changed. Some new potential of the tourism has available in India with special reference of Himachal Pradesh. Himachal Pradesh is one of the mountain state and delight for the visitors, particularly during the whole year. It has emerging new tourism like Tracking, Cultural, Rafting, Rural Tourism and Buddhist Monasteries etc. Tourism would bring many direct and indirect benefits to the local inhabitant. It has a huge capacity to create additional source of income and employment opportunities. This paper generally focus on the present tourism scenario of the country and its hidden and neglected potential of tourism sector in India on the basis of Himachal Pradesh with special reference of Buddhist culture, Monastery etc. An attempt has also been made to study the national and international tourist trends and its contribution towards foreign exchange.

Keywords: Tourism, Trends, Foreign Exchange and Hiddent and Neglegted Potentials.

Introduction

Tourism is now well recognised as an engine of growth in the various economies in the world. Several countries have transformed their economies by developing their tourism potential. Tourism has great capacity to generate large-scale employment and additional income sources. Today the concept of traditional tourism has been changed. Some new areas of the tourism have been emerged. It would bring many direct and indirect benefits to the people.

Tourism is simply defined as "the practice of traveling for recreation". As the largest business sector in the world economy, tourism employs 200 million people, generates $3.6 trillion in economic activity, and accounts for one in every 12 jobs worldwide. The tourism industry is especially important to developing countries since it is the principal foreign exchange earner for 83% of developing countries. The total contribution of Travel & Tourism to GDP was USD6,346.1bn (9.1% of GDP) in 2011, and was forecast to rise by 2.8% in 2012. The total contribution of Travel & Tourism to employment in 2011, including jobs indirectly supported by the industry, was 8.7%, of total employment (254,941,000 jobs). This was expected to raise by 2.0% in 2012 to 260,093,000 jobs. Travel & Tourism investment in 2011 was USD743.0bn, or 4.9% of total investment.

Tourism is often seen as a global phenomenon with an almost incomprehensibly massive infrastructure. Its importance is evident from the fact that its influence thoroughly penetrates society, politics, culture and, above all, the economy. Indeed, this is the branch of the global economy with the most vigorous growth: the World Tourism Organisation (WTO) estimates that in 2007 it encompassed 903 million tourists who spent 625 billion US dollars. They thereby supported a global system with roughly 100 million employees in the modern leisure and experience industry.

At first, the fields of business studies and economics dominated a study of tourism that was grounded in an institutional approach analyses from the cultural sciences and histori-cal surveys came conspicuously late. However, these are perceived differently to those stud-ies undertaken by economists and social scientists. At the same time, it is impossible to ig-nore the historical prerequisites and development of travelling habits and holidaying styles if one wants to understand the nature of tourism today. This is true not only of concepts and ideas associated with the topic, but also the specific insights which the disciplines employed aim to provide. Conducting historical research on tourism within the context of the discipline of history is not synonymous with the task of writing a history of tourism (or parts of it).

Concept of Modern Tourism

In the context of the history of tourism, the term "introductory phase" refers to all the developments, structures and innovations of modern. It prepared the way for a mass tourism recognisable to modern concepts of spending leisure time. The first step towards the development of a tourism industry in India was taken in 1945, when the government of India set up a committee under the Chairmanship of Sir John Sargent, Secretary, Department of Education, was appointed to advise the government on the development of tourism. The main objective of the committee was to survey the potential for the development of tourism in India. Initially four tourist offices were set up in Delhi, Calcutta, Chennai and Mumbai. The first tourist office overseas was set up in New York in 1952, "to carry out tourist publicity by sponsoring articles in the press, by television, radio programmes, by advertising campaign and participation in exhibitions etc. and supply correct information." However, in the year 1957 a separate department of Tourism was established.

The first tourism development council was formed in 1958 as an apex body of associate the state governments national carriers, hotels and the travel industry with the development of tourism in India. By March, 1997 the functions and responsibilities of the department became so important that the union government decided to elevate the department of Aviation and Tourism into the ministry of Tourism and Civil Aviation. In India the total contribution of Travel & Tourism to GDP was INR5,651.0bn (6.4% of GDP) in 2011, contribution of Travel & Tourism to employment, including jobs indirectly supported by the industry, was 7.8% of total employment (39,352,000 jobs). This is expected to rise by 2.8% in 2012 to 40,450,500 jobs and Travel & Tourism investment in 2011 was INR1, 253.9bn, or 5.1% of total investment. It should rise by 12.3% in 2012.The development progressed episodically and built upon a number of changing social conditions and factors. The most important undoubtedly include not only the advance of industrialisation, demographic changes, urbanisation and the revolution in transportation, but also the improvement of social and labour rights, the rise in real income and the resulting changes in consumer demand.

Tourism Attractions in India

India has an amazing variety of natural wealth, comprising the entire range of physical features mountains, hills and plains, forest and deserts, rivers, streams, valleys and meadows, trees, shrubs, plantations, flowers and orchids, lions, tiger, elephants, reptiles, birds, deer and rhino and also the diverse habitations required by such and array of flora and fauna. Few other countries of the world are blessed with such wealth of nature. The travelers who halt here would pass across the ice and snow bound mountain ranges of the Himalayas, some of the highest ranges of the world, down through the unforgettable valleys and dales of Kashmir and into the foot hills and tiger country, passing through some of the most picturesque setting ever. Through India has a long tradition of religious travel, international tourism in its present form is relatively of a recent origin.

Some of famous attractions in India's are given below:

The Taj Mahal: Situated at Agra in Uttar Pradesh.

The Red Fort: Situated in Delhi.

The Mahabodhi Temple: Situated at Bodh Gaya in Bihar.

The Brihadishwara Temple: Situated at Taliparamba in Kerala.

The Shore Temple: Situated at Mahabalipuram in Tamil Nadu.

The Airavateswara Temple: Situated at Darasuram in Tamil Nadu.

The Golden Temple: Situated at Amritsar in Punjab.

The Lotus Temple: Situated in Delhi.

The Victoria Memorial: Situated at Kolkata in West Bengal.

The Hawa Mahal: Situated at Jaipur in Rajasthan.

The Chhatrapati Shivaji Terminus: Situated at Mumbai in Maharashtra.

The Nalanda: Situated close to Patna in Bihar.

The Varanasi: Situated in Uttar Pradesh.

Glimpses of Religious Tourism in Himachal Pradesh

Himachal Pradesh is referred to as dev bhoomi or "land of God". The word "Hima" means snow when translated to Sanskrit, and the meaning of the term stands out to be an area that sits on the laps of the mountains. The state is covered with immense natural beauty and is, undoubtedly, one of the most popular tourist destinations in the world. A majority of the area is mountainous, and lofty ranges, deep valleys, swaying waterfalls and lush greenery symbolise the state. The climate varies extremely from one place to the other, providing heavy rainfalls to some area and no rainfall to others. State has so many other areas available for tourism industry. It would be very helpful to generate more income and employment to people residing surrounding areas. The remote valleys of Lahaul, Spiti and Kinnaur have strong Buddhist traditions. Splendid gompas, Buddhist monasteries, built along mountains seem to be a part of the rugged terrain. These are the repositories of a wealth of Buddhist art and culture. The dim, cool interiors of ancient monasteries glow with the brilliance of painted murals, stuccos and elaborate thangkas framed with rich borders of silk. Dharamsala, where the Dalai Lama has settled in exile, is a marvelous Tibetan township where an entire cultural tradition is being nurtured. It is a centre that attracts scholars, pilgrims and tourists. Buddhist Monasteries in Himachal Pradesh, Kye Monastery is situated 12 kms. North of Kaza in Lahaul-Spiti district and serves the western population of Spiti. It is the oldest and biggest monastery of the valley. It houses beautiful scriptures and paintings of Buddha and other goddesses. Lamas practice dance, sing and play on pipes and horns. Religious training to Lama's is imparted here. It has murals and books of high value.

Rewalsar is the most sacred spot for Buddhists in Himachal Pradesh, about 20 km south west of Mandi. According to legend, Guru Padmasambhava departed for Tibet from this beautiful spot, to spread the dharma. A pagoda-style monastery stands along the edge of the lake. Guru Ghantal Monastery is situated on the right bank of Chandra river about 4 kms. above Tandi and is believed to be the oldest Gompa of Lahaul having wooden structure with pyramidal roofs, wood carving, preserving the idols of Padmasambhava and Brajeshwari Devi. On the full moon night in mid-June a festival called "GHANTAL" is celebrated by Lamas and Thakurs together. Khardong Monastery is about 5 kms. from Keylong across Bhaga river. It is believed to be built in 12th century. This monastery has a large library of Kangyur and Tangyur volumes of Buddhist scriptures in Bhoti. Shashur Monastery is situated on a hill about 3 kms from Keylong in Lahaul and Spiti district towards north. During June/ July this monastery attracts a large number of visitors when Lamas perform the devil dance. It was founded in the 17th century AD. It belongs to red hat sect and is one of the oldest monasteries of the valley having a huge statue of Guru Padmasamhava about 5m high and houses library of Kangyur having 101 volumes. In Tibetan language Ta-Yul means the chosen place. Thang Yug Gompa is located 13 kms. above Kaza in Lahaul and Spiti serving western part of central Spiti. Situated in a secluded place in the narrow gauge of Kaza Nallah, it generally has a Lama from Tibet.

Kungri Gompa is situated in the Pin valley about 10 kms. from Attargo where Spiti river has to be crossed to enter Pin valley. It serves the population of Pinvalley. Dhankar Monastery is situated about 25 kms. east of Kaza and serves eastern part of central Spiti. Dhankar is a big village and erstwhile capital of Spiti King. On top of a hill there is a fort which used to be a prison in olden times. The Monastery has about 100 Lamas and is in position of Buddhist scriptures in Bhoti language. Principal figure is a Statue of "Vairochana" (Dhayan Buddha) consisting of 4 complete figures seated back to back. It has relics in the shape of paintings and sculptures. Tabo Monastery is another large gompa serving the population of eastern side. It has its origin in the tenth century old and is located 50 kms. from Kaza in Lahaul and Spiti district. In fame it is next to Tholing Gompa in Tibet. It has about 60 Lamas and houses a large collection of Scriptures, wall paintings etc. Murals of this gompa have similarity to that of the Ajanta paintings. Nako The legendary footprints of the Guru Padamsambhava are enshrined at the Lotsabaage Monastery at Nako. This high altitude village in Kinnaur is located near a limpid lake. Tashigang Gompa Tashigang Gompa can be visited by taking diversion from Khab to Namgya and then trekking to the Gompa.

These monasteries are situated in tribal areas of Himachal Pradesh, which are still hidden and untraced at national and international level for tourism sector. Besides these monasteries, the state has so many other prominent attractions such as; Water fall, Lakes, Cave, Heritage Temple, Local Fair and Festivals, Ancient Cultural, Wild life Sanctuary and Museum etc. Para gliding, River-rafting mountaineering and Rock climbing activities which fall in the purview of adventure tourism also attract the tourists globally. Tribal areas which remained cut off from the main stream of national life due to heavy snow fall do attract the tourists for skiing and Ice-Skating. It is recognized fact and proved in different studies that certain areas of the state are still neglected and hidden which needs to be tapped. Keeping in view these considerations, there is an apparent need to undertake a study which could explore those areas which are still hidden and neglected from tourism point of view and have the wide potential to develop them.

Review Literature

Sing, Prit, Pual, (1978) has concluded a study on economic potential of tourism in Himachal Pradesh with special reference to Shimla. Kuamr, Jaminder (2011) concluded study on "Tourism potential and its impact in Himachal Pradesh- A case study of Lahaul-Spiti and Una Districts. Chand, Subhash (2010) has studied the "Growth and potential of tourism industry in H.P. Kumar, Suneel (2011) has examine the study on "An analytical study of tourism development and tourist satisfaction in H.P.

Objectives of the Study

1. To study the tourism scenario of the country in general and Himachal in particular.
2. To analyse the flow of tourists visiting Himachal Pradesh on the basis of certain selected variables.
3. To examine the perception of tourists regarding Neglected and Hidden Tourism potentials in the state of Himachal Pradesh
4. To evaluate the opinion of tourists regarding their visit to Buddhist Circuits, Monasteries and also to know their version about the neglect of Buddhists circuits in Himachal Pradesh.
5. To identify the problems experienced by the tourists at different stages and advance suggestions to strengthen the tourism industry in the state.

Research Methodology

Questionnaire Design and Data collection: for this study, primary data was gathered with the help of a questionnaire and sampling elements comprised of 300 visitors, on simple convenient random sampling basis. The secondary relevant and required data was collected form various published sources like books, journal, magazine, reports, publications, and websites. The study areas keep limited up to most well-known tourism districts of Himachal Pradesh i.e., Kullu, Lahaul-Sipiti and Shimla. For the purpose of study domestic and international tourist considered. The Mathematical and statistical tools were used to make study more accurate and result oriented (Percentage and Chi-squares test).

Discussion and Results

Nationality and Gender wise Opinion of Tourists Regarding their Attractions of Visit

The table highlights the relationship between nationality of tourists and different attraction points in Himachal Pradesh. The responses of domestic tourist indicates that majority of them have attracted to know about art and culture, traditional values and also to enjoying the scenic beauty with 19% falling in each category. Thirteen percent of domestic visitor visit for monks and monasteries. However, some visitors visit such places as they are influenced by Buddhists religion and lord Dalai Lama.

In case of foreign tourists, most of them replied that they are attracted by the Indian traditional value (24%) and art & culture (20%). However, 16% of foreign tourists have

Table no. 1

Attraction point	Nationality		Total	Sex		Total
	Indian	Foreign		Male	Female	
Monks & Monasteries	26(13)	16(16)	**42(14)**	25(12.4)	17(17.3)	**42(14)**
Historical Places	17(8.5)	12(12)	**29(9.7)**	21(10.4)	8(8.2)	**29(9.7)**
Art & Culture	38(19)	20(20)	**58(19.3)**	38(18.8)	20(20.4)	**58(19.3)**
Traditional Status	38(19)	24(24)	**62(20.7)**	45(22.3)	17(17.3)	**62(20.7)**
Scenic Beauty	38(19)	14(14)	**52(17.3)**	33(16.3)	19(19.4)	**52(17.3)**
Peaceful and Good climate	22(11)	5(5)	**27(9)**	20(9.9)	7(7.1)	**27(9)**
Dalai Lama	14(7)	5(5)	**19(6.3)**	14(6.9)	5(5.1)	**19(6.3)**
Buddhist Religion	7(3.5)	4(4)	**11(3.7)**	6(3)	5(5.1)	**11(3.7)**
Total	**200(100)**	**100(100)**	**300(100)**	**202(100)**	**98(100)**	**300(100)**
X^2 Value	**=6.36**			**=4.45**		
P Value	**>0.05**			**>0.05**		

Attraction point	Na
	Indian
Monks & Monasteries	26(13)
Historical Places	17(8.5)
Art & Culture	38(19)
Traditional Status	38(19)
Scenic Beauty	38(19)
Peaceful and Good climate	22(11)
Dalai Lama	14(7)
Buddhist Religion	7(3.5)
Total	200(100
X^2 Value	
P Value	

Note: Figures in parentheses depict percentage.

Source: Data collected through questionnaires.

On application of Chi-Square test, its value is insignificant; hence null hypothesis is accepted at 5% level of significance. Attention towards monks and monasteries and small percentage of them visit these spots as they are fascinated by the Buddhist religion and by the teaching of lord Dalai Lama.

After the analyzing the table, It is evident that it reveals relationship among the sex of tourist and their attraction points.

The data signifies that a large number of the male tourists traveled in such places to know about traditional values (23%) and followed by those who visit to familiar about the Buddhist art and culture (18.8%). About 16% male tourists visit these spots for their scenic beauty and 12.4% visit to know about monks and monasteries. On the other hand incase of female tourists it can be seen that above 20% visit these spots due to their interest in art & culture followed by those visiting to witness the scenic beauty.

It is evident from the above table; the aggregate 40% of male and female visit such spots, being as art & culture and traditional values. Further the calculated X2 value is less than table value which means there is insignificant difference among the male and female tourist and their opinion regarding attraction points of tourist.

Age and educational qualifications of tourists and their attraction points

The table shows the age group of 15-30 year, It is seen that most of the tourists visit such spots to know about art & culture (21.8%) pursue by those visiting to see the traditional status (18.3%) and 14.9% for scenic beauty. While 14.4 % tourists from different age groups visit such spots to know about monks and monasteries. The analysis further shows that above eleven percent visit to be familiar with that Buddhist religion and lord Dalai Lama.

In the age group of 30-45 years, it is noticed that most of the tourists visit such spots due to their interest in traditional value 25% followed by those visiting such places for scenic beauty (19.4%) and to know about art and culture (15.3%). A good number of tourists from this age group have inclination for monks and monasteries (13.9%) and very few tourists are attracted by Buddhist religion and lord Dalai Lama. The tourists falling in the age group of 45years and above have shown a different trend as they mostly visit such spots for scenic beauty, traditional value, art and culture, monks and monasteries.

Table no. 2

Attraction point	Age				Total	Educational qualification					Total
	<15	15-30	30-45	>45		Below Matric	Matric	Graduate	P.G.	Above P.G.	
Monks & Monasteries	-	29(14.4)	10(13.9)	3(12.5)	**42(14)**	1(16.7)	3(16.7)	15(13.6)	20(18)	3(5.5)	**42(14)**
Historical Places	-	20(9.9)	6(8.3)	3(12.5)	**29(9.7)**	-	-	10(9.1)	15(13.5)	4(7.3)	**29(9.7)**
Art & Culture	-	44(21.8)	11(15.3)	3(12.5)	**58(19.3)**	2(33.3)	4(22.2)	15(13.6)	24(21.6)	13(23.6)	**58(19.3)**
Traditional Status	1(50)	37(38.3)	18(25)	6(6.2)	**62(20.7)**	2(33.3)	3(16.7)	26(23.6)	16(14.4)	15(27.3)	**62(20.7)**
Scenic Beauty	1(50)	30(14.9)	14(19.4)	7(29.9)	**52(17.3)**	1(16.7)	2(11.1)	19(17.3)	20(18)	10(18.2)	**52(17.3)**
Peaceful and Good climate	-	19(9.4)	7(9.7)	1(4.2)	**27(9)**	-	4(22.2)	9(8.3)	10(9)	4(7.3)	**27(9)**
Dalai Lama	-	16(7.9)	3(4.2)	-	**19(6.3)**	-	2(11.1)	8(7.3)	4(3.6)	5(9.1)	**19(6.3)**
Buddhist Religion	-	7(3.5)	3(4.2)	1(4.2)	**11(3.7)**	-	-	8(7.3)	2(1.8)	1(1.8)	**11(3.7)**
Total	**2(100)**	**202(100)**	**72(100)**	**24(100)**	**300(100)**	**6(100)**	**18(100)**	**110(100)**	**111(100)**	**55(100)**	**300(100)**
X^2 Value	=13.42					=30.6					
P Value	P>0.05					P>0.05					

Note: Figures in parentheses depict percentage.

Source: Data collected through questionnaires.

The X^2 test result depicts that there is no significant relationship between age of tourists and various places of attraction. So that, it can be concluded that there is insignificant relationship among different age groups tourists and the attraction point.

Table points out the relationship between educational qualification of tourists and different feature of attraction. It shows that in case of post graduate tourists, the prime reason to visit such spots in rich culture heritage (21.6%), simultaneously followed by equal portions visiting for scenic beauty and monks & monasteries (18% each). Above 14% from this group visit for traditional status while 13% mulls such spots as places of historical importance.

The responses of graduate tourist indicate highest preference for traditional status (23.6%) followed by 17.3% for scenic beauty. An equal percent of tourists 13% each like to sightsee for such places due to their interest in art and culture, and monks & monasteries.

It is also observed that in the group of above post graduate level, 27.3% visit such to know about traditional status followed by

23.6% who visit to know about art and culture. Above 18% consider these places as spots of scenic beauty. A small percent of tourists form this group visit such places due to monks and monasteries, historical places, Buddhist religion and his holiness Dalai Lama.

Further the Chi-Square value is insignificant at 5% level of significance. It means that hypothesis is accepted. It can further be interpreted that education qualification of the tourist does not make any influence by attraction points.

Tourist Opinion towards Buddhist Tourism and Other Neglected Buddhist Circuits.

Table no 3 Table depicts that in case of domestic tourists; highest 51% didn't have any idea about the Buddhist tourism. 26.5% refused to give their responses and 22.5% admitted that they have an idea About the Buddhist tourism followed by 32% refused to give their responses and 25% admitted that they have an idea about the Buddhist tourism. The table reveals that majority of tourists 48% haven't any cognizance about the Buddhist tourism. Further, on application of X2 test, the calculated value is less then table value which means, there exists insignificance difference among the tourist having different nationality and Buddhist Tourism.

Table no. 3

Responses	Idea about Buddhist Tourism		Total	Visits to the Monasteries		Total	Neglected Buddhist Circuits		Total
	Indian	Foreign		Indian	Foreign		Indian	Foreign	
Yes	45(22.5)	25(25)	**70(23.3)**	42(21)	20(20)	**62(20.7)**	112(50)	70(70)	**182(60.7)**
No	102(51)	43(43)	**145(48.3)**	130(65)	66(66)	**196(65.3)**	26(13)	11(11)	**37(12.3)**
Can't Say	53(26.5)	32(32)	**85(28.4)**	28(14)	14(14)	**42(14)**	62(31)	19(19)	**81(27)**
Total	**200(100)**	**100(100)**	**300(100)**	**200(100)**	**100(100)**	**300(100)**	**200(100)**	**100(100)**	**300(100)**
X^2 Value	= 1.74			= .042			= 5.90		
P Value	P> 0.05			P> 0.05			P> 0.05		

Note: Figures in parentheses depict percentage.

Source: Data collected through questionnaires.

Table depicts that, in case of domestic tourists, 65% did not visit the monastery followed by 21% admitted that they have visited the monastery and 14% refused to give their response about their visit. In case of foreign tourists, 66% did not visited the Monastery, 20% admitted that they have visited the monastery and 14% refused to give their responses about their visit. Further the X2 value is insignificant hence null hypothesis is accepted at 5% of significance.

After observing the table values, it seems to domestic tourists, 56% admitted that the Buddhist circuits are remained neglected and hidden, 31% refused to give their responses and 13% who did not believe that the Buddhist circuits are remained neglected and hidden from tourism point of view. In case of foreign tourists, 70% admitted that the Buddhist circuits are remained neglected and hidden followed by 19% refuse to give their responses and 11% who did not believe that the Buddhist circuits are remained neglected and hidden from tourism point of view in the state. Further, X2 value is insignificant hence null hypothesis accepted at 5% level of significance.

Perception of Tourists Regarding Hidden and Neglected Tourism Potentials

In this table tourists have given their perception regarding the tourism potential in Himachal Pradesh. Above the 50% of total domestic and foreign tourists have given their consent to yes and 25% of domestic visitor replied no and rest of domestic visitor said can't say any think about the hidden and neglected tourism potential in Himachal Pradesh. 16% of foreign tourists refused and 22% of overseas tourists said can't say anything.

Table no. 4

Nature of Responses	Nationality		Total
	Indian	Foreign	
Yes	130(65)	62(62)	192(64)
No	50(25)	16(16)	66(22)
Can't Say	20(10)	22(22)	42(14)
Total	200(100)	100(100)	300(100)
X2 Value= 9.40		P> 0.05	

Note: Figures in parentheses depict percentage.

Source: Data collected through questionnaires.

Chi-Square test, its value comes 9.40, which is less than the table value at the 5 percent level of significance. It means that there is insignificant difference in the opinion of tourists. It can further be interpreted that nationality of the visitors does not make any difference in perception of tourists regarding hidden and neglected tourism potentials.

Tapping of Neglected and Hidden Tourism Potential: Opinion of Respondents

Table shows that in case of domestic tourists 32.5% admitted that with the help of fairs and festivals the neglected and hidden tourism can be tapped simultaneously followed by tourist information centre (16%), proper marketing mix (14.5%) sufficient literature (16.5%) exploration of culture and tradition (9%) theme park (7%) the announcement of special tourist packages (5.5%) and putting up the exhibitions.

Table no. 5

Tourists Views Regarding Tapping of Neglected & Hidden Tourism Potential

Attribute	Nationality		Total
	Indian	Foreign	
Local fair & festivals	65(32.5)	28(28)	**93(31)**
Tourist information centre	32(16)	19(19)	**51(12)**
Proper Marketing Mix	29(14.5)	12(12)	**41(13.7)**
Exploration of culture & Traditional	18(9)	8(8)	**26(8.7)**
Theme Park	14(7)	11(11)	**25(8.3)**
Exhibitions	10(5)	6(6)	**16(5.3)**
Special tourist package	11(5.5)	7(7)	**18(6)**
Sufficient literature	21(10.5)	9(9)	**30(10)**
Total	200(100)	100(100)	**300(100)**
X^2 Value= 3.07		P> 0.05	

Note: Figures in parentheses depict percentage.

Source: Data collected through questionnaires.

In case of foreign tourists, 25% responded that with the help of local fair and festivals neglected and hidden tourism can be tapped followed by tourist information centre (19%), proper marketing mix (12%), theme park (11%), sufficient literature (9%), exploration of culture and tradition (8%) the announcement of special tourist packages (7%) and putting up the exhibition. On the application of Chi-Square test, the calculated value is less than the table value. It means that hypothesis is accepted with the supposition that there in not exists significant difference in the opinion of tourists Nationality wise and tapping of neglected & hidden tourism potential..

Finding, Conclusion and Suggestions

On the basis of analysis of data, it can be concluded that tourism has become a major social phenomenon of societies in H.P. It has driven a new experience urge among people for new experience. The importance of tourism, as an instrument of economic development and employment generations of particularly in remote and backward areas state. Tourism industry is a large service industry in terms of gross revenues as well as foreign exchange earnings. Tourism is playing an important and effective role in achieving the growth of state equity.

Findings

- It is noted that, major crowd of 57.3% tourists, domestic as well as foreign have attracted by Art & Culture, Scenic beauty and Traditional status of the state. Near nine percent of both resident have encouraged to take trip due to Historical places and Peaceful climate and just 3.7% visitor influenced by Buddhist Religion.
- 22.3% male, 20.4% female have given preference for attractions point, Traditional status and Art & Culture. Gender wise also given preference to point's Traditional status, Art & Culture and imitate by Scenic Beauty. Only 11 tourists (6 male & 5 female) out of 300 attracted by Buddhist Religion.
- On using statistical tool, Chi-square value is less than table value, it means there is no significant relationship among the nationality, gender wise opinion of tourists and attraction points.
- 57.3%, from different age groups of tourists, they have given consent that they are attracted by Traditional Status, Art & Culture

and Scenic Beauty. 6.3 percent of influenced by Dalai Lama and 3.7% Buddhist Religion.

- Out of 300 respondents having different educational qualifications, in the decreasing order, 62, 58 and 52 of total tourist replied that they are attracted to become familiar with Traditional status, Art & Culture and Scenic Beauty of the of state.
- Chi-Square value further confirms that there exists an insignificant difference in the opinion of tourists, regarding point of attraction and age wise and educational qualifications. Which depicts the no significant relationship has been noticed at 5% level of significance.
- Major chunk of domestic and foreign tourists replied that they haven't idea about Buddhist Tourism and they never visited any monastery in the state. A Small group of native and overseas tourists, 23.3% said that they have cognizance about Buddhist Tourism, 20.7% nodded they are now familiar with Monasteries and 60.7 percent tourists said that Buddhist Circuits are Neglected in H.P. Above 28 percent refuse to say anything about Buddhist Tourism 14 % reject to say about their trip in the Monasteries and twenty seven percent tourists not responded regarding Neglected Buddhist Circuits. On the application of Chi-Square test, the calculated value is less than the table value. It means that hypothesis is accepted with the inference that there exists insignificant difference in the opinion of tourists.
- 192 out of 300 travelers given their accord in yes and 22% said no, rest of total visitor refuse to say anything regarding hidden and neglected tourism potentials in Himachal Pradesh. On using Chi-square test, null hypothesis is rejected, it can be concluded that there is insignificant result.
- Maximum 31 percent domestic as well as overseas tourists said through the local fair & festivals help to tap neglected tourism in that state and 12% believed thorough the tourist information centre. Near 8 percent constant tourist said in the course of Theme park and Exploration of Cultural & Tradition will help to tap neglected tourism potential in the state. On the application of Chi-Square test, the calculated value is less than the table value. It means that hypothesis is accepted with the supposition that there

in not exists significant difference in the opinion of tourists Nationality wise and tapping of neglected & hidden tourism potential.

Suggestions

- Some of festivals should be organized by the tourism department, for main attractions to promote the neglected and hidden potential in Himachal Pradesh.
- Aggressive marketing of Himachal Pradesh as a tourists destination should be done in these countries from where the tourists arrival as substantial.
- There is need to carry out an extensive survey of the tourist resources of the state on scientific basis.
- The adventure sport, activities like, ballooning, hang gliding, Para-gliding, trekking etc. should be promoted through proper planning.
- Private sector investment should be encouraged to boost the tourism industry in the state.
- Development of new tourist roots to easily access the neglected tourist areas.
- In order to promote all parts of Himachal Pradesh as a tourists' destination, the emphasis should be given on above suggestions.

Refrences

Merriam-Webster Dictionary http://www.m-w.com/dictionary/tourism

http://www.ecotourism.org/webmodules/webarticlesnet/templates/eco_template.aspx?articleid=15&zoneid=2

A.K. Bhatia, "Tourism Development, Principle and Practices," Sterling Publisher P. Ltd, New Delhi, 1983, pp. 17-82.

S.P. Tewari, "Tourism Dimensoions," Atma Ram and Sons, Delhi, 1994, pp. 388-390.

www2.unwto.org

www.wttc.org

www.himachaltourism.gov.in

www.tourism.gov.in

SOCIO ECONOMIC BENEFITS OF TOURISM IN MAHARASHTRA: A CASE STUDY OF AURANGABAD DISTRICT

Varinder Singh Rana

Assistant Professor (School of Hotel Management & Tourism) Lovely Professional University Jalandhar-Delhi G.T.Road (NH-1), Phagwara, Punjab-144402 varinder.rana@lpu.co.in

Abstract: Tourism is service-oriented sector which has made rapid strides globally in terms of gross revenue and foreign exchange earnings. Tourism gives a financial incentive to preserve architectural heritages and helps the survival of art forms, crafts and culture. It is a composite of service providers, both public and private, which includes travel agents and tour operators; air, rail, and sea transportation operators; guides; owners of hotels and guest houses and inns, restaurants and shops; etc. Today, tourism is one of the largest and dynamically developing sectors of external economic activities. Its high growth and development rates, considerable volumes of foreign currency inflows, infrastructure development, and introduction of new management and educational experience actively affect various sectors of economy, which positively contribute to the social and economic development of the country as a whole. Most highly developed western countries, such as Switzerland, Austria, and France have accumulated a big deal of their social and economic welfare on profits from tourism.

Tourism in India is expected to play a key role in the country's economic growth, human resource, culture, wealth of the country in terms of foreign exchange earnings, etc. Simultaneously, it has a direct bearing on local culture, socio-economic patterns of life, traditions, food habits, language, values and ethics of the local people due to frequent visits of national and international tourists to attractive tourist destinations. Nel and Binns(2002) stated in their research that while pursuing the usage of tourism towards economic growth and poverty alleviation, it is important to consider the socio-economic impacts of tourism development. The social impacts of tourism are important as most local people are absorbed in the tourist industry in the various sub-sectors of the Industry. Maharashtra has a rich historical and cultural heritage, which has been under-explored by the tourism industry and the government agencies. The strong basic infrastructure availability throughout the state would provide a perfect platform for fresh private investments in development of tourism in the state, and in the process creating many direct and indirect employment opportunities to local residents. In the state of Maharashtra, the city of Aurangabad is known for its medieval monuments and cultural heritage. The objective of this research paper is to study the socio-economic benefit of tourism in Aurangabad district (Maharashtra) and to determine the nature of tourism and visitor resources present in Aurangabad and to find out the direct, indirect and induced effects of tourism spending. The research design used for this research is descriptive in nature.

Keywords: Tourism, Socio-Economic Benefit

Introduction

Tourism is service-oriented sector which has made rapid strides globally in terms of gross revenue and foreign exchange earnings. The tourism industry generates more employment opportunities (particularly in remote and backward areas) as well as develops necessary infrastructure like transportation and telecom in the economy. Tourism gives a financial incentive to preserve architectural heritages and helps the survival of art forms, crafts and culture. It is a composite of service providers, both public and private, which includes travel agents and tour operators; air, rail, and sea transportation operators; guides; owners of hotels and guest houses and inns, restaurants and shops; etc. Today, tourism is one of the largest and dynamically developing sectors of external economic activities. Its high growth and development rates, considerable volumes of foreign currency inflows, infrastructure development, and introduction of new management and educational experience actively affect various sectors of economy, which positively contribute to the social and economic development of the country as a whole. Most highly developed western countries, such as Switzerland, Austria, and France have accumulated a big deal of their social and economic welfare on profits from tourism. According to recent statistics, tourism provides about 10% of the world's income and employs almost one tenth of the world's workforce. All considered, tourism's actual and potential economic impact is astounding.

Tourism is likely to be a growing industry in India for some time. It has tremendous potential due to peoples' interest in travel and desire to explore nature and religious sites. Tourism in India is expected to play a key role in the country's economic growth, human resource, culture, wealth of the country in terms of foreign exchange earnings, etc. Simultaneously, it has a direct bearing on local culture, socio-economic patterns of life, traditions, food habits, language, values and ethics of the local people due to frequent visits of national and international tourists to attractive tourist destinations. People visit tourist locations to have a flavour of pilgrimage, cultural heritage, and nature. Sometimes they simply wish to get away from the monotony of routine life. People not only rejuvenate from these visits but also directly contribute for the growth of the local economy through the hospitality industry, handicraft industry and secondary occupations including tourists guide, carriers, etc. Tourism is defined as one among many social and economic players in the state. It encompasses an industry that manages and markets a range of products and experiences to the visitors who have a wide range of motivations, preference and cultural perspectives and are involved in a social exchange with the host community.

Tourism industry in Maharashtra has a tremendous potential for growth, given the availability of basic infrastructure and the variety of tourist themes offered by various destinations in Maharashtra. Maharashtra has a rich historical and cultural heritage, which has been under-explored by the tourism industry and the government agencies. The strong basic infrastructure availability throughout the state would provide a perfect platform for fresh private investments in development of tourism in the state, and in the process creating many direct and indirect employment opportunities to local residents. The direction and magnitude of the flow of investments depends on the prioritization of destination and the nature of projects proposed in that region. In the first 5-10 years, the western region of Maharashtra, specifically Konkan and the Aurangabad region would be on priority in terms of expenses incurred on tourism projects, tourism infrastructure and promotion. In the state of Maharashtra, the city of Aurangabad is known for its medieval monuments and cultural heritage. It was the seat of the Mughal Empire for a short period. The city boasts of Bibi-ka-Makbara, a tomb that has some resemblance to the Taj Mahal. The importance of Aurangabad is great, owing to its proximity with world heritage sites of Ajanta and Ellora. These sites have Buddhist, Jain and Hindu temples. Aurangabad is also famous for its silk and cotton textiles. The historic city of Aurangabad, on the Deccan plateau, has many tourist attractions and could easily stand on its own charm were it not overshadowed by the world-famous Ajanta and Ellora Caves. The traces of the long artistic and cultural influences that a number of dynasties have cast upon it are present everywhere in Aurangabad. The city continues to attract tourists from all over the world who come to discover an old world carved in stone. Aurangabad District is blessed with 2 unparalleled world Heritage sites of Ajanta and Ellora. Ajanta also happens to be the first monument in the country along with Ellora and Taj Mahal to make it to the World Heritage site list of UNESCO in the year 1983 India has 27 properties of both cultural and natural significance out of which 4 are in Maharashtra and 2 in the District. There seems to be a huge gap in attaining the statement of Universal value. It's not Ajanta, Ellora but its World Heritage. This gap needs to be filled in. This research provides information of the current status of tourism in Aurangabad and presents the current status of economic development in the district. Aurangabad District is one of the 35 districts of Maharashtra state in western India. It is bordered by the districts of Nasik to the west, Jalgaon to the north, Jalna to the east, and Ahmednagar district to the south. Aurangabad is the headquarters and principal city. The district covers an area of 10,100 km^2, out of which 141.1 km^2 is urban area and 9,958.9 km^2 is rural. In 2006 the Ministry of Panchayati Raj named Aurangabad one of the country's 250 most backward districts (out of a total of 640). It is one of the twelve districts in Maharashtra currently receiving funds from the Backward Regions Grant Fund Programme (BRGF).

Nature of tourism

1. Aurangabad-Heritage tourism
2. Paithain-Pilgrimage Tourism
3. Pitalkhora-Heritage tourism
4. Mhaismal-Leisure tourism
5. Khultabad-Pilgrimage tourism
6. Vetalwadi fort-Heritage tourism
7. Daulatabad fort-Heritage tourism
8. Ajanta -Heritage tourism
9. Ellora caves -Heritage tourism
10. Gautala- Nature Tourism

Tourism employability (Current Situation)

- Direct Employment: - Estimated to be around 8,000 in the District as Airlines/ Travel Agents/ Tourist Taxi Drivers/ Hotel employees/ Handicraft Vendors/ Travel/ Related Services, Tourism aggregation etc.
- Indirect Employment: - Estimated to be around 90,000 people.
- Ongoing Scheme: - Capacity Building Programmers.
- Self-employment training 32
- Funding Pattern
- State Govt. through different empowerment schemes.
- Central Govt.
- MTDC's own plans

Tourist guides

Current situation - No of approved tour guides 60

Ongoing Scheme: - - Restricted training monopolized by Ministry of Tourism, Govt. of India to avoid saturation.

Development of local economy

Tourism empowers people, triggers local economy, alleviates poverty and raises the standard of living. The development of local economy through Tourism spending is not determined or as such is scattered or in other terms the benefactors are not evenly spread. A major analysis reveals that the Rural Heritage should have done that but instead the multiplier in economic terms seems to be central at Aurangabad.

Review of literature

Nel and Binns(2002)stated in their research that while pursuing the usage of tourism towards economic growth and poverty alleviation, it is important to consider the socio-economic impacts of tourism development. The social impacts of tourism are important as most local people are absorbed in the tourist industry in the various sub-sectors of the industry. Some of those areas will include working as servants, house maids, waiters, gardeners and other menial work that may give people a sense of inferiority while others may be entrepreneurs who owns their own tourism enterprise. The amount of taxes collected by government will also increase with the higher level of economic activity. Residents of a local community might have a better standard of living and higher income by tourism activities and economic empowerment

Scheyvens (1999) said that economic empowerment mean that tourism brings lasting economic gains to a local community. This is characterized by the fact that tourism brings long - term financial benefits to a destination community and money is spread throughout the community. There noticeable improvements in local service and infrastructure as well as educational opportunities for locals through the corporate social responsibility adopted by investors in the tourism industry.

True economic empowerment, however, requires more than corporate social responsibility approach to development (Milman and Pizam, 1988)

Dr.R.gopal, Ms.Shilpa Varma and Ms.Rashmi Gopinathan said that Maharashtra Global economic restructuring has created a climate in which many local economic have to adjust in order to maintain or enhance their socio economic viability. India has achieved great prosperity in tourism as a product .and it create direct and indirect job. Agri tourism in India innovative income generating activity for enterprising farmer .agriculture is backbone of Indian economy .this sector contribution towards GDP is decreasing farmer are finding it difficult to carry the agricultural activities without an addition income whereas tourism is gives employment generation and help to brings booming sector and its helps to provide facilities to poor and deserving women for earning their livelihood.

Gee et al (1997) A host nation will gain foreign exchange, which will contribute to improve the nations balance of payments Lane .B (1994) points out that "rural tourism should be -located at rural areas. Functionally rural i.e. .small scale enterprises, open space; natural contact, heritage, traditional, societal practices etc; rural in scale; traditional in character; take different forms representing the complex pattern of rural environment, tourists share in village life, and rural villages gain economic and other benefits from tourist activities. According to the Annual Report of Ramakrishna Mission and Pallimangal Kamarpukur, 2006-2007, tourism is more labor intensive than other sectors

Vanhoe (1980) noticed, "Five most commonly occurring economic variables affecting tourism demand are income level, population, relative prices, and exchange rate and travel costs.

Objectives of the study

1. To study the socio-economic benefit of tourism in Aurangabad district (Maharashtra)
2. To determine the nature of tourism and visitor resources present in Aurangabad and to find out the direct, indirect and induced effects of tourism spending.

3. To identify the principal socio-economic, community and tourism effects (both positive and negative) in Aurangabad district.

Research design

The research design used for this project is descriptive in nature. The survey approaches are predominantly based on qualitative methods. The sample is collected using Non Probabilistic Sampling as the respondents profile is unknown. Convenience sampling is used as the respondents are selected on the basis of availability and also this technique is more economical

Data Sources

Primary sources

The well structured questionnaire had been given to the respondents that include close ended questions.

Secondary sources

Secondary data was collected through research articles, journals, websites and magazines.

Sampling Size and Unit- 50 and sample size is composed of local people who are associated with tourism industry and tourists who are present in Aurangabad.

Sampling Technique- Convenient sampling and judgmental technique is used.

Tools of data collection

The study is based on the primary data, derived through sample survey using pre-tested structured instrument (questionnaire).

Findings

1. Research says that the impact of tourism on Aurangabad economy is positive .Tourism helps to promote Aurangabad economy
2. Through the research it has been found that the impact of tourism on Aurangabad society is good because tourism promotes Aurangabad culture.
3. Government helps a lot for promotion of tourism in Aurangabad
4. Through this research it has been found that because of interaction between local people and tourist, they learn so many things like language, culture, etc.

5. Community participates in promotion of tourism by conservation of natural resources' development of rural tourism and maintenance their culture.
6. The research shows that tourism industry in Aurangabad brings more foreign exchange into Maharastra.
7. Aurangabad district residents have better standard of living and high income due to tourism.
8. The new infrastructure development is happening due of tourism.
9. Government is also considering local community perception for development of Tourism
10. Research proves that the local people have not positive attitude towards the Tourism.
11. As per the perception of people, alcohol and smoking should be strictly prohibited in Aurangabad district.

Recommendation

1 Government of India has to make, more rules and regulations for the development of tourism in the country

2 Government has to make defined and strict rules for security of the tourist

3 Local people should maintain the beauty of tourist place

4 Local people should cooperate with the tourists and they should help the tourists and should not cheat them.

5 There should be more tourist offices for the help of tourist at the tourist places so that the tourist should not face any problem at the tourist place. Tourist offices should give maps of tourist place and brouchers

6 Government should develop and promote that tourist places which are not yet covered a lot.

7 Government should build rest houses in the way to the tourist places.

8 Government should help the people to set up business to promote culture and generate income.

9 Government should ban the alcohol in tourist destination in Aurangabad district.

10 Government should give the same employment opportunities to male and female

References

Angelsen, A., Fjeldstad, O., & Rashid-Sumaila, U. (1994). Project Appraisal and sustainability in lessdevelopecountries. Norway: BergenPrintServices.TourismManagement,Volume26,issue2 (April2005),p.157-172.ISSN:0261-517DOI:10.1016/j.tourman. 2003.11.005

Elsevier Science journals.ohiolink.edu/ejc/article.cgi?issn=02615177&issue.

Briedenhann and Wickens, (2004):"Tourism routes as a tool for the Economic Development of rural areas-vibrant hope and impossible dream?" Tourism

ijrcm.org.in/download.php?name=ijrcm-1-vol-3...5.

Cortés-Jiménez (2007) "Tourism, capital good imports and economic growth: theory and evidence for Spain", Tourism Economics, 13(4), pp 515-536

Chakraborty Subhasish (2007): A Project work of "Developing an integrated Tourism Circuit in the Land of Sri Ramakrishna Paramhansa

https://s3-eu-west-1.amazonaws.com/.../Religious+Tourism+Master+Plan

Dr.R.Gopal,M.S.ShilpaVermaAnd M.S.Rashmi Gopinathan(2002) Rural Tourism Development: Constraints and Possibilities with a special reference to Agri Tourism Case Study on Agri Tourism Destination - Malegoan Village, Taluka Baramati, District Pune, Maharashtra Conference on Tourism in India - Challenges Ahead, 15-17 May 2008, IIMK volume 23, Issue 4, August 2002, Pages 333-341 web-http://dspace.iimk.ac.in/bitstream/2259/596/1/512-523

Gee CY, Makens JC, Choy DJL (1997). The Travel Industry. 3rd ed. New York: Van Nostrand Reinhold www.opf.slu.cz/vvr/akce/turecko/pdf/Tatoglu.pdf

Liu JC, Var T (1986). "Resident attitudes toward tourism impacts in Hawaii". Ann. Tourism Res., 13: 193-214

Dogan HZ (1987). Socio-cultural foundations of tourism. ?zmir: U?ur Ofset- www.opf.slu.cz/vvr/akce/turecko/pdf/Tatoglu.pdf

Jenkins (1998): 'The policy dimensions of rural tourism and recreation' in R. Butler, C.M Hall and J.

Jenkins (Eds), Tourism Recreation in Rural Areas, Chichester: John Wiley and sons: pp19-42

www.business.otago.ac.nz/tourism/research/publications/1998.htm 7) - Lane. B. (1994): what is Rural Tourism? Journal of sustainable tourism. Vol.2, pp.7-12

Milman A, Pizam A (1988). Social impacts of tourism on Central Florida, Ann. Tourism Res., 15(2): 191-204

https://hospitality.ucf.edu/files/.../RESUME-PUBLICATIONS_9-12.p.

Nel ET, Binns T (2002). Healing the wounds of apartheid: evaluating 'developmental local government' in South Africa's cities. Paper presented at the Institute of British Geographers Conference, Belfast, and January, 2002.

ftp://ftp.puce.edu.ec/Facultades/.../estrategia local africa.pdf

N. Vanhoe (1980): Forecasting Tourism, Review de Tourisme vol.3, pp.2-7

Republic of South Africa (RSA) (1998). The White Paper on Local Government. Pretoria: Department of Constitutional Development

www.afesis.org.za/Local.../south-african-local-government-10-years-

Nel ET (1999). Regional and Local Economic Development in South Africa: The experience of the Eastern Cape. Ashgate Publishing Limited, England

www.wscholars.com/index.php/ajtr/article/download/106/61

Rogerson CM (1999b). Local economic development and urban poverty alleviation: the experience of post-apartheid South Africa. Habitat Int., 23: 511-34

TOURISM AND HOSPITALITY INDUSTRY: INITIATION TOWARDS GREEN PRACTICES

Vijay Kumar

Dept. of Tourism, Hotel, Hospitality and Heritage Studies, Jamia Millia Islamia, New Delhi 110025, India vkumar@jmi.ac.in

Abstract: Tourism and hospitality are among the growth industries of the world, with more and more jobs on offer. Covering a wide range of occupations in different organizations - many of them overlapping - they offer you the chance of an interesting career with many opportunities to progress.

Travel and tourism are intensive human resources, which directly and indirectly to 8 percent of the global workforce. It is estimated that a job in the tourism industry generates around a core and an additional means or indirect jobs in the tourism-related economy. It is expected that the greening of tourism, involving improvements in energy efficiency, water and waste systems, to enhance the employment potential of the sector with increased local hiring and sourcing and great opportunities in tourism oriented local culture and natural environment. Green Tourism Promotion supports sustainable tourism that protects the environment and local culture and provides livelihood for the locals. It care and conserve the nature and offer guests an authentic cultural and nature experience.

Many Hotels are now having plants to reuse water, like The Orchid Hotel, Mumbai; is now Asia's first hotel to maintain such plants successfully and it has been certified as GREEN HOTEL or ECO-Friendly hotel. GREEN Cements are now been used in the construction of hotels which is also eco- friendly Nalla Beach Resort, Puducherry, A Hotel with unique bio gas produced from kitchen & dinning waste water recycling plant technology, rain water harvesting system in the premises. Tourism Concern is campaigning for immediate action by the Kerala Department of Tourism to ensure beaches and waters of Alleppey for sustainable tourism for litter free and waste free for the benefit for local communities and Tourism resources.

Water Equity in Tourism' (WET) programme marked the beginning of the 'Zero Tolerance for Water Injustice' Campaign in Goa. This was a direct offshoot of the recommendations of the Tourism Concern for 'Reclaiming Water Rights - towards an Equitable Social Contract'also. This would also ensure the desired results in the reduction of pollutant levels as well as ensure the participation of the hoteliers in protection of water bodies. Government Departments such as the Department for Agriculture, as well the Goa State Pollution Control Board building up public opinion through print and electronic media. Other than press releases in the Campaign

Therefore, Tourism Concern's Water Equity in Tourism programme (WET) should strive to ensure that the water rights of communities living in tourism destinations are protected in the face of growing competition from the industry, and in a world where freshwater for many is becoming increasingly scarce and looked into implementation strategies through community action and advocacy with the Government and other relevant Departments.

Keywords: Tourism and Hospitality Industry, Tourism Concerns, Goa

Introduction

The equated tourism historically "green" with " eco-tourism " and both, sometimes by mistake, it is assumed widely to cover the vacation experience that relate to the natural environment, while at the same time to make sure that is the protection of the environment and is not affected by the holiday activity. Must be discrimination, but since "green" tourism has in fact gone on to become a period that can be used widely and includes all. And can be applied to any form of tourism that relate to the natural environment and cultural heritage of the area (whether it be "comprehensive ," "alternative," "hard," "soft ," "nature-based", "cultural", or "based adventure"). By essence should demonstrate practices to prevent or minimize their impact on the environment, which should include:

- The wise use of resources such as raw materials, water and energy;
- Prevention of pollution (air, land and water) ;
- Protect and where possible enhance biodiversity.

In today's interconnected world, and stamp passports with increasing frequency. By 2020, will be an estimated 1.6 billion tourists travel the world every year, which is twice as many as in 2009. Whether trekking through the rain forest, wandering around ancient monuments, or diving near coral reefs, travelers gain unparalleled expertise and help strengthen local economies. However, tourism comes at a price : the impact on the ground. A lot of traffic can trample on the pristine environment, and air pollution, and the depletion of precious resources, emit gases that contribute to global warming. As awareness about the threat of climate change is growing, and there is an increase in demand for destinations - those "green" that make an active effort to improve environmental sustainability by addressing issues such as carbon emissions, and the preservation of biodiversity, waste management, and water supply. Tourism and environmental sustainability is rapidly becoming a natural partners .

Tourists, especially those environmentally savvy in major source markets such as Western Europe are increasingly wanting green spaces. A study by the county of Devon in the United Kingdom in 2005 that 54 percent of respondents consider environmental issues when booking a trip and 82 percent are willing to pay more for green services and products, and 72 % believe are green business is likely to be quality conscious .

In response, in an attempt to stay both environmentally sustainable and competitive, the leading tour operators such as TUI AG and Thomas Cook and demanding higher standards of hotels and Marketing and Booking give preference to destinations environmentally sustainable. Thomas Cook recently partnered with

UK-based Federation of Tour Operators (FTO) in order to launch awards Trave life, which recognizes hotels and other business partners that achieve high levels of environmental management .

Tourist destinations are aware that in order to maintain its competitiveness, becoming green must be the main component of the trademark policies and marketing. Failure to adopt such an approach may mean the loss of a loyal customer base. In addition, the regulations are being implemented strict carbon as all over the world, and start investing in green tourism provide economic benefits to the countries that host or trips to have another goal to keep in mind : the financial rewards for the adoption of sustainable policies.

The power of the totalitarian approach to the green

Destinations that must aspire to be sustainable considering the following four elements :

1. Carbon emissions: The tourism industry is currently responsible for about 5 percent of global carbon emissions, largely as a result of air travel and accommodation. The study estimates the global final of the World Economic Forum and Booz & Company that these emissions will double by 2035 if left unchecked.

Carbon mitigation efforts, and therefore, is the key to green policy. And should include these efforts and the elimination and reduction of emissions, and replacement practices harmful to the environment more sustainable ones, and balancing the remaining emissions. Destinations can also reduce the effects of carbon through their choice of goods and materials from sustainable sources .

Through the implementation of technologies and policies such as solar panels, compact fluorescent lighting, and energy-efficient appliances, building insulation, and renewable fuels, and carbon sequestration of green trees, and can dramatically reduce their carbon emissions destinations. Resort AquaCity popular Slovakia, which was named recently "Leading Green Resort in the World" by the World Travel Awards, and prevents an estimated 27 tons of CO_2 from entering the atmosphere every day by using underground water and solar energy policies that saved millions resort of euros each year. Mitigation options such as these increase the " double bottom line " by providing economic and environmental benefits to both, and they have a return on investment period is relatively short. It should also be investing in destinations and encourage guests to choose the means of transport and energy-saving activities. Depending on the location, visitors can be led toward collective smart transportation options such as trains, buses, hybrid electric or individual choices such as hybrid cars, bicycles, and sailboats instead of SUVs and boats.

In addition, it can motivate tourists destinations to compensate for the remaining emissions through local programs that invest in renewable energy technologies such as wind power .

2. Biodiversity conservation : site unique natural asset in the beaches, rivers, forests, mountains, coral reefs, deserts, and wildlife is the key to its value as a tourist destination. Thus maintaining these assets is a critical component of sustainable tourism. Over the past two decades, tourism in hot spots of biodiversity increased more than 100 percent, making conservation more urgent.

Without proper conservation efforts, tourism can contribute to the damage and destruction of plants and animals. The scared wildlife viewing unregulated away animals and disrupted nesting sites and feeding their own. Have been damaged coral reefs all over the world via cruise ships, divers, and other human activity. Trafficked sites trips too, such as the Annapurna Circuit in Nepal, and experience serious soil erosion and damage to the plant. Without biodiversity conservation or for flights leaving the most valuable possessions unprotected. Shielding of these assets is a high-yielding investment in the future. Policymakers must develop national parks and wildlife corridors, and regulate access to areas likely to be fragile, and the protection of native species, and pest control. Must be designed efforts to maintain the biological diversity of the needs of the regional and local specific. After all, you may not operate a policy that works in the rainforest in the desert, and vice versa .

3. Waste Management : Effective liquid and solid waste management is the key to " visualize clean" from the point. As a major pollution and waste affects the entire ecosystem, including land degradation,

water quality, health and hygiene. Reducing potential waste streams, and reduce the amount of solid waste that ends up in landfills and incinerators, and recycling whenever possible are all crucial elements of the policy of environmentally sustainable tourism.

Global best practices for solid waste management, which should dictate the collection of waste in sealed bags or boxes and transported in closed trucks, sorted and recycled to the maximum extent possible, and then disposed of in sanitary landfills as a last resort. In addition, waste ideally should be used for power generation.

Best practices for waste liquid begins with reducing the amount created and managed better then with aerobic treatment and filtration, followed by cleansing and to destroy bacteria and viruses. Are then dealing with the waste to remove minerals and pollutants biodegradable small. Can be advanced methods of waste management such as waste-to- energy and enhance the reputation of the point of the green on the pitch .

4. Water : Water is a scarce resource, increasingly, with many countries facing severe shortages. An adequate supply of water and healthy is critical for achieving environmental sustainability point of the long-term. Because the water supply and desalination are usually important sources of energy use and emissions, water policy to maintain doubly important. Should be measured water consumption and reduce the minimum level needed to run enough. Wastewater reuse increases the availability of safe drinking water and sanitation and reduces hand and cleaning fee. In addition, wastewater management proper reduces water pollution, and reduces the risk of disease .

None of these components can be properly addressed and managed without major support structures in place and that enable and facilitate the greening efforts. Should be applied for each enable each of the elements that we have described. And just like the components of the green itself, consideration must be given to these factors help through a holistic lens.

1. Regulations and Governance : A destination can not successfully embark on a strategy of green without the laws and regulations in the right place, or the right management structure in supervision.

Legislation should protect the environment, and the reduction of development can be harmful, and the control of harmful practices, and encourage healthy behavior .

Maldives, which has an economy which is heavily dependent on tourism, began implementation of stringent environmental regulations. Tourism is shown for selected regions and uninhabited islands for fear of spoiling the fragile ecosystem in the country. Norway fjords region, Kootenay and Yoho National Parks in British Columbia, and the Gaspe Peninsula of Quebec got the highest scores in the National Geographic Center for the " Places Rated " Destination supervision survey of sustainable destinations in 2009 to oversee environmental .

It should be under the auspices of the sustainability program successful by the highest levels of government, with the appropriate governing bodies at the national, regional or local, which is responsible for the leadership of the program and facilitate its implementation. Should these entities, which should work adequately, and include representatives of all relevant ministries, including tourism, transportation, the environment, and aviation, as well as local government and private sector representatives .

2. Stakeholder Participation: Green Transformation Program requires a truly comprehensive participation of many different players. It is absolutely vital that the government and the private sector, and civil society collaborate to create and implement sustainable policies .

At the government level, should the Ministry of Tourism in cooperation with the ministries responsible for energy and the environment, and agriculture, transport, health, financial, security, and other related fields, as well as with local municipalities. By directing policy direction and lead the efforts of environmental sustainability, and the ministry can motivate and influence of other stakeholders, both public and private sectors to engage in behavior that promotes environmental sustainability on the destination. For example, policy-makers can provide incentives, such as tax cuts and preferential agreements marketing, green companies operating in the tourism sector. Ministry of Tourism can also create a service dependency recognize accommodation and sustainable services .

At the level of the private sector, can hoteliers and tour operators, and transport services play a key role in protecting the environment and the impact on tourists to take sustainable options. Hoteliers can offer accommodation with a smaller carbon footprint and sustainable waste, energy and water policies. The tour guides, who know the destination intimately, they are the perfect ambassadors for environmental awareness. They can also affect the tourists to choose transportation options and activities with low carbon emissions, and the rotation of the custon.er 's sites differen' environmental in an attempt to reduce the human impact on biodiversity, and the education of tourists for the treatment of environmental assets with care while they are visiting .

At the level of civil society, non-governmental organizations can and universities to provide critical research and advocacy, and education of locals and visitors alike. Destinations must begin a transition green actively involve stakeholders in all sectors .

3. Funding and Financing: destination will be thinking of the green initiative may be concerned about the possibility of funding. However, it should Destinations to consider not only the costs associated with making the transition green, but the social and economic impacts of tourism revenue lost, and if the destination does not protect assets such as marine life and the rain forest, and desert landscapes, they may lead to the deterioration of irreversible these sights. In addition, it can often views generate income by taking advantage of their own resources, such as charging tourists to visit protected sites. Many of the green programs, such as the implementation of energy-saving technology, has a strong financial returns and can be easily and successfully implemented a private for-profit investments. Many of the initiatives that require the payment of private funds quickly through savings in operating costs. Then it can be recycled these savings in other investment projects green.

However, not all green initiatives financially profitable for both sides to do, and places are not able to generate revenue through its own resources always. When these resources are insufficient

Holistic approach in the india green

Many hotels now and there are stations for re- use of water, such as Orchid Hotel, Mumbai ; is now the first hotel in Asia to keep these plants successfully .. And has been certified as a HOTEL green or eco-friendly hotel. And now has been the use of cement in the green building hotels that are also environmentally friendly .. Nalla Beach Resort, Puducherry, a hotel with a unique bio-gas produced from the kitchen and food technology recycling plant wastewater and rain water harvesting system in buildings.

Anxiety tourism campaign for immediate action by the Ministry of Tourism and Kerala to ensure the beaches and waters of Alleppey for Sustainable Tourism of the waste and the waste is free for the benefit of local communities and tourism resources .

The stock of water in tourism ' program (WET) marked the beginning of " zero tolerance for injustice water ' campaign in Goa. Was this branch of the recommendations of the direct concern of tourism for the ' water rights Reclamation - towards a just social contract " as well. This would also ensure that the desired results in reducing the levels of pollutants as well as to ensure the participation of hoteliers in the protection of water bodies .

Government departments such as the Ministry of Agriculture, as well as the construction of Pollution Control Board in the state of Goa and the mobilization of public opinion through the electronic media and print. Other press releases in the campaign

So, should the stock water tourism concern in the tourism program (WET) strive to ensure that the water rights of the communities that live in tourist destinations are protected in the face of growing competition from the industry, and that in a world where fresh water for many has become increasingly rare and considered strategies implementation through community action and advocacy with the government and other relevant departments.

To encourage green tourism in Panaji (Goa) Energy and Resources Institute (Teri) is in consultation with the hotels for conducting regular energy audits to measure the daily energy consumption in these hotels. Are energy audits to measure the power (energy) consumption in the hotels to assist in the evaluation of the amount of energy that is consumed and to identify ways to prevent energy waste.

As a first step in ensuring that "green tourism" in the state, has been approached Terry hotels five star, and energy consumption patterns are on the higher side. " Some of them have responded positively, and they agree that energy audits are useful in terms of reducing the effects not only on the environment, but also to generate revenue through the provision of cost ," said Associate Fellow with TERI Saltanat Kazi.

Authorities believe that Terry Green Go would help in attracting tourists responsible, who are aware of and take measures to make sure that they cause minimum impact on people and the environment they visit.

Besides, they also propose building rating system Terry (TERI-GRIHA) to assist in the design and evaluation of a new "green buildings" in the tourism sector, and that will help to improve the environment by reducing greenhouse gas (GHG) emissions, and improve energy security and reduce the pressure on natural resources.

The goal is to encourage "green tourism" as a form of sustainable tourism, with a focus on environmental sustainability and involves the application of practices and environmentally friendly technology in every stage of planning and operations to prevent, mitigate and reverse the adverse environmental effects .

- Green tourism creates a ripple effect also extends to the effects of the tourism sector, in the locality, in the tourist place of origin., Which also includes eco-tourism and rural tourism and heritage tourism ," said Kazi.
- This would take advantage of the tourism industry are also reduce the environmental footprint there from the tourism sector, which depends environmentally and socially friendly attitudes and initiatives. Along with tourist facilities can improve the reputation, business and market share," she said. Was the impact of tourism on areas such as environmental ecosystems, beaches, wetlands and mangrove lands, forests, mountains and coastal areas and groundwater source of concern for environmentalists in the state.

- As a concept, and auditing energy and green building is a positive sign, but linking it to the concept of "green tourism" is not justified until there is a clear definition of what is a green tourism," said an activist working on issues of tourism, Roland Martins .

Three-step strategy for green

Address both environmental issues and enable the systems and structures requires setting priorities and commitment, and they are intertwined everything, making the development of a coherent strategy and environmentally sustainable tourism challenging endeavor. Moreover, each different destination ; Kenya's history, culture, the environment, assets, and the obstacles are vastly different from those of the Maldives, for example. Must be allocated to each strategy for sustainable tourism. How, then, should start point to go towards the formulation of such a strategy ?

Step 1 : Assess the health of your environment. Policymakers must conduct the first analysis of the baseline and professional credibility, check all of the strengths and weaknesses in its ecosystem as a destination. Compare the environmental performance of the current country 's global best practices. Prioritize your needs, and set expectations for the results of short- and medium- and long-term accordingly. This analysis is the foundation and starting point for understanding the issues need to be addressed immediately, as well as those that can become obstacles on the path to the green shift.

Step 2: Set of green journey. The second step is to create a vision that includes the goals of your destination. This vision and help you to draw your own journey amid the spectrum of possibilities.

At one end, you can choose to simply "do no harm " - to prevent or avoid the destruction of natural assets and the environment, with a focus on proven techniques and affordable but instead of cutting-edge solutions. For countries or locations with political challenges or limited financial resources, to this end of the spectrum may be more appropriate.

If you have more capital economic or political, however, may be aiming for the other end of the spectrum : the innovative, and the choices leading radical stake a strong claim to leadership in the field of green tourism and reflect aggressive, wanting insight on the competition in the arena still under development by parameters. As with any spectrum, and multiple options lies between these two extremes.

Scenario planning process can be a powerful way for the formation of vision. Leaders - ideally from both the government and related companies - can come together to develop a set of policy scenarios green strategy : tracks full forward, each making a trade-off between the benefits of various environmental, and speed that can get the results, and the associated costs. Make sure that all the scenarios reflects the unique strengths and resources and your destination, and every detail and specific needs and challenges of your language, as specified in your evaluation of step 1. It should also be varied scenarios enough to address the concerns of all relevant stakeholders.

Then you have to consider the effects of trade and environmental, financial and each scenario. We recommend that you ask a series of questions that should, at a minimum, cover the following dimensions :

Environmental impact. How will the new programs the main environmental dimensions ? How the results will be put at your destination in the global arena ? And the government and the private sector to meet the mandates of regional or international force, or to be eligible for incentives, existing or proposed ?

Demand and customer impact. How will affect access to the target State tourism demand of current and future for your destination ? How can any short-term effect on the cost of the potential negative tourism operators, and consequently on demand, can be mitigated ? How much credibility you might expect revenue associated to increase? Economic and financial impact. The amount of capital required to achieve the desired results? Equally important, how much financial gain or savings may result from the implementation? How this scenario financially compared to business as usual approach? What will be the impact on the federal budget and other government funds? How will its way to becoming the point of affecting the living green local players, such as working in the field of tourism? Do they have the necessary skills to cope with such changes? Stakeholders and making the initial investment the same people who will benefit from the proceeds? If not, how can bridge this gap?

And the existence of these questions answered to make it more evident than scenarios are viable. Once you have chosen a particular approach, the answer to these questions will also be crucial for determining program priorities and set realistic expectations about the goals. They can also serve as a catalyst for change, arming decision-makers with the necessary information and to engage a wide range of stakeholders.

Step 3 : Achieving Green Vision. There is a vision that has been built on such a scenario the strategic planning process leads to sustainable change only if it is implemented. How do you make the leap necessary to virtual real? How can you make sure that the implementation is your vision as planned - especially in light of the practical limitations such as financial constraints and limited resources, and priorities of the current work? Start by writing a master plan sustainable projects that frames a particular strategy, supports these projects with appropriate investments, and puts the long-term planning steps. Must be linked to the plan to infrastructure initiatives and existing businesses, including real estate development.

Ideally, the governing body dedicated to oversee the implementation of sustainability projects that have been identified, smooth and speed up the implementation process, and to ensure that the master plan includes the needs and constraints of existing initiatives. Administrative body can also be crucial in gathering concrete buy-in from stakeholders and the leadership of public relations, marketing, and education entities.

More than any other stage in the implementation phase, and multi-sectoral approach is crucial. Must obtain the views of society in the purchase, with the active participation of the government and the private sector, and civil society.

Conclusion

With growing fears of the effects of climate change continue to mount, and the international community to intensify efforts to combat it, and the tourism industry is to realize that becoming environmentally sustainable is the key to staying competitive, and good for the bottom line double.

After the implementation of the strategic transformation of the green is by no means an easy task, and can not be achieved overnight. Decision -makers, a Tourism Authority of national or regional leader in the greening effort must be maintained on the following principles in mind when launching and implementation of the strategy point of Green:

First, it should Destinations analyze the environmental performance of their current across the main dimensions of the green, compared with global best practices. It should be for the government bodies tourism take the initiative to launch pilot projects and investigate issues that need urgent attention, so as to avoid a decline in tourism. Take proactive measures is key.

Second, you should not approach the city of green initiatives such as a marketing campaign, but as a serious effort to become a point of environmentally sustainable. Quality sells, and in the world of virtual communities and customers travel quickly learn. When a tourist destination does not decide to become a green hand, must ensure that the road map is a comprehensive and tailored to the long-term instead of the death penalty for customized solutions, quick random.

Third, we must Destinations seeks to become a green make sure they involve all relevant stakeholders. Tourism ministries should reach within and across sectors to transform their destination. Compliance with the guidelines and norms is critical to capture funding and support. By following these principles, as well as the strategies discussed above, can ensure Destinations green strategies are in fact sustainable. Go green allows destinations to take advantage of the potential well, which will feed the needs of today with the protection and promotion of those tomorrow.

References

Brohman, J. (1996). New directions in tourism for third world development. Annals of Tourism Research, 23(1), pp. 48-70.

Erdogan, N. and Tosun, C. (2009). Environmental performance of tourism accommodations in the protected areas: Case of Goreme Historical National Park. International Journal of Hospitality Management. (28), pp. 406-414.

Honey, M. and Rome, A. (2000). Ecotourism and Sustainable Tourism Certification. New York: Mohonk Mountain House.

Zhang, H.Q., Chong, K. and Ap, J. (1999). An analysis of tourism policy development in modern China. Tourism Management, 20, pp. 471-485.

http://articles.timesofindia.indiatimes.com/2008-08-19/goa/27936905_1_tourism-sector-energy-audits-energy-security

NICHE TOURISM (HELPING GREEN TOURISM)

Vishal Srivastava

Faculty, Manyawar Kanshiram Institute of Tourism Management (Uttar Pradesh Tourism) Vikalp Khand-II, Near CB-CID Office, Gomti Nagar, Lucknow-226010, U.P. vishal@up-tourism.com

Sunil Upadhyaya

Faculty, Manyawar Kanshiram Institute of Tourism Management (Uttar Pradesh Tourism) Vikalp Khand-II, Near CB-CID Office, Gomti Nagar, Lucknow-226010, U.P. sunilupadhyaya@gmail.com

Abstract: There are a variety of niche tourism markets that may be developed depending on supply and demand assessments. Niche markets might include Farm and Country Tourism, Ecotourism, Bird-Watching, Cycle Tourism, Indigenous Tourism, Adventure, Health (Wellness and Medical), Backpacking, Educational Tourism. The development of products and experiences to meet the needs of these markets should be based on an understanding of the markets characteristics, behaviours and preferences.

Based on Research produced by the Sustainable Tourism Cooperative Research Centre (STCRC) the main focus is on the niche markets of:

- Farm and Country Tourism - The success of rural tourism ventures is dependent on the nature of the locality, property characteristics, human resources, market characteristics, marketing and accessibility.
- Educational Tourism - Research has shown that pricing, accommodation availability and ease of access are key influencers in a study tourism visitor's destination choice.

- Bird-Watching - Research has shown that the core elements of a bird-watching tour or walk are the opportunities to identify birds, observe behavior and have social interaction.
- Cycle Tourism - Increasing interest in cycle tourism from both a visitor and government perspective has been identified in research, in particular with the growth of the touring market.
- Indigenous Tourism - Indigenous and aboriginal tourism is a growing tourism niche market for many destinations around the world. Indigenous involvement in tourism can provide significant economic development and social benefits for regional and remote communities and provide the opportunity for visitors to experience unique and tangible culture.

Keywords: Niche Tourism, Farm & Country Tourism, Niche products.

Introduction

Niche tourism refers to how a specific tourism product can be tailored to meet the needs of a particular audience/market segment. Locations with specific niche products are able to establish and position themselves, as niche tourism destinations. Niche tourism, through image creation, helps destinations to differentiate their tourism products and compete in an increasingly competitive and cluttered tourism environment. Theoretical literature has paid little attention to the role and positioning of niche tourism products. Through the use of the niche tourism life cycle it is clear that niche products will have different impacts, marketing challenges and contributions to destination development as they progress through it.Niche tourism is, therefore, seen to be a response to an increasing number of more refined tourists demanding specialist tourism products. It is a means by which destinations can focus their offerings to differentiate their tourism products and compete in an increasingly competitive and cluttered tourism environment (Sharpley and Telfer, 2002). This critical appraisal presents an exploration of various forms of niche tourism cruise, medical and film. How destinations develop themselves to create unique products and images, which appeal to the tourism market, is a critical component of the research.

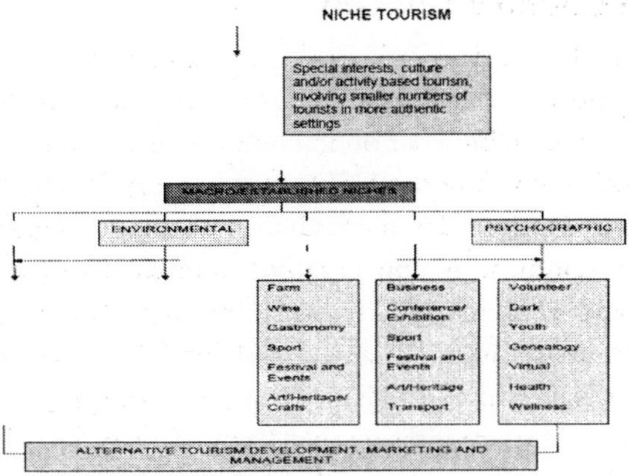

Source: Novelli (2005)

Positioning of Niche Tourism Products

Academic literature has paid little attention to the positioning of niche tourism products. Novelli considers 'the notion of an increasingly experienced group of tourists demanding specialist holidays to meet their specific desires' (Novelli, 2005, p.7), and how this has provided the conditions necessary to facilitate the growth of niche tourism. Sharpley and Telfer (2002) reflect on how tourist behaviour has produced a more segmented and sophisticated consumer market, and how niche tourism is a response to these specialised consumer needs and preferences. The development of niche tourism products has been a response by the tourism industry to diversify their product base to capture new, emergent tourist markets and build a more diverse customer base. Therefore, establishing very defined and individualised niches has allowed smaller independent tourism operators to compete in the highly price sensitive and competitive tourism marketplace.

The Ministry of Tourism has taken the initiative of identifying, diversifying, developing and promoting the nascent/upcoming niche products of the tourism industry. This is done in order to overcome the aspect of 'seasonality' to promote India as a 365 days destination, attract tourists with specific interests and to ensure repeat visits for the products in which India has comparative advantage.

Farm and Country Tourism

Many niche tourism programs are located in rural areas. From wine tours and eco-tourism, to agri tourism and seasonal events, tourism can be a viable economic component in rural community development. According the USDA, Cooperative State, Education and Extension Service, "Tourism is becoming increasingly important to the U.S. economy. A conservative estimate from the Federal Reserve Board in Kansas, based on 2000 data, shows that basic travel and tourism industries accounted for 3.6 percent of all U.S. employment. Even more telling, data from the Travel Industry Association of America indicate that 1 out of every 18 people in the U.S. has a job directly resulting from travel expenditures.

The publication Promoting Tourism in Rural America explains the need for planning and marketing rural communities, as well as weighing the pros and cons of the impacts of tourism. Local citizen participation is helpful and should be included in starting any kind of a tourism program. Being prepared when planning tourism can assist in a successful program that enhances the community.

Educational Tourism

For many in the world of education, the months of May and June represent the end of the academic year and the start of tourism's high season. Thus, from the perspective of the tourism industry as the academic year wanes, new tourism educational opportunities begin to wax. Educational tourism is one of the fastest growing areas of the travel and tourism and one that is too often overlooked by tourism professionals and marketers is "educational tourism." For example, many meetings and conventions have either an educational component to them or serve their members by being educational instruments. Often educational tourism is called by other names, such as career enhancement, job development or self-actualization experiences. Educational tourism then comes in a wide variety of formats, yet despite the differences all forms of educational tourism have a number of points in common. Among these are, the idea that travel is as much about self-improvement as it is about relaxation, that learning can be fun, and that learning is for people of all ages. Here are just some of the opportunities for your location to attract educational tourism income.

- School trips. It may pay your community to create reasons for school children to visit. While these trips rarely translate directly into overnight stays, they can help promote your tourism product in two ways: (1) children may bring their parents back for a longer visit and (2) they aid the local restaurant business.
- Alternative 'spring break" travel experiences. This form of educational travel may be the most controversial form, so much so that some may argue that Spring Break travel has nothing to do with education. This form of travel only works if you have a geography that lends itself, be it snow covered mountains or beaches with palm trees. In either case consider the pros and cons of Spring Break tourism. Often Spring breakers add extra tourism costs in the form or police and sanitation overtime.
- Study abroad experiences. Most major universities around the world promote some form of foreign travel for their students. Study abroad experiences provide students with anything from 6-week intensive study sessions to a full year of cultural and linguistic immersion. US universities that have long seen themselves as student-exporters have now come to realize that non-English speaking students seek US study abroad adventures too. Students often travel not only within their destination country of choice but throughout that county and even to neighboring lands. The goal here is to widen the educational experience so that university students do not only know their own culture but also that of at least one other nation.
- Seminar Vacations and Senior seminars. These types of travel experience especially appeal to those who have recently retired. Programs such as elder hostel provide senior citizens with everything from a chance to learn about the arts to physics lectures or astronomy. They are conducted at camps and on campuses around the world. Closely related to seminar vacations are "hands-on enhanced experience" vacations. For example, each year thousands of people travel to Israel to learn something about an archeological dig and then pay to participate on such a dig.

- Skill enhancement vacations. These are trips that range from learning how to build houses to how to protect the ecology. Nations such as Costa Rica have been extremely successful with eco-tourism in which they combine lessons on how to protect the world's ecology with the travel experience.
- Educational cruises. These cruises combine all of the fun of a cruise with lectures on specific subjects. Educational cruises have the advantage that people who take them tend to have a common interest and therefore have a greater possibility of making new friends while acquiring new knowledge.

Educational tourism offers another major advantage. It does not need to be weather dependent, a community does not need special geography and usually most of the needed infrastructure is already in place In order to take advantage of these educational tourism products consider

- Develop a tourism educational inventory. Work with local schools and universities to know what is of educational interest to visitors. While historical sites are an important part of educational tourism, do not neglect other aspects. For example, can you incorporate a local science lab into your list of educational offerings? Is there a way to work with a local school in order to teach an athletic skill? For example, Portugal's Pierre de Coubertin Soccer Academy, located just outside of Oporto will teach individual how to incorporate the art of soccer into a person's business life. While there adult students can learn soccer, get in shape, sample Portuguese wine, and visit Portugal's grape and wine country. These skill enhancement trips are a great way for working people to de-stress while learning a new skill or perfecting an older one.
- Find local people who would be willing to teach others a skill or impart some form of knowledge. These people become local attractions and the tourism industry can help them to earn extra money at the same time.
- Make sure that conference planners know that you can offer local educational experiences as a way to enhance their conference. Offer local experiences to conferences and seminars that add

both professional knowledge and personal growth. Indicate that you are willing to include family members who may also be attending the conference.

- Be careful of who works in educational tourism. Often tour guides and other educational tourism staff members forget that educational tourism is based around people on vacation. These people do not want to be treated as children. Never forget that they are paying guests.
- Establish regional tourism study groups. One of the best ways to promote educational tourism is to be involved in it yourself. Pick a topic for the year and help hotels and other tourism establishments know that visitors are welcome to come for one or more sessions.

Bird watching

You probably hear birds every day, but can you tell one bird song from the next? Bird watching, or birding, is an increasingly popular hobby in many parts of the world. Venturing out to look for and listen to various species of birds in your locality can be both enriching and relaxing. All you need is a pair of binoculars, a field guide, and a willingness to observe.

A pair with reasonable magnification (e.g. 7x or 8x) and lighter weight often works better in cluttered environments like forest or woodland. Higher magnification (10x or 12x; and heavier weight) glasses are better for open country and wetland birding; but some people will find them more difficult to hand hold and therefore suffer a more shaky image.

Some people prefer the guides with illustrations because photographs can lead to confusion due to poor lighting, flash, posture, etc. Get into the habit of studying the birds' habits, calls, and field marks before birding. This way, you will be ready to identify a particular bird the instant you see it.

If you really enjoy bird watching, search online for birding groups and chapters near you. Many lead bird walks that you can attend. Contact local universities or parks to find out whether classes or walks are being offered. The more sets of eyes and ears there are, the more birds you'll find, especially if you go with bird watchers who are more experienced than you are.

Most of the time, you will be surrounded by bird calls and songs, but will not have a single bird in sight. Look for movement in trees, and bring your binoculars to your eyes. Don't try to find the bird through your binoculars.

- If you can't go to the birds, bring the birds to you. Putting up bird feeders and keeping them filled with fresh bird food is an effective way to attract birds to your own yard. Do some reading to determine which type of feeds will attract any birds you are particularly interested in observing. Sunflower seeds will attract quite a few varieties and might be nice to start with. You can also install a bird fountain. Most things that can hold shallow water will do! Running or dripping water especially interests birds.
- Dress appropriately, as you would for hiking. Colours that blend